SPREADING
MY WINGS

SPREADING MY WINGS

One of Britain's top women pilots
tells her remarkable story
from pre-war flying to breaking
the sound barrier

DIANA BARNATO WALKER

FOREWORD BY RT HON LORD SHAWCROSS

GRUB STREET · LONDON

Published by
Grub Street
4 Rainham Close
London SW11 6SS

First published in hardback by Patrick Stephens Ltd,
an imprint of Haynes Publishing

Copyright this edition © 2003 Grub Street, London
Text copyright © Diana Barnato Walker MBE 2003

Reprinted 2004, 2005

British Library Cataloguing in Publication Data
Walker, Diana Barnato
  1. Walker, Diana Barnato   2. Women air pilots – Great Britain – Biography
  I. Title
  692.1¢ 3¢ 092

ISBN 1 904010 31 8

All rights reserved. No part of this publication may be reproduced,
stored in a retrieval system, or transmitted in any form or by any means,
electronic, mechanical, photocopying, recording, or otherwise, without
the prior permission of the copyright owner.

Cover design by Hugh Adams, AB3 Design

Typeset by G&M, Raunds, Northamptonshire

Printed and bound in Great Britain by
Biddles Ltd, King's Lynn, Norfolk

Contents

Dedication

TO JILL AND Laddie Lucas, whose continual encouragement made me turn my flying stories into this book. They wagered me a fiver I wouldn't do it . . . I've won!

DBW, Horne Grange, Surrey

Acknowledgements

I HAVE DONE my best to trace the copyright holders of all the pictures used in this book, and apologize to any I may have missed out. I would like to thank the following good friends for their help, advice and photographs: Jeffrey Quill OBE AFC FRAeS, the famous Spitfire test pilot; Air Chief Marshal Sir Denis Smallwood GBE KCB DSO DFC; Air Marshal Sir Patrick Dunn KBE CB DFC; Wing Commander Eric Viles MBE of the ATA Association; Squadron Leader A. C. Bartley DFC & bar; Mike Tagg of the RAF Museum, Hendon; Elwyn Blacker, of Pardoe Blacker, Lingfield; and Bill Port of the Bentley Drivers Club. Wing Commander P. B. 'Laddie' Lucas CBE DSO DFC galvanized me into approaching my desk and introduced me to the aviation author and historian Norman Franks, who guided me through the pitfalls of writing and whose knowledge of military aviation history and his own writing skills were invaluable.

Lastly, my dear friend Hartley Shawcross, for taking the time and trouble to write the flattering foreword to my book.

Foreword

by The Rt. Hon. Lord Shawcross GBE QC

DIANA BARNATO WALKER occupied an almost legendary position in the world of flying during the Second World War. She says in her flying autobiography that her childhood interest in aeroplanes was a forerunner to learning to fly them. She flew solo after only six hours' instruction at Brooklands Flying Club in 1938. In 1941 she joined the Air Transport Auxiliary, at that time under the direction of Gerard d'Erlanger, then a young banker, a private pilot and a director of British Airways who had conceived the plan of assisting the war effort by setting up a service to carry mail and important passengers to their destinations during the war. The first recruits to this organization (which was known as the ATA) included farmers, publicans, journalists and First World War pilots, all of whom soon found themselves in action delivering light aircraft from factories and maintenance units to the Royal Naval Fleet Air Arm and RAF squadrons. During these war years I was myself the Regional Commissioner for No. 5 Region in the North West of England which included some of the leading aircraft manufacturers and I soon became acquainted with these arrangements for delivering aircraft. The organization grew speedily and in January 1940 eight women were recruited, soon to be joined by others, including the famous pre-war pilot Amy Johnson, who met her death ferrying an Oxford in 1941. Having started with light aircraft, the ATA pilots were soon delivering fighters, twin-engined and four-engined machines and flying-boats – and indeed the early jets. Diana delivered fighter planes and twin-engined bombers in all weathers without radio or navigation aids. During the Battle of Britain the demand for ferrying Spitfires and Hurricanes to airfields in South East England became enormous and required ATA pilots to operate often during German attacks. Diana had flown 220 Spitfires before she was 22, delivering 260 of them in all as well as some 80 other different types of planes – without damaging any! She has now flown over 100 varied makes of aircraft. ATA operated throughout the war and was not disbanded until November 1945. The following year

Diana obtained a commercial flying licence and was appointed Corps Pilot for the Women's Junior Air Corps (now the Girls' Venture Corps).

Diana was awarded the Jean Lennox Bird Trophy in 1962 for a noteworthy achievement in aviation. In 1963 she flew an RAF Lightning at 1,262 mph, gaining the women's unofficial speed record and beating Jacqueline Cochrane of the USA and Jacqueline Auriol of France.

In recognition of all this – and not *just* this, for Diana had been a Red Cross nurse in the early months of the war and also an ambulance driver attached to headquarters in Belgrave Square, driving people and supplies in and out of blitzed areas – she was decorated, being awarded the MBE in 1965. On official occasions she proudly wears her wartime medals – the 1939–45 Star, the France and Germany Star, the Defence Medal and the War Medal given to her for flying various aircraft into Holland, Belgium, France and Germany.

I think I first met Diana Barnato Walker when we danced at a party at a riverside pub one very wet night, long years ago. She used to hunt with the Mid-Surrey Draghounds and the Old Surrey and Burstow, as did my late wife, and we enjoyed a neighbourly social contact during my many years in Sussex. Diana gives delightful small dinner parties (at which she is usually the excellent cook) and she has often dined with me at Friston Place. I am glad to have had the opportunity of knowing her as a neighbour and a friend, and commend her book for its good account of an interesting and eventful life.

Hartley Shawcross

◆ Chapter 1 ◆

Rigmarole about Early Days

I DON'T LIKE cellars! I was very nearly born in one . . . As cellars go, I suppose it wasn't bad, as it was our wine-cellar at No. 39, Elsworthy Road, by Primrose Hill, Hampstead, in North London. On 15 January 1918 there was a warning about a German Zeppelin or aeroplane overhead, so my mama was sheltering in the cellar. She was terrified that a bomb might be dropped nearby and got upstairs to the spare bedroom just in time for my arrival three-and-a-half weeks early.

I don't like looking stupid in front of other people, but even in my advanced years I cannot go down alone into a cellar: I have to have someone to accompany me. I don't think I am really frightened of anything else at all!

Only once in my life did I go down one alone, and that was in my present house, where the cellar is below the level of the water table. To keep the floor dry, there is an electric pump which empties the water from a well before it slops over onto the concrete floor. The oil-fired boiler is also down there.

One night when there were floods everywhere, I found myself alone in the house and just about to go to bed, when I suddenly realized that I hadn't heard the electric pump making its usual regular emptying-water noises during the evening. The boiler was still rumbling away, and I became worried that the water level would rise above its platform if the pump had conked out.

Anxiety eventually overcame my usual fear and, gathering myself together, I opened the cellar door, only to be greeted with the sight and sound of water gently lapping over the bottom steps. I retreated, put on my gumboots, then, hitching up my old blue dressing-gown, descended to the depths. With much bravery I waded along the basement corridor, with its cobwebs, towards the boiler and pump room . . . The pump had, as I'd guessed, stopped, but I could see what was wrong: the extra height of the water had made the float come off its wire. I could soon fix that!

I sloshed into the boiler room, quite forgetting that there was a step down, now under water, which makes that room 6 inches lower than the corridor. As I slipped down without warning, the water came over the top of my gumboots and, as the strikingly cold water poured in, I lost my balance and fell headlong into the 2½ feet of water. It wasn't even clean water!

So you see, dear reader, there is still something about cellars that does not appeal to me.

On the way down into that original wine-cellar where I was so nearly born was an iron bannister, while on the wall opposite was a brass light switch. The voltage in those days was only 110 DC – dangerous, but not necessarily a killer, unlike the 240 volts AC that is used in England today. Under some circumstances the 110 volts would have been enough to prove fatal. In our case there must have been a leakage of current because of a fault. As we (my elder sister Virginia and I) grew up, one of our party games was for us to take our various friends – 'friends?' – down to the cellars.

All the children were supposed to hold on to each other, because we said the steps were steep. Virginia would hold on to the bannisters whilst I switched on the light while with my other hand keeping hold of the hand of the unsuspecting friend (victim). Immediately the 110-volt electric current would go through all the children in the line – much to our amusement. We, of course, were always ready for the shock, but our little friends would nearly fall down the stairs with terror. We thought it awfully funny, but when my mama found out about it through some misguided child's parents, we got spanked – and quite rightly so, too.

In those far-off days we were always guarded by nannies, then by governesses and companions, and finally by various chaperones. Our mama would rarely be seen except for a loving peck on the cheek as we departed for school, although she always insisted on hearing our prayers before we tumbled into bed at night. We were never left alone, even inside our house.

The first 'keeper' was Nurse Gowing. She refused to be called a nanny and was thin and starchy. She wore sharply pointed hat-pins in her scratchy bonnet . . . I am amazed that those spikes didn't put our eyes out.

One day, Nurse Gowing made some treacle toffee on the nursery burner which stood behind the tall brass-edged fender which protected us from the always-plopping gas fire. She held me up to let me stir it with a wooden spoon, then, when it was cooked, she poured the still-boiling toffee into a carefully buttered old white soup plate that had a black-and-white chequered edge. Part of the coloured linen tablecloth was turned back on the large, round, wooden-topped nursery table and she then drew lines on the toffee. I thought we were about to play noughts and crosses on it.

I remember asking her if I could have some of the toffee, but instead of saying something like, 'No, it's too hot! Wait until it cools,' she replied, 'No you can't, it's all for your sister Virginia!' That was too much! Jealousy and greed were my motives as I grabbed two handfuls of the still-steaming toffee from the soup plate. Oh-dear-oh-dear! I learnt a lesson that day: don't grab; try guile!

When she heard my screams, my mama came rushing upstairs to the nursery. When my burnt hands and fingers had been seen to, Nurse Gowing got the sack. I was quite pleased.

I was nearly three years old when Nanny Brown turned up. She was gentle but wheezy with asthma. She brought very good references from Ralph Peacock, the artist, whose three sons she had lovingly nurtured. My American grandmother was horrified at the idea of an asthmatic nanny, adding that we children might also pick up her soft Suffolk accent; but Mama was adamant about engaging her. 'She's kind, and quite unlike Nurse Gowing,' I heard her say.

Nanny Brown was a great comfort after Nurse Gowing's starchiness – and so was her asthma, which caused her to sit up every night and cough. If we woke up, it was reassuring to hear that she was there, wheezing about in the gloom. We were not in the least bit worried by her breathlessness.

My mother and father parted when I was four, following my father's affair with a beautiful actress named June. I believe my parents would not have parted but for my mother's puritanical American parents, who told Mama that my father's romance could not be tolerated. A few years later my mama married again, Richard Butler Wainwright, who had been a pilot in the Great War and had won the Distinguished Flying Cross. Both my sister and I were bridesmaids. Thus my mama became Mrs Dorothy Maitland Wainwright while my father, Woolf Barnato, went on his way. To my later joy, they remained good friends. When I was a débutante, I used to see my parents sitting cosily in a corner of a ballroom at a grand dance, talking away like the old friends they had remained. Other people failed to understand it.

Much later on, my father told me that they very nearly 'got back together', but then they had their one and only real row over who was going to get the grand piano from the drawing-room if they did part. So they parted. The stupid thing about all this was that at the time, neither of them even played the piano.

It may well have been the association with stepfather Dick Wainwright that later got me interested in flying, although I was also to discover that I had an uncle, Jack Barnato, who had served in the Royal Naval Air Service in the First World War. Sadly, he died in the great influenza epidemic of 1918–19, so I never met him, but there was obviously flying somewhere in the Barnato blood.

My stepfather had been wounded in the war, having been hit in the right temple. Despite the severity of the injury and a lump of metal sticking out of his head, he had managed to fly his aeroplane – and his observer – back across the German lines, landing at his airfield before passing out. Mama kept the piece of shrapnel, which he later gave her, in her jewel box. It was all of 1½ inches long and very jagged.

He could have had a plate put in to cover the hole in his forehead, but the operation was a bit tricky in those days, so he didn't. He had to be extremely careful not to bump his head, I remember, and one could see what I took to be his brain, pulsating in and out of the dent. Fascinating for us when we were kids!

Even later, as an old man, he was into everything new. He had the first deep-freeze company, making freezers and containers. He also had the first video that I had ever seen and knew how it worked the day he got it. When he lived by himself later, he was always immaculately turned out – no egg on his ties – and one could see one's reflection in his toe-caps. He drove his own car all over the place and was way over 90 when he died.

Although he and my mama parted after 27 years of marriage and he married someone else, they still met from time to time, and I know my mama was still in love with him. By the time he died, so had his second wife, so we scattered his ashes in the little churchyard at Nutfield in Surrey, near 'Kentwyns', where he and my mother had both lived, and beside Mama's ashes. He had kept up his flying in his later years, at Redhill, and a formation of four Tiger Moths from there flew over at the moment we scattered the ashes. He would have liked that. I gave his flying log-books to the RAF Museum at Hendon.

Our house in London was on the edge of Primrose Hill in Regent's Park. There were no tall buildings in those days so when we looked out of the windows we felt we were in the country. We could see only the trees and grass of the large park. Our garden went down to the park where there was a hole in the fence which saved us a long walk.

We kept lots of pets: Alsatian dogs, chinchilla rabbits, a canary and two pink-cheeked waxbills. These were tiny brown finches with red beaks. They sometimes flew freely and were trained to come back when called, to sit on a stick when one was held aloft. One day, in mid-winter, their cage was on the window-sill in the night nursery and Nanny was out. The maid drew the thick curtains, forgetting to move the cage into the warmth of the room. In the morning I drew open the curtains and there were two little plops as the two dead and frozen waxbills fell off their perch onto the sand underneath.

I also had a tortoise which lived in the garden all summer. It too came when called. It died because I woke it up once too often from its winter hibernation. The beautiful grey chinchilla rabbits bred far too many babies (we once had quite a game standing them in flower pots in order to photograph them), so some were made into hand-muffs for Virginia and me! Knowing of its origin, I never liked using mine and always tried to lose it.

There was also a long-coated guinea-pig I had as a pet. I used to pick him up and cuddle him, stroking his whiskers and kissing him on the nose. I don't think he minded at all. One day I failed to latch his cage properly and one of the Alsatians ate him. Our gardener came up to the nursery, plonked a bunch of flowers on the table and told me the sad news. I burst into tears and he said, 'Now, now, Miss Diana! Don't take on so. Everything dies, like these flowers will; and you and me. It's the common denominator of everything that lives.'

His speech was a bit above my head and was of little comfort to my pets, who up till now had either been eaten, woken-to-death, made into hand-warmers or been left out to freeze!

Every Sunday, when we were young, Nanny used to walk us across Primrose Hill to the London Zoo. We used to get back in time for lunch which was always roast beef and Yorkshire pudding, followed by vanilla ice-cream and hot chocolate sauce. There were waffles and maple syrup for tea.

Our American grandmother Florence Maud Falk (neé Whittaker) always came to tea on Sundays when she was this side of the Atlantic. She was called 'Gra' because when I was a baby I couldn't say 'Grandma'. The name stuck and everyone always tended to call her Gra. She lived three streets away in Eton Avenue, by Swiss Cottage, but she never walked and usually arrived driven in one of her various American limousines. I should add that despite her dainty figure and tiny bones, she had a very loud voice and a temperament that was able to send out a lot of very noisy words very frequently and about all sorts of things.

One day the doorbell rang and the three Alsatians that we had then jumped up at the door and barked. They were quite frightening to people who did not know them but in reality were friendly dogs when they were not doing their watch-dogs act. I opened the door and Gra was there. She was about five feet tall and had a 'puff' of grey hair. She was wearing a beige crêpe-de-chine pleated dress with a lace jabot and tiny cream kid instep-strapped shoes. She knelt down to hug me and I noticed as she did so that she was not wearing her single-stone diamond ear-rings. I said, 'Gra – you aren't Gra without your ear-rings!' She turned her head and I saw she had an ear-ring on one ear only.

She was dismayed and said that somehow she must have dropped it on the way and that it was extremely unlucky that she had not come in her own car this time, but had taken a taxi. We looked down the garden path and outside her own door, but to no avail. Gra hadn't even taken a taxi from the usual taxi-rank, merely hailed one that had been passing her house. We would never find it again.

We had a sombre first course and then the front doorbell rang. Before anyone could stop me, I rushed out, saying, 'It's the ear-ring, I know it's the ear-ring!' I opened the front door to find a taxi-man standing outside. Without a word to him, I pushed by him, tore down the drive to his cab to find, on the coconut matting floor, Gra's missing diamond ear-ring.

The taxi-driver had followed me, amazed at the small hurricane of a child doing a war-dance of delight! My mama came out to collect me and I heard the man say to her, 'Excuse me, Madam, I hope you will forgive me, but the lady I dropped here nearly an hour ago gave me a penny instead of half-a-crown.' (Gra was very short-sighted.) 'When I went to get some tea just now, I found that all I had on me was that one penny. I hope the lady won't mind if I ask her for the correct money, but I haven't had any other fares since then, so I know it must be that lady.'

As you can imagine, the man got more than half-a-crown!

From the time I was six until I was ten, we went to Frognal School at the top of Fitzjohn's Avenue, which runs between Swiss Cottage and Hampstead. We walked the distance of three miles there and back again afterwards. The Avenue is a steep hill but I was never late for school. Virginia was; she was a fat child, puffed a lot, but didn't hurry.

Nanny, with her asthma, sometimes came to the last major road that we had to cross, saw us across it, then left us. When collecting us she only came to that same road, usually bringing the Alsatian, 'Dugan of Deloraine', with her. He was perfectly trained, walking to heel without needing a lead.

One day we had nearly reached the road while Nanny was still some way down Fitzjohn's Avenue. Dugan saw us and left Nanny to rush uphill to greet us. He jumped up at me to lick my face. Nanny called him, whereupon he wheeled round, circling out into the road. As he did so, a small black car with two people in it was coming down the hill. All four wheels went bump-bump-bump-bump over Dugan, who then got up and galloped back down the hill to Nanny. I thought he was alright but the couple in the car stopped and drove us home. Dugan was laid on the sofa in the front hall. About an hour later he quietly died, from internal haemorrhage I suppose. Another pet down the drain!

My mama came in just before he died. Nanny greeted her at the door with '. . . something awful has happened, Madam!' My mama thought at first it was one of us who had been run over but then didn't seem to mind about Dugan, being so relieved we children were alright.

I had been very fond of Dugan . . . At the time I wished it had been me . . .

We usually went to stay with our father for half the holidays in his far grander home, 'Ardenrun', near Lingfield, in Surrey. Sometimes we went for long weekends as well. The chauffeur, du Heaume, collected us in one Bentley or another, my father being not only the Chairman of Bentley Motors, but a member of the crack Bentley racing team as well. On the way out of London, du Heaume always stopped at Lyons Corner

House by Marble Arch and, to keep us quiet, bought us some large square lemon drops coated with rough sugar, which we sucked during the drive down. We always arrived with yellow tongues.

The housekeeper at Ardenrun had been governess to my cousins, Dudley, Stanhope and Eileen Joel. She was a small French lady who always dressed in black and wore a round diamanté and jet brooch at her throat. She had her own room on the way between the dining room, the kitchen and the servants' quarters. The room was filled with white Persian cats, who regularly moulted long white hairs all over us.

All along the side of that room was the store cupboard, to which we were allowed unlimited access. It was crammed with large boxes of Fuller's chocolates and walnut cakes and held huge quantities of sugared almonds and chestnuts in syrup, not to mention the lacquered boxes of crystallized fruits . . . So we went home, not only with yellow tongues but with yellow faces.

We were allowed to stay up for dinner at my father's house, which we thought was very grand and grown up. One evening all the 'Bentley Boys' – the nickname given to the drivers of W. O. Bentley's racing cars who drove in all races such as the Le Mans 24-hours, Essex 6-hours, German, French, Irish and Ulster TTs, as well as at the British racing track at Brooklands, near Weybridge in Surrey – were there celebrating one of their victories. I was put on a chair with two cushions next to Doctor Benjafield, who was one of the Bentley Boys. Even at a comparatively young age he was bald.

The first course arrived which was a clear consommé with alphabet letters floating about in it. I could just spell my own name then so was trying to fish out the appropriate letters to spell DIANA, around the rim of the soup plate, when I noticed 'Benjie', on my right, with his eyes closed, slowly leaning further and further forward towards his soup. The soup was almost too hot to drink and I thought that at any minute he would topple into it and burn his nose. I didn't know quite what to do.

Nobody else appeared to have noticed, so I took my hot soup spoon and put it right on the top of Benjie's bald head, which woke him up with quite a start! Then everyone saw what had happened and roared with laughter. I was very put out and not sure if I would be scolded. However, I needn't have worried, for after dinner, Benjie presented me with a lovely pale grey cashmere scarf and thanked me for saving him from drowning in his soup.

I wound Benjie's gift about my neck and went around to everyone present to kiss them goodnight before Virginia and I went up to bed. Amongst the company was June, the 'infamous' actress who had been the cause of my parents' divorce. Although I was polite enough to say goodnight to her, I purposely did not kiss her. I was just escaping out of the drawing-room door when June called me back, saying that I hadn't kissed her.

This was a problem nearly insoluble for a youngster of my tender years and experience. Mama had told me that I must not kiss June whilst I was at Ardenrun but not why I should not do so; although I knew without her having to tell me. June got up from her chair in all her beauty, crouched down beside me with her arms outstretched and again said, 'Kiss me goodnight, too?'

I could feel a surge of heat suffusing my body. This was a very difficult situation; someone was going to be very angry with me but I had to tell the truth. 'Mama said I wasn't to kiss you,' I blurted out. June only laughed, as I added, 'Because you are a very wicked woman!' and fled out of the room in tears.

A little later my father came up to the night nursery to hear our prayers and to tuck us in. I was afraid that I had upset him and, having got away that night without being ticked off for putting the hot soup spoon on Benjie's bald head, I was now in for a proper scolding for being so impolite to one of my father's friends. However, I was lucky, for he merely remarked, 'You're very small but you were quite right; and I like it that you are so honest.'

◇   ◇   ◇

Our nursery and night nursery at Ardenrun were on the top floor. There was a little toy house that we children could get right inside, as well as a hurdy-gurdy with cardboard records with pieces cut out here and there in order to make tunes. There was a huge white rocking-horse, too. We were spoiled, of course, having far better toys there than we had at our mother's house.

In the mornings we were woken up with hot milk and water biscuits on a lace-covered tray, brought to us by Berthe, a little old Swiss maid who wore a black-and-white checked dress with an organdie apron. She moved about silently wearing brown carpet-slippers.

There was also a cellar at Ardenrun! This never seemed spooky as it was always filled with my father's pals eating eggs and bacon on their way home after hunting – or just filled with my father's other drinking friends. The cellar had been converted into a pseudo-Tudor pub which they called 'The Ardenrun Arms'. It had a large oak-beamed open fireplace with a whole load of pewter mugs hung around which my father's friends kept giving to him.

There were two little Elizabethan-paned windows – leaded lights – with ivy growing up the white-washed alcove walls opposite. There always seemed to be bright sunlight outside, even in the winter evenings, and it was a long time before I was tall enough to be able to see that the sunshine was, in reality, electric light. We did not get, nor did we give, any electric shocks to our small friends in that cellar; the wiring was much better.

My father was a great sportsman. Amongst other things he was wicket-keeper for Surrey. At Ardenrun he had practice nets on the lowest of the five terraces of the garden. All the 1930 Surrey team, including Percy Fender and Jack Hobbs, as well as all of Don Bradman's Australian touring team, came to stay. They taught me how to play cricket at the nets, so by the age of 12 I found I was much in demand to join the teams of my little schoolboy friends. Not long ago I discovered my old childhood autograph book in the loft with all the signatures of both teams in it.

My father was also a top shot as well as being able to beat everyone at tennis up to 'country house' standard. He rode, he swam, he skied like a bomb and he played golf. He was, without doubt, a most well-co-ordinated human being.

When he was 35, and already over half-way through his life, he had a great friend, T. A. Bourn, known as 'Dale' to his pals, who acted as his social secretary. Dale was a fine amateur golfer who won the English Championships in 1930 and was runner-up three years later, the same year he reached the final of the British Amateur at Hoylake. My father usually played golf with a handicap of 18, but one day he and Dale struck up a wager of £5 to £500 – my father waging the larger sum – that he would achieve a scratch handicap in just one year.

So determined was my father to win the bet that he played golf virtually every day. Even when he went on a trip to America he still managed a game most days. He took lessons at Coombe Hill from Archie Compston and from all the famous golf professionals of those times.

His game improved rapidly until the 364th night, when the culmination of the wager drew near. The evening before the match was due to be played, my father's 'friends' sabotaged him. They took him out to dinner and over-wined him, over-dined him, then produced a gorgeous girl who over-seduced him.

The next morning, the 365th day, still in a daze, he played for the wager – and lost. He did not get down to scratch and every catty pal said that this was only because Dale was hard up at the time and my father did not want to take the fiver off him, but wanted to give him £500 instead.*

Two weeks later my father got his handicap down, not to scratch but even better – to +2. He played off that handicap until the day before he died. A year and a fortnight from 18 to +2 . . . Some application! Some sportsman!

Although Chairman of Bentley Motors, he did as he was told by W. O. Bentley and didn't commandeer the best car by virtue of his position in the company. He won the Le Mans 24-hour race three times running, in 1928, 1929 and 1930, in the days when only the drivers could refuel or service the cars when they drove into the pits. W. O. Bentley said that he was the best driver in the world.

We were not taken over to France to watch my father winning these three successive races, but we sometimes went to the motor-racing track at Brooklands, with its famous banked circuit, to see him driving there.

One day, Clive Dunfree, one of the original Bentley Boys, was driving 'Old Number One', one of my father's cars, while I was standing next to my father with the beautiful actress Jane Baxter, who was a great girlfriend of Clive's. The Bentley was being driven very fast and high up on the great curved concrete banking. Suddenly the huge car disappeared over

* Dale was killed in the Second World War whilst flying training in a Tiger Moth.

the edge into the trees, and there was Clive, rolling over and over, then sliding down the steep sides of the track.

There were a lot of pine trees around the top of the track and it was believed that a branch must have hit Clive as he drove along. Jane must have been a supreme actress or had enormous control of her feelings. She never even cried but my father had tears rolling down his face at the death of his great friend.

One weekend whilst I was at Ardenrun, a lot of small blue racing Bugattis turned up. Ettiore Bugatti was there too – he was a great friend of my father's. There must have been about eight cars so 'races' were quickly organized. The 'course' ran from the big house, down the front drive to the pond by the farmhouse, over the bridge, then down the half-mile-long straight back drive. At the end, they turned round quickly and drove back again.

On the return leg, the cars were supposed to go another way round the pond and past the stables and kennel buildings, because the timing, which was started by someone with a very old stop-watch, was arranged so as to enable the next starter to go along one side of the pond whilst the car which had started before him was coming back on the other side.

All seemed to be going well and my father acquiesced to my entreaties to be given a ride with him when it was his turn. It was a bit of a squash for two of us in the Bugatti but we managed. As we got to the bottom of the front drive, speeding through the entrance gateway, with the pond dead ahead of us, we saw a cloud of dust zooming towards us – on the wrong side of the pond! It was on 'our' going-down side!!

There was no possibility of two cars passing each other in that narrow space, so my father turned the steering wheel sharply to the left and went through a farm gate onto a cinder track. From there we careered around the grass field beside the front drive whilst the other car hurtled through the entrance gates beside us. He then drove calmly, but fast, back through the farm gate, turned left and carried on past the pond, over the bridge, as if nothing had happened. In spite of our extra route, my father's driving time was the quickest of the lot.

Later on, when I used to drive up to London with him, I saw that he drove so smoothly, with no apparent rush or hurry, that I never realized how fast we were going. Even on that short run and without exceeding any speed limits, we were always at least ten minutes faster than anyone else.

Virginia went to the boarding school Benenden, but I was too fond of my home comforts, so was allowed to go to a day school: Queens' College in Harley Street was the one selected. I liked school, where I enjoyed the various sports, being pretty good at swimming, hockey and netball. I was a thin, wiry, undersized ball of energy. I went to ballet and tap as well as acrobatic dance classes, also doing extra gym – anything to use up my seemingly boundless energy.

By the time I was ten, I was beginning to stay with my father more and more, for we were fast becoming like two friends rather than father and daughter. He let me ride his 18½-hand hunters, even taking me hunting with the Old Surrey and Burstow Foxhounds. He rode Punch whilst I was put onto Conqueror. My father could never lose me because the horses were stablemates, so wherever he went with Punch, my Conqueror was certain to follow – even when going into a wood to spend a penny! (As a matter of interest, my father could attend to this call of nature without getting off his horse. Unfortunately I could not.)

Whatever he jumped, I jumped it after him. Those two horses were beautifully trained. Conqueror would gallop across a field until he approached a hedge or fence, when he would slow to a canter and then, with perfect timing, would always take one long stride, then a short stride, then jump, all in nearly slow motion. It was as if he was saying to me, 'One, two-three, pop!' I did nothing, and he looked after me. My father was asked by his horrified friends why he allowed a 'pimple' to ride on the back of an 18½-hand heavyweight hunter. All he would say was, 'She is far safer there than on anything else . . .' And so I was.

Chapter 2

The Barnatos and Joels

I SUPPOSE I had better jot down something of my antecedents before I go much farther. In any event, they are far too interesting to ignore. For my paternal grandpa, it really was a case of poor boy makes good, which is always a good story. Grandpa Barney was very poor and made very, very good.

Barnet Isaacs – as he began life – showed promise at an early age in the East End of London as a trader and juggler – now there's a combination! The trading was mostly apples from a barrow, while his brother Harry and he made a little money juggling in the streets. The family was hard up and lived near the Mile End Road. They were devout Jews, not too proud to do varied tasks to make ends meet.

The members of the East End community, including Barney and Harry, were asked to do a turn in the local music hall. Barney fancied himself as a straight actor, so elected to play Othello. Nothing was more incongruous than Barney, a diminutive, extremely blond youth of about 17, who wore pince-nez spectacles, playing the great dark Moor. There were titters from his family and friends in the front rows and by the end of his performance he had brought the house down. They laughed, cheered and clapped, thinking Barney had been burlesquing the act. He hadn't. He was mortified, hating being laughed at.

By the time the other acts finished, he was crying in the wings and wouldn't come on stage with the rest of the entertainers to take a bow. The audience kept shouting, 'Barnet too! Barnet too! Barnet too!', until at last Barney saw the funny side himself, swallowed his damaged pride and took his bow. From then on, he and Harry were no longer known as the Isaac boys, but as the Barnetoo brothers, which soon became Barnato. Barney adopted the new surname which was later taken by his diamond firm.

◇ ◇ ◇

When news of the diamond finds in Kimberley trickled through, Harry, the eldest brother, went to South Africa. He wrote back with glowing tales to the family about how the streets were paved with diamonds, and how he was living in luxury – a far cry from life in the Mile End Road.

Barney's imagination was fired. He saved up £50, a vast sum for a young Eastender in those days. His brother-in-law, Joel Joel, who had married Barney's sister Kate and kept the pub 'The King of Prussia' round the corner, gave him 40 boxes of bad cigars as a send-off gift for his momentous journey. So with his £50 and the cigars as his only means of support, Barney set sail for fame and – hopefully – fortune.

When he arrived at the South African port of entry, he did not have enough money for the drive in a covered wagon to Kimberley, but for £3 he arranged with a drover to walk all the way (around 300 miles), keeping an eye on the company's cattle. At night he slept under the wagon as an extra watch-dog. When he finally reached Kimberley he found brother Harry, not living in a palace of luxury, but in the worst part of the shanty town, in the very last torn tent of a row, asleep in the middle of the day, his toes coming out of his socks.

Barney began to do the only thing he knew – trade. He swapped some of his bad cigars for a chicken, the chicken for a goat, the goat for a donkey, then finally, the donkey for a pony that belonged to the post-master; always trading upwards. The idea of getting hold of the postman's pony was that the pony went on all the mail rounds, stopping at all the diggings and claims. The pony knew the route on its own and, very soon, so did Barney.

In the early days, the diggers scratched the surface of the ground to find their diamonds, never going very deep. When they reached the blue ground, they gave up and moved on to a new claim. First of all, Barney asked for the right to 'glean' the deserted claims. He found a few small stones and set up as a trader. Gradually he was able to buy more and more of the disused claims. He believed that most diamonds could also be found in the blue ground, which was opposite to the then-prevailing theory. When he had collected a big enough area of claims, he brought in mining machinery and mined deeply – and successfully. The Primrose Diamond Mine was his first large venture and he incorporated a primrose into his much later acquired crest, with *Industria atque Fortuna* as the motto.

Stories about Grandfather Barney are legion. Shortly after he arrived in Kimberley, a visiting showman, a hefty bare-fisted pugilist, offered a golden sovereign to anybody who could knock him out in the boxing ring. Barney took up the challenge amongst ribald laughter from the rough onlookers that such a tiny, short-sighted man could even contemplate vanquishing the visiting hero.

Barney wasn't only fighting for one golden sovereign; he effected a mass of side bets on himself, for nobody believed he had a chance against this giant of a man. Barney took off his pince-nez glasses, laid them down carefully, and his opponent didn't know what hit him. Barney said later, 'If a fellow's going to hit you, you hit him first' – and collected a lot of money.

After the failure of the 'Jameson Raid' in early 1896 (resulting from a dispute over heavy taxation and poor treatment of immigrant workers), some of Barney's diamond magnate friends were put into jail for treason. Barney was not implicated, but he went to the President of the Transvaal, Paul Kruger, to ask him to show leniency. Kruger liked Barney. They sat on the stoop – a porch – outside the President's house to talk. Kruger was wearing his stove-pipe top hat as usual, but was unmoved by Barney's pleading, so Barney said he would close all his mines if Kruger didn't acquiesce and let his friends out.

Barney went straight back and began to paste up notices himself, on all his vast quantity of mines, saying that all the workers would be sacked the next day. The mines were the centre of the South African economy so Kruger saw reason and gave in. All the participants were let off with the payment of a £25,000 fine – a huge sum in those days.

Barney met and fell in love with a beautiful dark-haired girl called Fanny Bees. She and her sister Emily, who married a brave and upright army officer, Robert Finlayson, had trekked up from the Cape in a covered wagon with their father, who was a tailor. He was of German extraction. Colonel Finlayson owned the local hotel in Kimberley and both Emily and Fanny helped in the family concern.

Barney's parents in London would not accept Fanny until she was received into the Jewish faith. She was unable to convert in South Africa, so after 12 years they finally married and had three children: Leah, Jack and Woolf, my father.

In her later years, Grandma Barnato was blackmailed. She couldn't have got through so much money otherwise. My father tried desperately to find out why or who, but to no avail. In the end, he gave her a monthly, then a vast weekly 'allowance', but she still used it all up in spite of a simple living standard.

After her death at 96, we found that all her jewellery had disappeared except the three-strand pearl necklace she always wore and a gold chain bracelet, which was found mixed up with a lot of junk beads. There were some coins on it – a Kruger sovereign and half-sovereign. The sovereign was the one Barney had won in the boxing ring. There was also a soft lead bullet in a little case that was made to look like a bullet. Grandma was shot in the leg sometime, in some altercation, but I never discovered the story.

Having become firmly established in the diamond mining business, Barney progressed. Later, however, he became embroiled in a battle between himself and Cecil Rhodes over the amalgamation of Barney's Kimberley mines to form the new company of De Beers. Both had to raise money. Rhodes was more able to acquire it from his ally Alfred Beit and other influential friends, but he needed time to get some more, via London. Telegraphic communications were slow.

All the diamond stock was sorted and laid out pending valuation. Rhodes and Barney inspected it, Rhodes then saying to Barney, 'Those diamonds would fill a bucket, wouldn't they?' Barney took the bait and, showman that he was, had all the sorted and graded diamonds shovelled into a large bucket and swaggered down the street with it. It took four days to sort them all out again and until that was done, the company's value could not be admitted. Meanwhile, the delay allowed Rhodes to get the rest of the capital and promises that he needed.

Barney received around £8 million for the company; for many years the original cheque, suitably framed, hung in the company offices. He became a life governor of De Beers and was later elected to the Cape Parliament.

When the business in diamonds and gold expanded in Kimberley and Johannesburg, Barney, always family-minded, asked his nephews Jack, Solly and Woolf Joel to join him and brother Harry. Many people involved in building up the mining and financial side of South Africa in those early days had a tough time, living violent lives and many of them died violent deaths.

Solly Joel had ambition. His ultimate goal was to get control of the company. It was said that he master-minded the organizing of a phoney indictment of illicit diamond buying on brother Jack Joel (whose son would become the venerable and respected racehorse owner and breeder, Jim Joel. Uncle Jim remained much loved by the family until his death in 1992 at the age of 97.) Illicit diamond buying was considered a serious offence: if one was black, the penalty was death, but if white, it meant flogging and terrible prison conditions.

My Uncle Jack didn't wait for the case to come up, but hopped it back to England, out of the jurisdiction of the courts, where he continued to run the English side of the business well out of Solly's hair. Jack later married the sister of Tommy Sopwith, the famous aeroplane designer. It was unfortunate that Jack took it upon himself to be against virtually every person who took a loving interest in his children, which was probably why Uncle Jim never married. May, one daughter, had all her suitors scared off. Only Jack's daughter Katherine managed to escape her father's clutches, ran away from home and married a Gentile, a Mr Freeman, later giving up the Jewish faith. That sent Jack into permanent mourning and I well remember him in later life, all in black and wearing a tall stove-pipe hat. Jack never forgave her infidelity to their religion and her name was never mentioned. He died in 1940.

One of Solly's children was Doris – 'Auntie Dorrie'. She was his favourite until she married a Mr Walters, of whom Solly disapproved. Solly warned her that if she married him she would be cut off. She did so and so Solly did cut her off. Also, he never spoke to her again either, even when she had a child, which died. Solly and Jack were certainly an uncompromising pair of brothers.

Solly's yacht was called *Doris* but after her marriage he renamed it *Eileen* instead, after his other daughter. All the things that had 'Doris' on them – dinner service, tea cups, silver, linen, blankets, deck-chairs –

were thrown overboard on Solly's orders and replaced with another lot with 'Eileen' on them.

Aunt Doris was one of my godmothers. She, like my other godmother Dorothe, never forgot my birthday or Christmas. When Aunt Dorrie died she left me a lovely bit of jewellery, a sapphire and diamond clip like her racing colours. Dorothe gave me a sapphire and diamond bangle for my 21st birthday.

After Jack's return to England, the only people left to thwart Solly were my Grandfather Barney and his nephew Woolf Joel. It was many years later that I heard the full story of what then developed, from my cousin Stanhope. I remember being at my father's house, Ridgemead, when Stan and I got talking about South Africa and Grandpa Barney. I said something like, 'When Barney Barnato committed suicide . . .' and Stanhope looked up sharply and said, 'Or Solly pushed him!' Which was astonishing, as Solly was Stan's father! 'He gave him the heave-ho overboard,' Stan went on.

Over the years I had heard about Barney's drowning on a trip back to England on the *SS Christiana*, but it had happened a long time ago, so at my tender age, I hadn't really listened. Now I did, as Stan told the story.

In 1897 a journey to England was arranged for Barney. It was said he had been overworking and no doubt he had. He liked his drink, too. Barney and Grandma Barnato, the three kidlets, Leah, Jack, and my father Woolf – then aged one year – were all aboard the liner, and so was Solly.

Apparently Barney was promenading round the deck one day with Solly. A steward was stacking chairs nearby. Barney asked Solly the time; 'Three fifteen,' said Solly, looking at the large watch on his waistcoat chain. Suddenly there was a cry of 'Murder!' The steward looked up to see . . . 'Mr Joel and Mr Barnato at the rails of the ship'. What happened next is a bit fluffy. Whether Solly was hanging on to Barney's coat tails to stop him going over, or helping him to do so is not at all clear. Sufficient to say that after the shout of 'Man overboard!' went up, the ship stopped and put down a boat to pick up Barney, who was floating in the water.

'If you flounder about and drown,' said Stanhope in telling his story, 'the body usually submerges as the lungs fill up with water. If you go in unconscious, then your lungs are still full of air, so you float.'

Barney floated; so he was unconscious when he went in. Did they have a fight? Did Solly biff him, or vice versa? We know Barney was pretty good with his fists . . . but what could they have had a row about – if they did?

When the boat got to him he was dead. They brought him back on board. By the time the decomposing body reached England, the verdict was that Barney had committed suicide whilst the balance of his mind was temporarily impaired. But why would he commit suicide? He had everything to live for – a beautiful wife, three lovely children, lots and lots of money. He was coming home to receive all sorts of accolades that a poor-boy-made-good would be delighted to be given. He had got there by his own hard work and canniness. Why should he jump overboard? Not he . . . he had a lot more mileage in him. He was only 45.

The steward did all right. He became quite a friend of Solly's and went shooting with him on his English estate. But if you want a motive, it's not far to look.

But what of brother Woolf? Woolf suddenly became the victim of a blackmailer, a known counterfeiter and villain called Von Veltheim. Woolf had nothing to hide or to fear, so he told the police, who asked him to call Von Veltheim's bluff, and they would nab him red-handed whilst he was asking for money. The trap was duly laid with the police hiding behind a screen in Woolf's office. Von Veltheim was shown in, Woolf sitting behind his huge desk. Von Veltheim threatened Woolf with a gun if he didn't get paid to keep his mouth shut about something (the family never did discover what). Woolf stood up and Von Veltheim shot him dead before the police could jump out from behind the screen. The murderer got off with two years as he pleaded self-defence. It so happened that there was a gun, albeit unloaded, in the top drawer of Woolf's desk.

When I was told this story by my cousin Stanhope, Solly's son, I heard for the first time all about how hard Solly tried to get his hands on the company and all the loot. He was something of a brigand, and Stan even suggested that Solly probably paid for Von Veltheim's defence. He would have been quite happy to do so because the tragedy had got Woolf out of his way. In order to realize his ambitions, Solly had needed to oust his nephew from the South African end of the company.

In my mother's jewel box was a letter from my godmother, Aunt Dorothe, my Uncle Jack Barnato's widow, who subsequently married Lord Plunket, which had been addressed to my Aunt Leah. It said in essence: 'If Pa Falk [my mother's father] wants to try to find out, I for one won't stop him, and if he wants 20% of anything he may find, let him have it if he's so sure something is wrong. If he finds anything, then we have a chance of the rest of it between you and me and Dot [my mother].' This letter referred to the rumours, still abounding in the 1920s, that Barney and Solly had had a row on that fateful day. Only one thing concerned both of them – money! In his barrow-boy days, Barney would not have paid tuppence for an apple when a penny would do. Yes, he and Solly had come up the hard way. Having had nothing, and then having made a lot, meant a good deal to them, putting it mildly. These men were now seriously rich by the standards of the day, and raking in the shekels hourly.

Pa Falk, my American grandfather (originally Von Falk whose great-grandparents had emigrated to America from Germany), was a Wall Street broker with the famous firm of J. S. Balche & Son. He was a great mathematician, one stage away from being a genius, I'd say. He made a proposition to Aunt Dorothe, Aunt Leah and my mother, that he would look into the situation to see if there was anything he could find in the finances of the company at that time which could have led to a disagreement between Barney and his nephew Solly. The three ladies agreed – which was something in itself, for they seldom did. They didn't always see eye to eye: Leah drank, Dorothe was social and my mother was somewhat puritanical – an unlikely mix.

To do this, Pa Falk had to retire from his job. The firm regretted his departure and presented him with an enormous engraved, embellished silver punch bowl with swan's heads as the handles, and all gold inside. It comes out of the bank vault for parties or when the Old Surrey & Burstow Foxhounds (of which I was Master for 13 seasons) meet at my present house at Horne, in Surrey. It makes the rum punch taste and look much better.

It was hard work. Pa Falk certainly burnt the midnight oil. The research and calculations took him over two years. He travelled to South Africa several times and, despite every conceivable difficulty being put in his way, got permission to see the company's books. When he finally got to the very page he really needed, he found it had been torn out . . . He had then to start again but doggedly went on and on.

A court case provided access to other books and finally he got the answer he sought. As from a day just prior to Barney's strange and sudden demise, Solly had been diddling Barney out of well nigh £1 million. That wasn't much to those boys even then, but it was enough to have a row about, when Barney had made it all from nothing, with Solly helped along on his back.

Under the terms of Barney Barnato's will, after due provision for Grandma Barnato, Uncle Jack, Aunt Leah and my father, the sole survivor of the company took the kitty – and that was eventually Solly. So he did all right, didn't he?

Solly enjoyed litigation and in his long life went to court over sundry trivialities. This time, thanks to Pa Falk, the issue was the £1 million owed to Barney's heirs by Solly. My father didn't want to have a court case at all, let alone to represent the three usually squabblesome ladies. He and Solly's sons and daughters, Stanhope, Dudley, Doris and Eileen, were the greatest of friends, but he was overruled by the ladies.

The case went to court and was settled amicably after lunch on the second day of the hearing. Solly was forced to pay the Barnato side £960,000, which, I suppose, was the million less legal fees. Pa Falk got his 20 per cent.

A short time later, some of my father's pals said, 'Well, yer know, Babe [Babe was my father's nickname, being the youngest in his family], y'er missing out on the interest!' My father didn't want to pursue this conversation until they continued, 'Just think of the interest on a million over nearly 30 years.' That certainly caught my father's attention.

With a very bad grace, Solly, on a loser this time too, also settled that bit. More for the ladies and Pa Falk to share.

◆ Chapter 3 ◆

From Stirring Events to Flight

MY MAMA DID not talk to me or tell me much about my father, but she always allowed me to go down to hunt on Conqueror. Sometimes my father would collect me from Elsworthy Road, going down just for the day. Sometimes his chauffeur, du Heaume, fetched me, while at other times my cousin Eileen (Joel) and her husband John Rogerson drove me down and kept an eye on me while out hunting.

Mama always thought that my horse addiction was temporary so never got around to buying me decent riding clothes. My jodphurs sort of fitted but everything else was wrong – very wrong. I wore my school shoes, and was sent off wearing my school blazer with my white silk school blouse beneath it.

When I was out with the hunt I felt very shy about my get-up, surrounded as I was by everyone resplendent and beautifully turned out in full hunting kit. The solace was that great horse of mine. He would go over anything, so we were always able to be near enough to hounds to see what they were doing and he was so well behaved that no grown-ups took exception to us being there. In those days, children were supposed to keep behind the grown-up members of the hunt.

One day I overheard two snooty people saying, 'I really do wonder why Babe's kid comes out looking like that . . .' I was mortified, although secretly I absolutely agreed with them. On my way home I confided all this to Eileen and John.

The very next time I went hunting with them, they drove me first to their large house in Trevor Square, just off Hyde Park. Taking me up to their bedroom, they took off my horrid blazer, turned the points of my soft school blouse inside its own neckline, then tied a crisp white hunting stock on top, securing it with the loan of a gold tiepin on which was a fox's head. Eileen found a proper riding coat that she had had when she was a child, gave me a pair of yellow string gloves and a hunting crop. Now I felt the part!

My father happened to be in America on that occasion, but that day, in 1932, Conqueror and I were standing beside a covert when one of his old friends, gloriously bedecked in hunting pink, rode up and stopped beside us. 'Ha!' he began, 'I see your father's done it again.' I hadn't a clue what he meant, so to save answering, I gave Conqueror a little kick in the ribs on the side that was out of sight of the information-bearer. My horse obligingly wheeled his huge backside around and bumped into the bloke, and by the time we had sorted ourselves out, as well as apologizing for Conqueror's (!) misdemeanour, hounds had found and we were away.

As we galloped across the fields, someone else rode alongside. 'Nice picture of your father in the paper,' he shouted. This time I didn't have to try to answer because of the wind in my ears and because I was busy choosing where to point Conqueror at the next hedge. However, I began to wonder what my father had been up to.

When we checked, a third man turned to me. 'She's very pretty, isn't she?' I gave up. It was something that everyone thought I knew about, yet I had not the slightest idea what it was. I felt a little worried but just said, 'Yes', and took a large swig from the small hunting flask in its cylindrical leather case that was attached to my saddle. Most people had something very uplifting in their flasks – mine was filled with orange juice.

Eileen and John didn't say anything about the mystery on the drive home, but as soon as I got back to Elsworthy Road, I went into the study to look at the day's newspapers. There, on the front page, was a large picture of my father, while on his arm was the daughter of a Californian coal magnate, Jacqueline Queagly of San Francisco, the beautiful girl he had just married. I was very hurt and not a little jealous, wishing that my mama and stepfather had told me the news before I went hunting.

When I was about 12, Nanny Brown left Elsworthy Road for a while, to return to Suffolk to take care of her own ailing mother, who can't have been all that ailing because she survived until just before the war, when Old Nanny returned to us again. By this time we had the farm at Nutfield, near Redhill in Surrey.

Whilst Old Nanny was away, we had a succession of governesses. Virginia was still at boarding school and only saw them during the holidays, but I came into contact with them all the time. I thoroughly resented Old Nanny having left me, so I took it out on the various governesses. I often wonder how they stayed as long as they did.

There was only one lady whom I deigned to like, called Miss Pester. She had four spinster sisters who lived in a wonderful Elizabethan manor house at Bearley, four miles from Stratford-on-Avon. The house had a priest's hole, while the garden had a long lavender walk and a dovecote full of beautiful white-feathered things. We went to stay, Virginia and I being allowed to cycle the four miles to see a Shakespearian play every afternoon. One day, for a special treat, we were allowed to go to an evening performance. Unfortunately for my literary education, we had also seen another Shakespearian play that afternoon. Even now, I still get muddled up between *Much Ado About Nothing* and *As You Like It*.

Virginia and our little local friends decided to act the witches' scene from Macbeth. Virginia made a gruesome-looking old hag out of herself. 'Double, double, toil and trouble; Fire burn and cauldron bubble . . .,' she hissed. The 'cauldron' was a flowered chamber-pot from under one of our beds, beneath which I had lit a real fire. I was not allowed to act.

My sister had said, 'You're no good at all at remembering things.' She had a photographic memory (she was able to read a page of poetry or prose only once, then recite it word for word). So I was relegated to 'props' girl.

We played our scene in one of the barns, charging our friends a halfpenny to come in. One day, I made the fire burn too brightly and the triangle of sticks holding the 'cauldron' collapsed in a shower of sparks. The chamber-pot was cracked and broken, the fire brigade had to be called, and I was in trouble. Miss Pester was terribly peeved about her pottie.

The house at Bearley had a ghost. It really did have one! Virginia and I shared a room. At night, each of us put a chair for our clothes at the end of our beds. The chairs stood in direct line between the bedroom door and a door which led down to the priest's hole. If anyone wanted to walk from the door to the priest's hole, or vice versa, our chairs would have been in the way.

Every morning (and I do mean every morning!), when we awoke, the chairs had always been moved into the gaps beside our beds. I thought that Virginia was teasing me, whilst she thought it was me who was moving them. When we eventually told Miss Pester about it, she said almost casually, 'It's only the ghost.' So after that, we put the chairs where the ghost wouldn't be likely to bump into them during his nocturnal prowls!

My sister Virginia and I were luckier than many children of that era, in that we were always taken abroad for our holidays. Very few of our school chums went out of England. They seemed to be taken to the English seaside or to Scotland, whereas we always went skiing over Christmas, or were sometimes taken to America in the summer in order to visit our grandparents, who had homes in both London and New York. (They paid taxes in neither country because they stayed just under the six months' legal limit in both places, the extra few days being taken up on the voyages across the Atlantic in one of the large Cunard liners.) If we were not taken to New York, then we went to the South of France. So, at the beginning of every school term, Virginia and I usually lauded it over our classmates.

We had an American first cousin, Pomeroy, who was, in age, exactly between Virginia and me. He came over to stay with us during one of his long summer vacations. He was tall for his age, blue-eyed, fair-haired, but with a long face. He was 'American looking' and extremely serious,

and I thought him a bit of a nincompoop. I expect he didn't warm to
his British cousins' humour either.

It was suggested one day that the forthcoming holidays should be
spent in Norway, so itineraries were discussed by my mama and
stepfather. In those days it always meant going by boat, so pictures of
liners and photographs of Norway were left spread out on the sofa in
the study. Nothing was finally decided, which left the whole holiday still
under consideration.

Also, to my dismay, Pomeroy was coming along with us, as well as
our American grandmother, who had been widowed when Grandpa Falk
died of hardening of the arteries at the age of 40 – no doubt having been
brought on by overwork of his financial brain. Gra was to be included in
the party along with her maid and chauffeur. The others were my mother,
stepfather, our mother's ladies' maid, our chauffeur, Nanny, Virginia
and me. Two cars would be taken over on the same boat with us – my
grandmother's American Franklyn and our Hispano-Suiza – as we
planned to drive to several different parts of Norway.

Early one morning, soon after the talk about the proposed Norwegian
holiday, I was lying half asleep, half awake, when I saw a vivid picture.
It was not a nightmare as such, and I was fully conscious that it was not
a dream because I was not asleep. It was a shattering experience. I saw
the liner we were on being pulled sideways towards a Norwegian quay
by the fore and aft hawsers, whilst we three children, with Gra, were
leaning on the iron rails watching the manoeuvre. Suddenly, Gra wasn't
beside me anymore. I went tense when I saw her in the dark oily water,
squashed between the side of the boat and the wooden sleepers of the
dock.

The next night I 'saw' the same picture, only this time I was standing
between Gra and her maid; otherwise, the details were the same. I didn't
know what to do. I felt that this was going to happen to Gra if we went
to Norway. After all, I had seen it twice; I had to stop us going there.

I made myself as unpleasant to my parents as only an adolescent child
can. I said I did NOT want to go to nasty, cold Norway; I wanted to go
to lovely sunny southern beaches to swim, to fish and to play on the
golden sands of the then unspoilt South of France. I kept it up, causing
lots of lovely rows, so that my mother's friends began to say, 'What a
difficult child Diana has suddenly become.'

In the end there was a change of plan, though I don't expect it had
anything to do with my tantrums. The holiday, as it had been for the
previous three years, was to be a trip to Le Lavandou, which was still
quite unspoilt, boasting but one small hotel plus miles of sandy beaches.

I was delighted but told Virginia under a sworn oath of secrecy about
my 'visions' of Gra's 'squashing'. She said, 'She'll be alright now. Sorry
your dream wasn't about Pomeroy!'

We took the two cars. My stepfather shared the driving of the Hispano-
Suiza with our chauffeur, Hugget, who had carried me up the garden
path when I was one year old. Gra's chauffeur had nobody to help him
with the Franklyn. We three children took it in turns to ride in Gra's

car. I didn't really like my turn because the soft springing of the American Franklyn made me feel sick. On the other hand, it was nice to be clear of cousin Pomeroy and Virginia's ceaseless chatterings.

On the way, we all met for lunch at Montelimar (where they make nougat). We were taken around the factory after lunch, being presented with boxes of the stuff when we left. I had been in the Franklyn all morning so felt distinctly queasy. It was very, very hot. Virginia and I had come to blows about some of the nougat – a proper row it was! I remember it well.

We were in the village square near a café which had coloured enamel tables with slatted chairs outside on the dusty, sandy ground. I pushed Virginia, not very hard, but hard enough for her to fall and roll over in the dust. Her dear little white straw hat with its pink ribbons and white daisies came off, finishing up between the hind feet of the last in the line of a row of waiting cabbies' horses. The animal was undoubtedly frightened out of its three-legged lethargy, for it promptly made a mess on the hat. I thought it quite hilarious, doubling up with mirth.

Not so, anyone else. Certainly not so, Virginia.

It was Pomeroy's turn to drive with Gra. As Virginia and I got into the Hispano, my mama said, 'I won't have both those squabbling brats together in the same car at the same time – it will ruin the journey.' We were made to draw lots to see who was to be the 'fortunate' girl to take over Pomeroy's place. Unfortunately, I won, although I begged Virginia to go instead as she wasn't ever car-sick and liked Gra more than I did, but she declined to take up my offer. She knew that I always felt sick but she was getting her own back after the hat incident.

My stepfather asked Gra's chauffeur before we left if he was not too tired to go on driving; then I was put in the back seat between the maid on my left and Gra on my right. The Hispano-Suiza, with the others in it, went on ahead to the next stopping-place, a village on a hill, where we were going to have tea.

There was a partition in Gra's car between the chauffeur and us, as well as glass sliding windows halfway up to the roof. Behind the glass on our side was a beige silk net, tacked onto the roof by gold buttons, where all sorts of things were stored. There was my beribboned daisied hat, the maid's knitting with needles sticking out, Gra's jewellery case, her embroidery, plus a chess set in a wooden box. Pomeroy and Virginia played chess, but I wasn't bright enough to join in, they said.

It was still extremely hot so we had all the windows open. I had made a fuss about having to go in Gra's car, one of my reasons being that it was so draughty. To appease me, my mama had put her beautiful brown-and-white large batique silk scarf around my shoulders; it smelt of her perfume.

We were driving along the wide straight road, lined with large trunked plane trees. I felt awful after all that lunch, followed by the nougat, not to mention the heat. I could see the village on the hill where we were going to stop. It was not far away, I thought, my purgatory was nearly over.

Suddenly the wooden chess men in the net above began to rattle and slurp about in their box as the net began to swing wildly. I saw that we were no longer being driven in a straight line at a boring 60 miles per hour, but were going all over the road at a considerably faster speed . . .

I came to in a field, lying beside a stook of corn. The stook in front of that one was completely flattened where I had first landed, then I must have rolled against the other. My arms and legs were covered in scratches from the stubble, while I had lumps out of one knee and another out of my elbow. I felt the back of my head and didn't like it – my hand came away covered in blood. I was nearly 100 yards away from the road. It was later thought that I had cannoned out through the roof of the (closed) Franklyn, as some shreds of the beautiful batique scarf were found on the metal supporting spars. The rest of the scarf had somehow blown over my face, protecting it, as there were no marks on it. Being a very small, wiry little girl, I had somehow gone out between those narrow bars.

I walked back through the field towards the road, finding the maid picking up pieces of Gra's jewellery which were scattered about the road from her broken jewellery case. I saw the Franklyn upside down with its dark oily underside gleaming. Gra was lying squashed beneath it.

In spite of that horrific scene I didn't have nightmares. On the contrary, I was only too happy to show off the shaved patch with its scar and stitch marks on the back of my head, recounting the gory details to my open-mouthed little schoolfriends. I suppose I didn't really like Gra all that much.

Virginia came to see me later in the American Hospital in Cannes and said, 'Hmph! In spite of you being so nasty to everyone, your dream came off, didn't it?'

In her will, Gra left me those diamond ear-rings, one of which she had so nearly lost in that taxi-cab incident. They were very nice but my ears were not pierced and my large face would have swamped the studs, so later I had them incorporated into a clip made by Messrs Cartier Ltd of Bond Street.

It was a beautiful thing, two-coloured gold, including the diamond studs and other little bits of diamonds. I wore it more than any other piece of jewellery but so nearly lost it one Christmas Eve. After a party, I went to church and, feeling a little over-dressed, wrapped the clip in a piece of tissue paper and put it into my handbag.

The next day I could not find the clip anywhere. We hunted high and low for several days but to no avail. The tissue and clip were eventually discovered outside the house by my maid on 2 January, having been there since Christmas Eve, covered in snow. She walked the dog, it lifted its leg in the gutter, the snow melted – and there was the clip. Gra's diamonds lost and found twice.

On my 15th birthday, no early-morning telegram arrived at Elsworthy Road from my father. This was most unusual and I was extremely upset to think that he had forgotten me. When I got downstairs to the study I opened the papers, only to see a picture of my father wearing a teddy-bear coat with his striped pyjama trouser legs showing underneath. He was standing beside the old well by the front door of Ardenrun, holding a garden hose in his hand from which water appeared to be merely trickling. A lot of icicles had formed down the pipe under his hand. The caption read: 'Woolf Barnato's Mansion Gutted'. . . It had happened the day before. No wonder he hadn't got around to sending me a wire. Everyone had had a lot of fun at Ardenrun. Sad it had now gone up in smoke.

In 1934 we were taken to Honolulu for a six-week holiday. Our Uncle Phil Thurber, who had married my mother's sister, Aunt Muriel, producing my cousins Pomeroy, Dorothe and Muriel, was a colonel in the US Army. The American Army was not mechanized in those days and to our delight we found we had the choice of some 420 cavalry horses to ride. We had a splendid time, and stayed at the Officers' Club.

Every day we rode around some of the fire-break trails, which were areas cleared of vegetation about halfway up each mountainside or hill. Guavas grew wild – we would pick them to have 'pip-spitting on horseback' competitions. The furthest spat-out pip won the contest. If you had a horse that stood still, the winning odds were better.

Colonel Philip Thurber was a stickler for time; I suppose he wouldn't have been in command of the US Army's Oahu Base if he hadn't been. One day I was late. There was Uncle Phil shooting his shirt cuffs to see his wrist-watch, saying, 'You've kept the horses waiting four minutes in the sun.'

We went surf-riding, spear fishing and pineapple snitching with our cousins plus other officers' children. Pineapple snitching was a rodeo act done at a sharp trot or slow canter, leaning down to grab a pineapple from the edge of a field as you rode past. The Army horses were not as tall as Conqueror, but for an undersized girl it was extraordinarily difficult not to fall off. A pineapple could be bought for 5 cents, but a thief was fined $5. The dishonesty did not appeal to me, especially when I found that the only pineapple I ever managed to snitch wasn't very ripe.

In 1936 I was a débutante and thoroughly enjoyed all the fuss. The presentation at Court was a fiasco, or should I say it went off like a damp squib? Edward VIII had not yet been crowned, so a garden party was held instead of the usual ceremony inside Buckingham Palace. We lined up to go forward, one by one, to curtsey, but when there were only three girls left in front of me, the heavens suddenly opened with a torrential downpour. Everyone scurried to the tea tents where I consoled myself with some strawberry ice-cream, thinking it was far more original to have been presented at Court and not to have made my carefully practised curtsey.

My mama decked me out in beautiful evening dresses made by Madam Emilienne in Grafton Street, W1. I made a host of new friends and went to wonderful balls. I met many young men, all of whom had been thoroughly vetted by the various mothers. They were called 'Debs' Delights', which meant they were both acceptable and eligible. One or two became unacceptable, one being the young and handsome Paul Richey.

Paul later had a marvellous record as a wartime fighter pilot, becoming famous for his book which was entitled *Fighter Pilot*, published in 1942. He had fought in France, won the DFC, been wounded and was back on operations again by that time.

He started out as a Debs' Delight, being attractive, dashing, and a good dancer. He wore an opera hat with his white tie and tails, instead of the customary top hat . . . Oh dear. He used to make a lot of noise and get drunk now and then, so was crossed off the Debs' list, which meant that he was no longer invited to the pre-dance dinner parties nor to the dances. Not that that stopped Paul. I was delighted to find him every evening in the bar of all the best dances that he deigned to gate-crash. That took some bravery, so I was not at all surprised that he flew with equal bravery with the RAF during the Second World War.

Mama always chaperoned me and brought me home at the end of the evening, or should I say, in the early hours of the morning? If I went to a dinner party before a dance, then that hostess was responsible for seeing her various débutante guests to their homes. However, I was 18, and didn't like all that molly-coddling any more, so thought the only way to get away was to learn to fly. At least Nannies, Governesses, Companions and Chaperones wouldn't be able to come along.

Germany was re-arming and there was a growing fear of the Hitler regime. Some far-thinking people saw the need to train more pilots in England, as there were but a handful over here compared to the multitudes in Germany.

Harold Balfour (later Lord Balfour of Inchrye PC MC), who had been a successful fighter pilot in the Great War and was later an MP, Minister of Aviation and Under-Secretary of State for Air in Neville Chamberlain's government, played a major part in the RAF's expansion plans and later in the Commonwealth Air Training Schemes, as well as starting the Civil Air Guard. This was formed so that young people could learn to fly for just 7/6d an hour. If war had not come when it did, the Civil Air Guard would soon have outpaced the German Youth Flying Club Movement. There were also a few flying clubs which were not heavily patronized. Although there was no direct government subsidy, the clubs were given a certain sum for every pilot who got his or her flying licence.

In those days I was far too much of a snob to go to learn to fly with what I thought would be the *hoi polloi*, even though it cost only 7/6d an hour. So I took myself off to the top flying club, which was situated in the very centre of the Brooklands racing track where I had often watched my father race Bentleys and other cars in his hey-day. If he had driven there, then I would fly there.

At Brooklands Flying Club, an hour's flying cost £3 (!), so I very soon ran out of pocket money. My parents certainly had no intention of helping out as they were sure I would break my neck.

I learnt in a Tiger Moth with Ken Waller, who later became an instructor with the Cinque Ports Flying Club. I had absolutely no idea at all what I was doing when I got near to the ground. I just jiggled the stick, but we always landed safely. No doubt Ken had control. Ken was about 26 or so, and a good pilot. I was a very bumptious girl, so I thought he was sick of me when, after six hours' flying time, which had been spread out over several weeks, Ken got out. There was no statutory number of hours before a pilot was allowed to fly solo. The average was around nine hours. It simply depended upon the instructor assessing the pilot's efficiency.

It was quite a foggy day, I remember, and as he climbed down he simply told me to go off solo, the short way of Brooklands, towards the sewers. By then, I thought he wouldn't have minded if I'd landed in them, but he did say, 'Take care of this Tiger – it's the only club aeroplane with an instrument panel in it!' I didn't know what he meant; I had never used the full instrument panel. While I was flying I had been using the 'U-tube' of coloured liquid which showed the climb or descent according to how much coloured liquid was in either part of the 'U', and the wind speed arrow indicator on the right hand of the wing spar.

As I taxied to the take-off point, concentrating on the great task ahead, you can imagine how I felt when I was waved to a standstill and a couple of knarled and ugly hands appeared on the edge of the cockpit, while an equally hideous face appeared at the same height as mine.

Taken aback at this most critical of times, I heard the man implore me not to fly. He had been a flyer, had crashed and a burning aeroplane had seared and burnt his flesh. He didn't want this to happen to anyone else, far less a pretty young girl. I didn't take any notice of his words and took off.

FIRST SOLO – BROOKLANDS, 1938

As I was taxying out to try
To keep the Tiger in the sky,
A little man with wave and leer
Came running to the cockpit's side.
He put his claws upon the wing
Impelling me to turn to him,
And said, above the engine's din,
'Don't fly! Don't fly Miss! Look and see
What aviation's done to me.'
I scanned his scarred and broken face
And horror shuddered in my mind
What flying now could do to me,
And I would end up same as he.
'Don't spoil your beauty, dear Lydie,
I'm only meaning to be kind.'

He was . . . And as the years rolled by
All stupid stunts did I escry,
Because of that burnt canny man
Whose wounds I saw before my eyes
When scary things were in the skies.
I was quite competent, 'twas said –
But for that frightening damaged chap,
It's certain I'd be dead.

I had to stop flying very soon after going solo – which I achieved without
breaking anything, either aeroplane or me. There was no pocket money
left to pay the £3 hourly rate, but the very great shock of seeing that
terribly burnt man just when I was about to go solo made me become a
very careful pilot. Later, whenever I was tempted to do something really
rash or unnecessary, I 'saw' that little man and heeded his warning. I
didn't mind the idea of being bumped off, but I didn't want to be
maimed. A wounded man is a hero, but a damaged and disfigured
woman is . . . nothing, as I found out later.

That little man may have done his old flying club out of a few
government grants because he scared some would-be pilots from going
solo or stopped their training, but whoever he was, he certainly did me
a good turn.

Few pilots can honestly claim to have eschewed a beat-up over their
own, or their girlfriends', homes, and I must admit, in spite of the grim
picture in my mind of that little man's face, during the war I did once do
a really unnecessary beat-up.

Beforehand, however, I had, in anticipation, made a careful survey –
from the ground – of the route that I would fly past my father's new
house, Ridgemead, on the edge of Windsor Great Park. The garden had
a lot of trees in it. There was a paved terrace at the back of the house
with a line of linked goldfish ponds, which the local heron used to fish
regularly, to the detriment of the neat lines of goldfish which he left on
the edge. It also had two cottages, a garage block and stables with grooms
living over.

There was a balcony along the outside of my father's bedroom which
ran around most of the house and past some of the guest rooms. The
balcony was on the first floor of this long, low, Spanish–American-style
country house, which had been built by the architect Robert Lutyens
(1901–72) to my father and stepmother's specifications. Today it is an
old people's home, while the cottages are separate households.

Because the house originally showed up so much from the air, with
its green tiled roof and white walls, it was camouflaged in the war, and
after that we called it King Kong's castle. It looked dreadful but we got
used to it. Some important archives or secret things of some kind were
stored there. It was extremely difficult, after the war ended, to remove the
camouflage paint.

Despite this camouflage, the house was still quite simple to find from the air and I thought I could fly at the same level as the balcony, so long as I lined up with and flew between certain trees. At the other end of my proposed run were some high beech trees, which made a picture frame for a view of distant Windsor Castle. I knew I could easily fly through this 'picture frame'!

One sunny morning I was given a Hawker Tempest fighter, flying it out of Langley. It was early 1945 and by then I was an experienced pilot who should have known better. As Ridgemead was on the way, I did my carefully thought-out flypast. Several weekend guests were still there and waved across at me as I went by the first-floor balcony for the second time – at their level. They said later that I was so close to them that when they put out their hands to wave, they could almost touch me as I went past.

A Tempest V, with its huge Sabre IIA engine (a Mark II Tempest had a 5000 hp Centaurus V engine), was a very noisy flying contraption. Although it may have been impressive to view, certainly at that height, it was an extremely silly thing to do.

My burnt man would not have approved.

Those last years of peace I remember well. There were parties and dances, skiing holidays in Switzerland, with all sorts of friends. I met and danced with any number of young men who, in just a few short years, would make names for themselves in the coming war.

Coming up to my 21st birthday (January 1939), my father said we were both going to Paris for the weekend. He needed a chaperone, he giggled. At that time he had the most beautiful Rumanian girlfriend who had the most gorgeous figure I had ever seen. I was somewhat jealous because I was encased in puppy fat, or should I just say fat?

We arrived at the Ritz where our first-floor suite, overlooking the Place Vendôme, was enormous, with two bathrooms and a huge sitting room. It was not then decorated in the modern Ritz Hotel manner with brass bedsteads, pink or blue shiny satin bedheads and curtains, but with old-fashioned dark Victorian furniture and lovely antique carpets, all having great charm.

Soon after our arrival, my father said, 'Let's go downstairs, I've got your birthday present . . .' Down we went. He led me out through the swing doors. There in the road was a most glamorous-looking, pinky-beige, slightly iridescent, open two-seater sports car – a Talbot Darracq.

Whew! I voiced my understated but surprised delight and thanks, then took the car out to dinner with an admirer, driving up the hill to Montmartre. The Darracq had an early kind of pre-selector gearbox which I just could not get the hang of. The appropriate gear was selected, then you pumped the clutch down – or was it the other way round? Anyway, by the time I got the car back to the Ritz, I had burnt the clutch out.

The next day my father was most understanding – can't think why. He said perhaps it wasn't quite the car for me, so he would give me his second-hand, four-month-old Bentley instead. It was for me to decide so, although the Bentley wasn't new, I accepted this latest offer.

The clutch on the buzz-box was fixed by Ettiore Bugatti's firm. My father then dined with Ettiore whilst I went out to dinner with the Darracq and a different admirer. The new clutch had a hard time and smelt a bit but by now I was getting more used to it.

By the time I got back to the Ritz after my second night out, I had changed my mind about having the Bentley. I was in love with that buzz-box by then. It was about 2 am in the morning, but the concierge organized a place for me and the car on an early cross-Channel ferry. My father and I had been due to return to England later that morning but to drive to Calais to catch the boat meant an early start for me. My father wasn't yet in, so I left a note on the floor outside his bedroom to tell him I had, after all, decided to keep the Darracq.

I arranged to be called at 5 am, but I was woken by a furious parent when he himself had been woken up with breakfast brought in to him instead of to me. He had probably only just got off to sleep after his night out. I soon found out he had other things on his mind too.

'I am going into the bathroom,' he yelled, 'and if, by the time I pull the plug, you haven't decided on the Bentley, well, you shan't have either car!'

That settled it. Having remade my decision, I thankfully was able to turn over for a bit more sleep, instead of running the risk of re-burning out the two-seater's clutch in a hurry to get to the port of departure on time.

Later on, my father told me it wasn't being called too early which had annoyed him, for which he apologized . . . no need . . . but that he had done a deal over dinner with Ettiore Bugatti to take the Darracq in part-exchange for a new Bugatti and didn't want to 'unscramble the egg'.

So, I got my first Bentley, CXF 114, a silver-grey Park Ward 4^1/$_2$ litre. Fancy being given a Bentley for a 21st, and nearly turning my nose up at it. Times have changed. Now I even add up the milk bill.

♦ Chapter 4 ♦

War – and the Air Transport Auxiliary

WHEN THE SECOND World War erupted in Europe in the late summer of 1939, it changed everybody's life, not the least mine. No doubt I would have continued to chug through life pretty much as I had been doing in recent years had it not been for Adolf Hitler and his dreams of world domination. Not that I didn't continue in like vein initially, which, when one looks back on it today, seems incredible.

The war still hadn't touched many people by the beginning of 1940. The 'Phoney War' was on and life too went on much as before, except for the blackout and some rationing, including petrol rationing which made driving about something to be planned carefully. Britain was frantically gearing up production of war materials of every kind, and people were being called up into the Services or drafted into factories. Some women had turned into 'land girls' while others, like me, into nurses. I volunteered to be a Red Cross nurse, but as yet the expected flush of casualties had not materialized, so was told I would not be needed for a while.

I had a birthday party on 15 January in the Embassy Club in Bond Street, then a fashionable restaurant with a fine band. The next morning I took the Bentley over to France, following exactly the same procedure as before the war began. The AA looked after me at Dover, there seemed to be no problems aboard the ferry and the unloading at the French port was trouble-free. As a bonus, petrol was not on ration in France.

I was accompanied by a great friend, Lorna Harmsworth, a lovely, blue-eyed blonde. She had acquired a Press Pass from her father, Lord Rothermere, who owned the *Daily Mail*. Lord Rothermere, of course, was famous for many things, not least being the driving force behind the building and development of an aeroplane – the Bristol Blenheim – which he pushed forward as a private venture until it was taken over by the RAF when it proved to be a faster light bomber than the fighters of the day! Not that I knew much of that on my trip to France, but I would later know all about the Blenheim.

I had been given a Pass from the French Embassy by Count John de Caraman. We were told passes were needed to enter France, but no-one asked to see them.

The idea behind our trip was to go to Megève, a skiing resort on the other side of Mont Blanc from Chamonix where the Scots Guards were in training, learning to ski prior to proposed sorties or invasions into Finland or Norway. We stopped the first night with the de Caramans, Johnnie and Nada, in their Château de Courson at Brugères-le-Chatel, 25 miles south-east of Paris. I cannot remember anything about the interior of the place except that the bathroom was freezing. I was so tired after the nearly-all-night birthday party, the early start from England followed by the long drive after only a few minutes' sleep. I needed a hot bath before dinner to warm me up.

There was a really huge ornate lead bath, large enough for several people at once. The only thing was, the hot water obviously had a long journey, so it arrived with the chill only just taken off, and the lead was very cold to sit on.

So the blonde Lorna and the brunette, Diana, both skied for ten days in Megève and Chamonix, then I left to drive quietly home. On the way I stopped in Paris, staying with Gogo Schiaparelli. Her mother owned the fabulous couture dress establishment. During the five days that I was with them, the House of Schiaparelli made me a collection of clothes the like of which I had not owned before – or since, for that matter. There was a heavy wool tweed coat lined with patriotic red, white and blue silk, a navy blue crêpe pintucked dress, and two silk afternoon dresses, one pink patterned with flowers, the other duck-egg blue with little red and blue striped marks on it. Two hats were included, one a velvet bonnet with white broderie anglaise trimming, the other made of red straw. Then there was a heavy pink satin long evening dress. The satin was so soft it caught the rough edges of my fingers when I touched it . . . People were beginning to die for their country whilst I was buying clothes.

France was in some ways already more geared up to the imminent dangers of war and invasion than the isolated islanders of Britain. They were closer to the enemy and had seen it all 25 years earlier. They didn't have the Channel to protect them, just the Maginot Line, which in the event proved totally useless.

In France, cars did not have such extreme blackout covers on their headlamps as the English had. We drove on sidelights and headlight hoods were only allowed to show tiny slits of light. I changed my English headlamp covers for French ones whilst I was over there.

Unlike Britain, the French had a curfew. Everyone had to be indoors by 11 o'clock at night. Gogo and our various friends came back after our evenings out to the play room in the basement of the Schiaparelli home in the Rue du Berri, just off the Champs Elysées. The room had a bar, a gramophone and was edged all around the walls with emerald green sofa seats. Here we, plus our young friends, would congregate. If we forgot the time, then some of the timid who did not dare risk being caught in the streets after 11 pm used to sleep there on the narrow sofas.

When my clothes were finished, I left for England, stopping on the way for lunch at Amiens with Bruce Shand and Charles Banbury, who were with the 12th Lancers there, and Count Henri de la Falaise, a friend of Gogo's, who was the French Liaison Officer to the 12th. Henri, of course, was bilingual, having lived in Hollywood; he married in succession two lovely film stars.

We ate marvellous duck paté in the Café Godebert in the beautiful square of Amiens. Sadly, that café no longer exists. When the bombing began in May, Amiens was bombed flat. No more duck paté.

From Paris I had telephoned my father, who said he would leave my February ration of petrol coupons with the Automobile Association at Folkestone, where the ferry was supposed to dock. Only two gallons of fuel were allowed to be left in the car's tank for the Channel crossing. But my ferry zig-zagged across in case of submarines, arriving not at Folkestone, but at Dover. No petrol without coupons at Dover!

The Bentley had twin S.U. carburetters which ticked a warning a mile or so before they ran quite dry. Ticking away, I free-wheeled into a small garage near Maidstone. Explaining my plight to the old man running the pumps (all the young men had been called up by then), he agreed to fill the car if I posted my coupons on to him when I got home. Whilst he was away getting some change, a tiny puppy climbed into the car, settling down on my lap between me and the steering wheel. Near the pumps was a large brown cardboard notice, on which, written in chalk, was 'Cairns for Sale'. When the man returned, I asked him if the tiny dog was a cairn and was it for sale? He said yes, but seemed reluctant to sell it because it went with him when he drove his lorry. I asked how much, and he replied, 7/6d. To my dismay I found, even with the change from the petrol, I hadn't got enough English money to make up this sum. All I had was French francs.

In spite of this he let me drive away with his cairn, owing him the money as well as the coupons. The puppy I called 'P-nut', which was the name of Gogo's dog. I have had cairns as constant companions ever since.

The 'Phoney War' ended on 10 May 1940. The serious lurch towards the Battle of Britain had begun. Back from France, I returned to my Red Cross duties, wondering, like everyone else, what our futures might be. I was soon to find out.

The Air Transport Auxiliary was the brain-child of Gerard d'Erlanger, born out of an idea of his at the time of Munich in 1938. A member of a respected banking family, as well as a director of British Airways, the forerunner of BEA (British European Airways), he thought that Britain could use the help of her many young and not-so-young amateur aviators in a war which seemed to be inevitable.

At first he wrote to Harold Balfour, and then to the Director General of Civil Aviation, Sir Francis Shelmerdine, setting forth his idea and scheme, by which these aviators could, perhaps, assist in the delivery of light aircraft, or the carrying of mail, dispatches, medical or other light supplies. He received some initial encouragement, but when war finally began in September 1939, his scheme was rushed ahead with some alacrity.

In the beginning it came under the general wing of British Airways itself, which had moved from Croydon to Bristol upon the outbreak of war. Just days before the official declaration, about 1,000 holders of 'A' and 'B' flying licences up and down the country were written to, some 100 of whom responded. After flight testing of these people, who came from many different walks of civilian life, the first 30 were selected. A dark blue uniform was designed and made, looking a little like the uniform of some of the airlines, but single-breasted. With it came a forage cap, distinctive buttons and pilot's 'wings' in gold. The provisional name Air Transport Auxiliary stuck, so the wings sprouted from a circle within which the letters ATA were prominent.

Those first pilots, keen for the most part to do something for the war effort, had a variety of experience. Some had been airmen in the First World War, like the one-armed, one-eyed Stewart Keith-Jopp, who, despite his obvious handicaps, as well as being over 50 years old, proved nevertheless to be an exceptional pilot who was destined to remain with ATA for the whole war. Others came from the general sport flying fraternity – company directors, racing drivers, aviation journalists, antique dealers – you name it, they had it! There was even a conjuror and a bookmaker.

Although not fully envisaged by d'Erlanger, the RAF believed the ATA would be useful in delivering Service aeroplanes from factories or maintenance units to airfields and squadrons. The RAF did have its own ferry pools of pilots for this task, but with the increase in aircraft needed at the start of the war, and the necessity of releasing some of the pilots for front-line duties, it seemed best to get the men of the ATA to handle this important task.

I say men, but of course, one very early innovation was that despite the period – far away from the days of equal opportunity that we enjoy today – it was recognized that a number of women held 'A' and 'B' licences. Indeed, many household names of the 1930s in the field of aviation included women. People such as Britain's Amy Johnson, the famous record-breaking pilot of the 1930s, and her American equivalent, Amelia Earhart, had shown that aviation was no longer just a man's domain. Thus it was that the Under Secretary of State made the historic and memorable decision that lady pilots with similar experience to men would be accepted for work with the ATA.

To this end, Pauline Gower was given the task of organizing the women's section of the ATA. Pauline was the daughter of Sir Robert Gower MP, and had herself clocked up something like 2,000 flying hours and carried over 30,000 joy-riding passengers. In January 1940 she was given permission to recruit eight experienced female pilots to ferry Tiger Moth two-seat biplane training aeroplanes from the de Havilland factory at Hatfield, north of London. These initial eight women pilots were: Winifred Crossley, daughter of a doctor from Huntingdon; Margaret Cunnison; Mona Friedlander, the ice-hockey international; Joan Hughes, who at the age of 17 had been Britain's youngest pilot; Gabrielle Patterson, a member of the National Women's Air Reserve; Rosemary Rees; Marion Wilberforce; and Margaret Gore. Perhaps it should be noted that five of them, plus Pauline, were to complete nearly six years of continuous ferrying with ATA, being still with the organization when it was finally disbanded.

By 1944 there were 108 women pilots together with 551 male pilots and 22 UK bases, but Pauline Gower and her first eight women accepted to fly with ATA in the early days had a tough time. A ferry pool was set up at Hatfield. Despite the supposed glamour, the life was hard for all ATA pilots, not least the women, who had to prove themselves able to do the job as well as the men.

Even with the 600 flying hours that they had to have to be accepted, they were only allowed to fly light single-engined aircraft. They were expected to ferry Tiger Moths, the open-cockpit trainer, all the way to Scotland at the height of the bad, cold weather of that first winter of the war, then travel back home at night in an unheated, darkened train, usually choc-a-bloc with troops, so that the only seat was on their parachute bags in the freezing corridors. Wartime travel by train had to be experienced to be believed, especially during the blitz periods.

Aircraft could be required in any corner of the British Isles, and had to be flown there through all sorts of weathers, followed by a slow, exhausting journey back to base to start the same thing the next day. The women got very tired but they stuck it out.

Later on the 'taxi' programme was organized, whereby all pilots were dumped, then collected, or ferried between jobs. Initially this was by Puss Moths, then American Fairchilds and the old workhorse, the Avro Anson. Some days a pilot could be ferrying, and the other days he or she could be a taxi pilot.

Gradually, Pauline Gower pulled strings to get permission for the women to fly twin-engined aircraft after a course on the Airspeed Oxford at the Central Flying School at Upavon, but still they were only allowed to fly single- and twin-engined training planes and not any operational ones, though there was scarcely any difference in the aptitude required to fly, say, a training Master or an operational fighter, or for that matter, an Oxford trainer compared to a light twin bomber like the Hampden. But things were looking up.

Pauline engineered a bit more permission. Everyone watched with bated breath when Winifred Crossley was finally let loose on a Hurricane for circuits and bumps around Hatfield. She got away with it . . . Another hurdle had been jumped by the women, so now they could fly operational singles and twins as well as the various trainers.

But still the men did not allow the women to fly some new types right away. Even much later, there was a lot of humming and hawing before Lettice Curtis, a tall, blue-eyed blond girl, an excellent pilot in No. 1

Ferry Pool at White Waltham, was allowed to ferry a Typhoon on 24 June 1942. Soon so many aircraft were being churned out of the factories that everyone was needed to ferry them. Initially the Typhoon was made Class II 'plus', to pretend it was a bit more difficult to fly than the other fighters. It wasn't, just heavier, more powerful, faster and noisier, and a bit of a finger-burner for the ground crews if they had to reload it with starter cartridges if it didn't start first go.

Lettice was also the first woman allowed to fly a four-engined bomber, the Avro Lancaster, and tiny little Joan Hughes, the youngest and prettiest pilot, a blue saucer-eyed brunette, was the first woman to fly the four-engined Handley-Page Halifax.

Even the ATA big-wigs themselves, let alone the RAF or Air Ministry high-ups, had not quite got used to the idea that women could easily and efficiently operate any aircraft they were given. By the end of the war, the women's accident rate was lower than the men's. Perhaps this was because the women ATA were able to choose for those duties, were of a better physical standard, many of them being much younger and fitter than the available men, who in the main were not eligible for RAF or Fleet Air Arm flying duties because initially men could not fly with the RAF if over 25. Maybe the women were more careful, or maybe they were luckier.

Lois Butler was one of the early ATA women. She was the wife of Alan, the head of de Havilland. When I was wondering whether to join ATA, she and I had a quick lunch together in the 500 Club in South Molton Street. She tried to dissuade me from trying to join ATA, explaining, 'You know, you won't have time for any other life at all. Not like you are used to now . . !'

What she didn't know was that I was already working with the Red Cross. If she had looked outside, she would have seen my Red Cross Headquarters Ambulance, for I was grabbing this lunch between jobs. In any event, I hadn't had much time over recent months, having first been a VAD nurse at Botley's Park, Chertsey. This had been a lunatic asylum, and within a month we VADs were taking out stitches and giving injections. Later still, with the Red Cross, working under Lady Limerick from Belgrave Square, I would drive about in my green ambulance, collecting people for hospitals or delivering stores.

One day the ambulance went wrong. There were four very pregnant ladies to take out of the London blitz area to a country hospital. I agreed to drive them in my Bentley, the Red Cross providing petrol coupons. On the way, driving far too fast along the empty bypass towards Maidstone, there was a large bang: the Bentley's engine had blown up. A connecting rod had gone through the side of the crank case – a very embarrassing thing to happen when I was responsible for these ladies who had been dug out of their blitzed houses. They didn't need any more frights or delays when they were about to give birth. Apart from these sort of moments, my days with the Red Cross were not very exciting, but it was a valuable job.

Lois pointed out other pitfalls, too, but they only made me able to concentrate my mind on the possibility of getting into the ATA, even with my infinitesimal qualifications compared to those of the first ATA women.

Dick Fairey, the son of the founder of Fairey Aviation, based at Hayes, Middlesex, who made so many of the aircraft I was later to fly, and Bobby Loewenstein, a Belgian whose financier father had disappeared in mysterious circumstances from an aeroplane over the English Channel in 1928, were already ferry pilots. They were both great friends of mine and, knowing that I had learnt to fly, they suggested that I ought to join.

They cooked up a plan but kept it secret. They arranged to ride with me in Windsor Park one Sunday morning. Bobby rode Tommy the Twin, a dark brown thoroughbred twin racehorse that George Duller, the trainer, had given to my father because it was too small to go into training, while Dick rode my father's heavyweight hunter, Lottery. I rode Bright and Early, a horse in a million, a thoroughbred which had belonged to my stepmother Jackie. She and my father had divorced in May 1940, Jackie having then gone to America with my two baby half-brothers – '. . . to escape the bombs . . .' – so the mare became mine.

This dark mare was really beautiful. She pointed her toes, was elegant, graceful and a comfortable ride – the perfect show-off ladies' hack. She had been taught a wonderful trick. My stepmother had had a fear of being run away with, so this mare had been taught to stop dead when the reins were thrown up to her ears. Even at a canter. I never dared to do it at a gallop. Dick and Bobby said we looked beautiful together – the horse and I, that is, not I and them!

As if by chance, but actually well organized by my two gallant friends, we met A.R.O. Macmillan near the Copper Horse. Macmillan was a former reserve air force officer, now the Chief Flying Instructor for ATA. The boys knew he always rode on a Sunday morning, and knew his timetable. I must say I expect I looked super on that marvellous mare, but the CFI looked very ordinary on a very old rough cob. He wore brown boots with no garters and rough clothes, while the tops of his ears stuck out where he had crammed his bowler hat down on them. I was certainly better at riding a horse than he was, but I knew that I could never ever catch up, or even try to match, his expertise in the air.

During that ride, Dick and Bobby 'sold' him the idea of giving me a flight test. They made it perfectly clear that I had learnt to fly, but carefully omitted to tell the great man that I had only notched up a grand total of ten flying hours.

◇   ◇   ◇

It was now early 1941. Pearl Harbor had not yet taken place, so America had not come into the war. England was still alone and, following the Battle of Britain, was desperately short of pilots of all sorts. So they scraped the bottom of the barrel and out popped me.

The ATA thought that young girls who had started to learn to fly (which was very unusual in those days) had probably picked up quite a lot of extra knowledge whilst hanging around their various flying clubs. Anyway, they had at least had some initiative, which was one of the things the ATA was looking for in their future ferry pilots.

The test with A.R.O. Macmillan was arranged for the following Wednesday, so we had two days of feverish activity. My tiny amount of flying had all been done at Brooklands two years before, and what I might have learnt had long since been forgotten. Luckily the test was to be in a Tiger Moth, which was the type I had flown.

I looked up the speeds for take-off, approach and landing, then took the silver-grey 4$^1/_2$ litre 1936 Bentley up and down the Egham bypass. I opened all the windows and pretended I was seated in a Tiger, looking out of the side windows at the grass verges so that I could judge what the waving grass looked like when I would be easing off the ground or trying to land again at these exact speeds.

Bobby and Dick, together with an RAF admirer of whom I was extremely fond, named Claud Strickland – a fighter pilot with 615 Auxiliary Squadron – sat beside me on the large orange sofa in the outer pannelled hall at Ridgemead and, one after the other, went through those exact speeds, as well as everything else about flying the Tiger Moth. These ranged from switch-on to switch-off; in fact we 'flew' the sofa until I got everything right. Surprisingly they didn't laugh at me, in fact they were very serious. Although Link trainers for blind flying instruction were around, flight simulators had yet to be invented. That sofa was the first one I met!

So arrived the morning of the anticipated entrance test flight, but the aerodrome was waterlogged by a continuous deluge, so the flight was cancelled. There followed another few days of anxious waiting, although it gave me a few more hours to fly the sofa. I became quite proficient – or so I thought.

The great day arrived at last, 9 March 1941. I felt quite detached from reality when I finally found myself flying in the circuit of White Waltham, near Maidenhead. 'Go down the railway line towards Reading,' boomed the CFI's voice in my ears through the Gosport tube – an ingenious contraption whereby an instructor in the rear cockpit could yell into the ears of the pupil. It had nothing to do with radio.

I didn't even know what a railway line looked like from the air, having done 'all' my flying in the circuit of Brooklands where I could always see the large concrete racing track. I suppose I must have got to Reading, then I remember flying back over White Waltham to make a surprisingly good landing after half an hour's flight. So the sofa had been a good simulator.

Macmillan said my application would be considered and that he would write to me in a few days. Dick and Bobby drove me home, cheering me up by saying I had a very scared and white face. I'm sure they were right.

The day after the test, Bobby suggested that I went up with him to hunt in Leicestershire where he had a house near Thorpe Satchville, but the next day the Quorn cancelled its hunt, also due to waterlogging. Bobby said we would ride his horses around his point-to-point course instead.

His groom wheeled out two beautiful point-to-pointers, then we did a circuit of the course. Out came a second pair which looked even more superb, with my horse taking the jumps faultlessly, as did Bobby's. The third pair arrived, but Bobby wanted to go round again on the second lot, so off we went. At the first fence, my horse jumped badly – he wasn't really trying any more. He was obviously used to going round just once, then back to his stable, obviously disliking today's routine. At the second jump he didn't try at all but crashed right through it, and part of him bashed my face in.

I woke up in bed at Bobby's house. I asked the housekeeper to send someone to pick up the broken bits of my teeth if they could be found, so that the dentist could copy them. Funny how the mind works at such times, for I certainly didn't know how badly I was injured.

I was taken to London in an ambulance with Bobby sitting crying beside me, because he said he felt so responsible for messing me up. He also told me that he loved me and wanted to marry me, no matter what I looked like. That was encouraging . . . or was it? What did he mean, no matter what I looked like?

I was patched up in the London Clinic, where one of the most painful things was being bumped down to the cellars on a trolley every night because of air raids. After a while I refused to be taken down, saying I preferred to be bombed in my bed upstairs. I felt sure it wouldn't have hurt any less. After various operations for the broken-up jaw, a tooth was taken out from my mashed-up sinuses just beneath my right eye. The jaws were wired up and as the risk of blindness receded I was allowed to see my friends.

Claud Strickland took one look at me and never came back. Having been my most important love, this was devastating. He moved on to another, more attractive girl, but I didn't blame him. I thought things weren't so bad, as Bobby had told me that he would put up with me and my future ugliness.

Every evening when he finished flying, Bobby drove to London in order to see me in hospital between six and seven o'clock. He went out round the town afterwards then used to drive back to his house near White Waltham to be ready to fly the next day. After ten days of this, in the early hours of one morning, he drove his Bentley into a wall on the way back. The car was a write-off, but Bobby went flying that very next day and died in a twin-engined Blenheim bomber. Coming in to land at White Waltham under single-engine safety speed, he pulled the idle cut-out on one engine instead of the pitch change and flipped over into the deck. Pilot's error. Not to be wondered at.

Once more I was devastated. No Claud, no Bobby, plus no face. Then to rub it all in, the letter arrived from Macmillan to say that ATA would accept me as a ferry pilot and would I report as soon as convenient.

Part of me wanted to report next day, but that would have frightened everyone to death. Instead I had to write a letter. 'Dear Mister Macmillan . . .'

In the event it took me six months to mend. During that time, the wonderful ATA training programme was set up. If I had joined them six months earlier I could not have survived with the little knowledge I had of the air. I was given another test flight by the head of the Training Pool, Captain A. D. Pickup, who told me 40-odd years later that I had turned up wearing a leopard-skin coat. It had belonged to my stepmother but she had left her furs behind when she went to sunny California, so I used to raid her wardrobe. I must have impressed him, or perhaps it was only the coat?

Captain Pickup said I looked far too attractive to know anything about flying – I didn't – but his flattery on my new looks boosted my confidence. It was nice of him not to mention my scars. He passed me out anyway, so I was able to join the Air Transport Auxiliary.

Meanwhile, Claud had been shot down and killed in his Hurricane towards the end of October 1941, while Dick Fairey had lost his wife in the London blitz. He then lost both legs when his ship was torpedoed on the way to the USA to take up a test pilot job over there. He had to endure four days in an open boat before being rescued. The war was reaching out and tearing at my heart.

Dick's story was particularly tragic. A childhood friend, he was still flying with ATA when his father, Richard, was in Washington, USA, with the Exchange Control Commission. Crossing the Atlantic in those early wartime days meant either freezing in the back of an unheated four-engined aeroplane or going by boat. Dick elected to go by sea – he thought it would be more comfortable. Little did he know . . .

Ships and their naval escort vessels always kept together in convoy, to afford some protection against marauding U-boats, but the skipper of Dick's ship went ahead of the convoy. He was smuggling gold, Dick later told me, so wanted to get to his destination early to get a good price. He had done it all before, apparently, but if he got away with this final voyage he would have been financially set up for life.

All alone, they were picked off by a U-boat. When the torpedo struck, the ship heeled over sideways. Dick was on the loo, wearing shirt, trousers and bedroom slippers. With difficulty he crawled along the wall of the corridor to his cabin and managed to reach down to the hook behind the door to grab his flying coat, but he couldn't risk dropping down into the cabin beneath him or he wouldn't have been able to climb out again. His shoes and flying boots had slid to the bottom of the wall out of reach.

When he emerged on deck, he found it had only been possible to launch the lifeboats from one side because of the angle of the ship. All possible boats had been dropped into the water, some turning over on impact. All were overfilled with people and only one was still attached to the ship. Dick shinned down its ropes to land in the last floating, over-filled, open lifeboat.

The Germans in the submarine, which had surfaced, jeered and shot at some of the other boats and sank them. Dick's boat included some Lascars, the Captain and an Alsatian dog.

They were in quite a spot, for it was the height of winter, and they were some 350 miles from Newfoundland. There was a compass aboard and, after noticing a certain inefficiency in navigation, Dick took over to steer the boat back into the shipping lanes. There should have been 'iron rations' of biscuits, chocolate and so on, but these had been lost or stolen prior to launch. There was nothing to eat except a couple of packets of (rationed) fruit drops that Dick happened to have in his pocket.

It was freezing in the open boat. Dick kept first one finger and then another warm by sticking his hands between his legs, but his toes froze in his bedroom slippers.

Meanwhile, his father, having heard the news about his son's ship being overdue, pulled all available strings. After a while, Dick had steered back into the shipping lanes. Finally, a Catalina flying-boat sighted the tiny boat after four days and four nights. They were picked up by a ship coming away from America and taken to Greenland.

In those days not so much was known about frostbite as is understood today. It is said that very frozen people were laid on deck outside as they weren't expected to survive anyhow, but most of them did: whereas the less frozen people were warmed up inside, to their detriment.

Dick only had frozen toes, so was heated up inside, as were all his other shipmates – and the dog. Like meat out of a deep-freeze, they should have been defrosted gradually, so they all went bad before reaching Greenland. The Lascar who had been on the tiller lost his hands.

Dick was brought to London. I went to see him in the London Clinic, by which time it was necessary for his gangrenous feet to come off. Dick decided on a full amputation of the legs at a certain distance under the knees, because although a longer leg only without feet might have seemed more attractive, it would have made a second amputation later in life more probable because of the lack of circulation around the lower limbs encased in artificial legs.

In spite of losing both legs, Dick still flew, drove his Lagonda and other cars, learnt to fly a post-war Sikorsky S.54 helicopter, shot and played golf. The only thing he gave up doing was dancing, but he didn't like that anyhow.

He also used his artificial legs to advantage after the war, for when the Socialist government decreed that people could only take £45 with them when going abroad, he would fly his Rapide to his destination with his tin legs stuffed with pound notes so he could have a good evening out.

Chapter 5

The Blue-Nosed Spitfire

THE ATA TRAINING was second to none. It was thorough and extremely well worked out. The flying training was the best ever provided anywhere for any pilots, before or since. How else could the myriad of individuals of all shapes and sizes, including 28 nationalities, of all different upbringings, occupations and intellectual capacities, have been moulded together into such an efficient organization as the ATA became?

By the time I joined in late 1941, the system was as follows. After we had had medical checks and signed a form saying we wouldn't pass on secrets, our lessons began in a classroom. Subjects covered included meteorology, balloons that surrounded towns and factories, map reading, signals, technical data, engines and, of course, navigation. The last was, to me, the most important: I was to fly fast aircraft without radio to assist me (radios were not installed in some of the aircraft straight out of a factory) in all weathers, just with a map and compass. Some of the early aircraft didn't even have a gyro.

We were not taught to fly on instruments because we were not supposed to fly above cloud. We had some short-range aircraft and might not be able to get down before running out of fuel. This happened to Amy Johnson.

The next stage after passing out from the classroom stuff was dual and then solo flight in an open-cockpit Magister light aircraft, followed by 30 cross-country flights, some of them in a Hawker Hart. After getting away with that, the next stage was dual, then solo, in a Miles Master, a training aircraft which had a tendency to drop a wing if care was not taken on a turn. One of the women spun in that way.

The next stage was the North American Harvard trainer. Its Wasp engine sounded like an angry bumble-bee but noisier. This time the instructor sat in the back seat so one felt more on one's own for the first time. No comforting head in front to clear up one's mistakes, only the heavy breathing down the speaking tubes connected to my helmet. For all these aircraft there were technical and engine lessons before flying began.

There were also technical courses given by a dark, beady-eyed man from BOAC (British Overseas Airways Corporation, today once more British Airways) by the name of Gribble. He really could not understand how dumb some people like me were when it came to understanding the most simple of his explanations about engines, airframes, aerodynamics, etc, etc. I didn't even know how my car worked when I started flying with ATA, so most of his carefully explained data was far above my head.

When we had completed all 30 cross-countries and finished listening to all that Gribble had to tell us, we were ceremoniously presented with our 'wings'. A great moment.

The reasons for making us do so many cross-countries were for us to gain general flying experience, become familiar with the country, and see for ourselves the actual whereabouts of the many hazards such as balloon barrage areas. These were enormous hydrogen gas-filled silver balloons on very heavy cables which went up to cloud base or to 5,000 feet, placed around sensitive areas such as factories, certain aerodromes, towns and cities to keep German aeroplanes high up, accurate bombing being difficult through cloud or from altitude, nor could their fighters' ground-straffing come off. It was also easier for our early radar tracking and anti-aircraft defences to target higher flying intruders. We marked these barrages on our maps in heavy red pencil so that we could decide routes to give them a wide berth. The cables were dangerous to fly into; I think they got more of us than the Germans.

By landing at various aerodromes, we soon found out exactly where we would have to take our aircraft and get our delivery chits signed when we later needed to deliver an aeroplane there.

Many of the early wartime RAF fighters overheated on the ground. The 'kettle boiling' on a Spitfire frequently happened when we had to taxi a long distance, due to lack of airflow through the radiator duct which was under the starboard wing. This duct was a clever aerodynamic design, making the radiator much smaller and with less drag than it would otherwise have had.

All Rolls-Royce engines from First World War Falcons and Eagles were liquid-cooled. The Merlins in the Spitfires used ethylene glycol. This allowed the water temperature to increase to 120°C. Higher than that, steam blew out from the header tank behind the propeller. Sometimes, in combat above 25,000 feet, fighter pilots using a lot of power could overheat, steam then blowing back over their windscreens and freezing out the visibility. That did not happen to me, but twice I had to switch off to cool the engine . . . Most embarrassing, leaving overheated Spits lying around blocking busy taxi tracks, so it was essential, after landing, to taxi in to the dispersal area in as short a time as possible.

Finally came the three hours in the school Hurricanes. All alone. No instructor's head in front or behind. On my own. Up to me. Break my neck, or the aircraft – or both.

After this it was Ferry Flight, also at White Waltham in March 1942, with the first deliveries, followed by a trial posting for a few weeks to one of the several ferry pools around the country – '. . . to see how you get on'. I was sent to No. 15 Ferry Pool, Hamble, the first all-women ferry pool, and did a lot of taxi-pilot work in Fairchilds to gain flying experience by fetching and delivering other more senior pilots to and from their jobs.

The next stage was a solid assignment to a pool. As luck would have it, I got back to White Waltham, to No. 1 Ferry Pool. It was a happy posting for me as it was close to my father's house at Englefield Green, so I could live at home and drive to the airfield each day.

After a little more ferrying, and a few new types of light and fighter aircraft (Class I & II), I was back at school to move on to light twins. We learnt on the Airspeed Oxford (Class III). Again the same programme was followed: first the classroom, then on to dual and solo flights. In this way the pilot progressed gradually and, in my case, smoothly, without anxiety.

Every type of aircraft – training, operational Royal Air Force or Fleet Air Arm, or American – was put into a category or class. Pilots learnt to fly one aircraft in each class and they could then safely operate any other aircraft in that same class. They moved steadily upward to more complicated things, going back to their pools between courses and ferrying everything as well as the machines in their newly qualified class. So once a pilot became a dab hand at the latest aircraft in each class, he or she moved back to their relative pool.

ATA pilots could not have flown so many different types of aircraft without their ATA handling notes. This little cardboard-covered, loose-leaf book measuring 6 inches by 4¼ inches had every conceivable aircraft in it that we might be expected to fly, each on a separate page. For every aircraft there were potted details of what it was necessary to know before and during a flight. It contained all the take-off, climb, cruise and landing speeds, plus revs and boost, temperatures and consumption: everything under the sun that we needed to know.

We sometimes flew several different types in one day, so it was not possible to remember all the relevant speeds, etc. I used to mug up the take-off, climb and cruise details and then, when I got to the other end, read up the landing details whilst in the circuit. If we were given a new type, we were supposed to read the maker's full handling notes but there wasn't always time. The ATA ferry pilot's handling notes were sufficient.

The various classes of aircraft that we flew all through the war were:

Class I –   light: such as Magister, Swordfish, Gladiator;
Class II –   fighter: such as Hurricane, Spitfire, Defiant, Mustang;
Class II+ –   'difficult' singles: like Tomahawk, Typhoon, Tempest, Sea Otter and Walrus;
Class III –   light twins: like Oxford, Whitley, Anson, Hampden and Blenheim;
Class IV –   heavy twins: Wellington, Manchester;
Class IV+ –   'difficult' twins: such as Hudson, Marauder;

Class V – tricycle undercarriage: Albemarle, Boston, Havoc,
Aircobra and Mitchell;
Class VI – large flying-boats, off the water:
four-engined aircraft, Lancaster, Halifax, Stirling,
Fortress or Liberator.

We learnt a code that covered every aircraft likely to be flown by us, a drill of vital actions to be used by ATA pilots on all flights. I still remember them:

Before take-off:

H – Hydraulics
T – Trimmers
T – Throttle friction
M – Mixture
P – Pitch
P – Petrol
F – Flaps
G – Gills (including temperature, carb heat and icers)
G – Gauges check
F – Fuel boosters
U – Unlock controls
S – Superchargers
T – Tail wheel lock

In the landing circuit:

P – Petrol
B – Brakes
F – Fuel boosters on
H – Hydraulics
U – Undercarriage
M – Mixture
F – Flaps
P – Pitch
G – Gills (and carb heat)

After landing:

T – Tail wheel unlocked
G – Gills open. Gauges check
F – Flaps up (half-a-crown fine if you forgot)

And, of course, little things like turning off the petrol, caging the gyro, shutting the hood or doors, and not leaving your maps and overnight bag in the cockpit before going to get the delivery chit signed.

When the operations officers worked out the programme in the morning before the pilots reported in, they reckoned an hour on the ground for each collection and another hour for delivery. If we were held up with one of our flights, something went U/S (unserviceable), and the nearest pool could not fix us up with another suitable link-up job, then we usually got stuck out for the night. But fancy being given so many lovely things to fly, and be paid for it too! The women pilots were paid less then their male counterparts. This was considered to be perfectly natural and was accepted at the time. At least we were eventually allowed to wear trousers with our uniforms.

Women were still considered second-class material, even though they were doing exactly the same flying job and taking similar risks. We didn't mind at all. All we wanted to do was to fly, and most of our deliveries were absolutely brand new. Unfortunately, a few were very, very old indeed – clapped out and war-weary – and certified fit for one flight only. With those, I kept my fingers crossed and hoped it wouldn't be my last flight too.

As a matter of interest, our ATA Flight Instructions were as follows:

Pilots had to fly 'contact' – in sight of the ground. Originally we were cleared to fly in 1,000 yards' visibility with a 600-foot (vertical) ceiling, later extended to 1,500 yards and 800 feet clear of cloud as aircraft types got faster. This was extended again even later. In worse conditions than those laid down, pilots were supposed to put down or turn back. Of course, whether we did or not sometimes depended on the date waiting at the home base, or the star rating of the possible funk-hole ahead.

If from the ground the weather seemed nearly unflyable or beneath the weather minima laid down, most of us would take off to have a look. We did a circuit. It often didn't seem so bad once we were up in it. I used to do that, and then set my watch and a very accurate course from the centre of the aerodrome and proceed gingerly. Though that is hardly the right word for flying 'contact' in lousy conditions at several hundred miles an hour.

One misty morning very early in my ATA training, I was flying a Miles Magister into the sun on my way towards Gloucester, where there was a balloon barrage around the town and the nearby Gloster aeroplane factory. I was pretty certain I knew exactly where I was, but to be quite sure, not wanting to run into a cloud stuffed with a balloon or a mist-obscured balloon cable, I turned back on my reciprocal course. I could see better in the mist with the sun behind me. Whilst deciding on my course again, I looked at my maps at the same time as I circled.

Having pinpointed my position exactly, I saw an octagonal concrete structure below and flew around it whilst working out my new course. I saw a lot of RAF men on the concrete waving and pointing with feverish activity, although I couldn't work out why. Suddenly I noticed a huge, elephantine silver balloon coming down just above me, realizing in that same instant that I must have been flying round and round its cable. If I'd hit that it could have sliced through my 'plane like a cheese wire.

I had already become aware of the presence of some sort of guardian angel in my life who insisted on looking after me, and who now, since joining ATA, was having His work cut out trying to help me. I should certainly like to thank Him for keeping it up. He really has been busy. I knew *He* was trying to tell me that my flying career – not to mention my life – were going to go on after all. My guardian angel was a reassuring fellow.

The grass at White Waltham had taken quite a hammering from constant use by the school's aircraft, together with the taxi and other movements of No. 1 Ferry Pool. In the early spring of 1942 it was decided to put on a top surface dressing to improve the quality.

Immediately this had been done, we had a spate of tyre bursts on take-offs and landings. There was a production shortage of rubber tyres together with some dented aircraft and upset pilots, none of which was conducive towards the running of an efficient ATA. The top dressing, liberally scattered all over White Waltham, not only on those parts mainly used for take-offs and landings, but also on the surrounding parking and taxiway areas, was found to have contained tin-tacks, nails, nuts and bolts, as well as little bits of metal and glass – whether by negligence, or sabotage towards the ATA or the war effort, was not for us to decide.

ATA work was suspended. All of us were drafted to crawl on hands and knees in lines across the aerodrome to pick up the offending matter. It was hot and tiring work, and all to no avail. We missed so much that magnet-bearing and sweeping-up trucks were brought in. Meanwhile, the taxi-Ansons, in transit aircraft, delivery aircraft, etc were moved to '40 acres', a small collection of flat fields between White Waltham and Reading previously used for forced landing practice by the school.

ATA operated successfully if not without difficulty. Things were slowed up, the pilots driven first from HQ, No. 1 Pool, to their first jobs or in transits on '40 acres'. School training was in the way of the deliveries, so stopped. I was told to go somewhere else, anywhere, to practise my forced landings, having already done some with my instructor before White Waltham was closed.

Off I flew, found a delightful field surrounded with trees, pretended at various heights that my Tiger's engine had cut, avoided the trees and did several pretty arrivals. The inevitable happened: taxying to take off, I got bogged. Bright enough not to risk tipping up, I abandoned the Tiger and walked to the nearest farmhouse, whose owner gave me a lift to the Great Western Railway to return to the school.

I found my instructor, who was furious: 'You always get things wrong,' he yelled, 'you'll never make a ferry pilot. I told you to do precautionary landings. That does not mean *actually* landing, only down to the position to do so before going round again without the wheels on the ground.' Well, he hadn't explained that very clearly. We had always done complete practice landings together. But '40 acres' was different from any old boggy field.

The Tiger had to be brought back on a conveyor. Some cows which had been let into the field after milking had had a good lick at the doped wing edges, making the machine a flying hazard before repaint.

Many men who could not get into the Royal Air Force as bomber or fighter pilots because they could not pass the strict RAF medical or, as I have said before, because they were over 25, joined the ATA instead.

One day, when I was still a very new recruit, I opened the door into the Common Room at White Waltham, to hear a lot of noise going on inside. I peeped nervously round the door to see two of our one-armed pilots, R. A. Corrie and Charles Dutton, later Lord Sherborne, waving their respective single arms about while having the most furious row about which arm it was better not to have in order to fly. 'Oh, I can fly an Oxford!' said one. 'Ha – but you can't fly a Wimpy like I can!' retorted the other.

With twin-engined aeroplanes, because of their lack of (opposite) arms, it just depended on the positioning of various controls whether either of these two could manage to fly certain aircraft or not. All I know is, that whenever I have been temporarily incapacitated with one limb or other, it has been frighteningly inconvenient and downright awkward. Yet those two men delivered fighters, and some bombers, with only one arm each, when often I would have liked to have been an octopus.

Later on, when I got to know him better, I asked Charles Dutton however he managed with, say, a Spitfire? He said, 'Well, you see, Diana, I trim the aircraft and I set the friction nuts very tight on the throttle and boost levers, and I open up, with the control column between my knees, and if I've got the friction nuts right, the throttle and boost don't creep back on me. I take my (only!) hand off the throttle block and transfer it to the stick until I am airborne. Then once again, I put the stick between my knees, put up the undercarriage, throttle back to climbing revs and boost, then take the stick again for the climb. The same drill, of course, also goes for the cruise settings.'

'Yes,' I said, 'but what about setting the gyro, and so on?'

'Oh, that's easy,' he answered, 'but setting the compass is a bit tricky. I'm rather inclined to go into a dive when I lean forward to reach the compass [which is set low down between one's feet] because I can't open my knees which must hold the stick.'

'Well, how do you fly *and* hold your maps at the same time?' I continued.

'Well, I've got my mouth, you know; but I have dropped things now and then. It's a bit awkward sometimes to pick them up!'

How he was able to open and shut the cockpit hood was another question, for I always seemed to need both arms, plus a lot of strength, as hoods often stuck. And what about landings? 'Coming into land is easy,' he confided, 'I just pull the throttle and boost right back, then put everything down at once. I can't do a power-assisted approach and landing in anything – it has to be like engine-off! I don't usually have a problem with hoods.'

'But what if you bodge it and have to go round again?' I persisted.

'Well, I don't!' he said.

A.T.A. Accident Report:
On the 26th April, 1942, First Officer the Hon. C. Dutton (a one-armed pilot) was ferrying a Spitfire from Lyneham to Biggin Hill. When he had got about a mile beyond Kenley he experienced a complete engine failure due to a broken connecting rod. He succeeded in lowering his undercarriage and flaps and in landing his aircraft at Kenley in a high cross-wind on the runway without further damage.

He received a Certificate of Commendation.

We also had that First World War veteran Stuart Keith-Jopp. He was a real workhorse in spite of his disabilities which I mentioned earlier. He flew many different types and I can't remember seeing his name in any of the accident reports. He was determined to fly a Tempest and was given a delivery chit for one out of Hawarden, a ferry pool and factory south of the River Dee near Chester.

Charlie Moore, the flight engineer there, helped get him into the Tempest, where he found the only thing Jopp couldn't manage was the tail wheel locking device in the cockpit. Charlie jacked up the Tempest's tail, but even with the weight off the tail wheel, Jopp still couldn't lock it. Impossible for a one-handed man.

So determined was Jopp to fly this fighter, which was a new type to him, that Charlie Moore walked out beside the aircraft to the top of the runway and, when it was turned into wind, leant into the cockpit before take-off and locked the tail wheel for him.

'You're on your own now,' he said and left him to get airborne. There was no accident report re taxying around after landing with a locked tail wheel, so Jopp must have found someone at the end of his delivery runway to unlock it for him before he turned off.

Another man who was at White Waltham while I was there was the actor Norman Shelley, also one of our ATA pilots. He used to suddenly disappear and seemed to get a lot of extra days off compared to the rest of us. We didn't know then, but it came out long after the war that he was frequently asked to pretend to be Winston Churchill on the radio when Churchill's pressure of work or secret absence abroad kept him from talking to the nation himself. No-one could tell the difference.

I certainly had no illusions about what I was letting myself in for in joining ATA. While I hoped it would be fun, I was also aware of the dangers. One of our American pilots, R. W. 'Bill' Reisert, had an experience in February 1942 of which he reminded me only recently, which shows some of the dangers we lived with.

Bill was flying a Defiant out of Prestwick, going south. He ran into bad weather so climbed to avoid the high hill by Millom, losing control in the cloud. He panicked and baled out. As he floated down, his right foot felt very cold and, glancing down, he found that the boot was missing. As he descended the boot came rolling past him, turning over and over. Looking down at it, he then saw the glow where his aircraft hit the ground and burnt for a few seconds. Moments later another glow appeared.

He landed safely, finding himself in the grounds of a hospital. Nurses rushed out, dusted him down, retrieved his flying boot which had landed a few feet away, and took him inside. After being seen by the doctors and pronounced fit, he wanted to get to the railway station, but the only transport available was an amubulance. He climbed in the back, taking great care of his bundled-up parachute, but then the driver said he had to go somewhere else first.

Bill was driven towards the high hill, passing his burnt-out Defiant on the way, to the scene of another aircraft crash. That was the second glow he had seen. There was nothing whole of this one left except the tail – which showed it to have been a Beaufighter – sticking out of the ground. The two-man Polish crew were both dead and the medics put the corpses on the floor of the ambulance, covering them up with Bill's parachute – much to his chagrin. He felt fond of that 'chute as it had just saved his life.

'Hop in,' they said.

He was then driven to the station, keeping company with the two stiffs in the back. It seems they too had been caught out by the same lump of weather, but they had hit the hill instead of jumping out.

On 6 April 1942, an extremely gusty, windy morning, I was told to do a cross-country in a Magister from White Waltham to Henlow, where I was to land. I was then to fly on to Debden, a Royal Air Force Fighter Station in Essex, turn over it, head on to Wattisham, a Norfolk aerodrome, then to Feltwell, before landing at Sywell, near Northampton. Taking off once more, I would then fly back to White Waltham.

When I got over Debden, the wind and gusts had really become strong. In fact it had quickly become a question of me or my breakfast – I must get down! Not being supposed to land there, only to circle it, I nevertheless made a good approach and touchdown, explained my problem, and was greeted in a friendly manner. I was taken to the Officers' Mess to wait until the weather sorted itself out.

As soon as I walked in, I saw an old acquaintance, 'Sas' de Mier, one of the only Mexicans then in our Air Force. His brother 'Mo' de Mier was the only Mexican in a kilt, being an officer in the Gordon Highlanders. Sas was an air gunner on a Boston III (*W8358* 'A'), which had force-landed there the day before after returning from a raid. He introduced me to his crew, Squadron Leader Anderson and Pilot Officer Young, and to a lot of Debden-based fighter pilots. I rang my CO and was told to go on with my cross-country when the wind dropped.

I had lunch in the Mess, sitting next to a squadron leader, the commander of No. 65 Fighter Squadron. He was a well-built, thickset young man, dark with blue eyes, but with one of the worst haircuts I had ever seen! None of his hair seemed to stay put, making the top of his head look completely square. We got along fine.

His name was Humphrey Gilbert, descendant of Sir Humphrey Gilbert of Revesby Abbey, Lincolnshire. Joining the RAF pre-war on a short-service commission, he had fought in the Battle of Britain, shot down several enemy aircraft and been shot down himself and wounded. The following year he had been a flight commander with the first American Eagle Squadron here at RAF Debden, before taking command of 65 Squadron on the same base. It was the time when Fighter Command was beginning to operate out over the Channel or over Northern France, and Gilbert was leading his men on these offensive operations.

After lunch the wind had dropped a bit, so I went down to the Magister, but try and try, the thing wouldn't start up. The ground crew said they'd take a look at it and give me a call at the Mess when it was fixed. They didn't, so I stayed the night, having a happy evening with Sas and his Boston crew, Squadron Leader Humphrey Gilbert, and some of the other pilots, including a dashing flying officer, Tony Bartley DFC, one of Gilbert's flight commanders. Tony had also fought in the Battle of Britain with 92 Squadron earlier over Dunkirk with another acquaintance of mine – Bob Tuck. Tony was to finish the war with a distinguished record of fighter operations both in England and in the Middle East. After the war he was to marry the film actress Deborah Kerr.

I had first met Tony at a dance at Stowe School, where he had been a pupil. I suppose I was about a year older than him. It was Tony who introduced me to his CO, Humphrey Gilbert; the two men were close friends as well as squadron and flight commander. Tony was known by his nickname of 'Bolshie'; he was a very attractive and lively young man who was to visit Ridgemead on occasions. Tony once did me an extremely good turn, though I don't think to this day he knows how good a turn it was.

My father, who during the war was an RAF wing commander working in Lord Beaverbrook's Ministry of Aircraft Production in London (he had been a captain in the Royal Artillery in the First World War, seeing action in France, Egypt and Palestine), had a girlfriend at that time called Vera Scott, who had been around for a couple of years. She was, no doubt, very sexy. She kept asking me about all my admirers. 'Is he rich?' was always the first query. If they weren't she left them alone, otherwise she usually set her cap at them and got them. So I loathed her and was obviously jealous of her presence in my father's life.

When I was at home, we also nearly came to blows every day when tea came in, over who would act as hostess and pour the tea. I usually grabbed the teapot first but sometimes Vera won. She was a top-class gold-digger and I didn't think her worthy of my father's attentions.

One sunny weekend we were all in the bar at Ridgemead when Tony and Vera went out into the garden. She returned later, somewhat ruffled, with smeared lipstick and with her blouse torn. My father saw this and as my jaw dropped he winked at me. I chalked up a score point and realized I should not have been so worried, nor have underestimated my father in relation to this current girlfriend.

Anyway, the next day at Debden, the weather was good but I still couldn't get the Magister to start! I hadn't understood much of the ATA technical lectures so had no idea what was wrong, and if the mechanics couldn't get it going, how could I? I telephoned my CO, explaining my problem, which he took very well considering the shortage of school aeroplanes.

Meantime, Sas's Boston had been repaired and the crew took me up with them on their test flight (1 hour 20 minutes), during which time I suddenly realized that in such an aeroplane, I was very close to the real war! Humphrey Gilbert also showed me his Spitfire. It had a blue nose and I admitted that I hoped one day to be able to fly a Spit.

By the afternoon, the Magister was still proving obstinate. All we could get out of it was a dull 'clank' from the trolley 'acc' battery. I hardly dared speak to my CO, who sounded, and I don't wonder, somewhat unbelieving of my story. However, Humphrey Gilbert talked to him for me, explained what was happening, and said that I should have to stay over yet another night. I rather gathered, from the other end of the telephone, that Diana Barnato had become extremely unpopular with her CO.

After three days, suddenly the Magister started. Without too much further delay, I was off to complete my cross-country flight. However, in those few days Humphrey and I had fallen head-over-heels in love with each other. In the following few weeks we met in London and danced all night. When I was due for a day's leave, Humphrey picked me up at Heathrow – then just a small grass 'factory' airfield belonging to Fairey Aviation – in another Magister (*T9883*) and flew me back to Debden. Two mornings later I was flown back to White Waltham in the same aircraft by a Bob Sarll.

Over the next couple of weeks, Flying Officer Sarll became the dogsbody who was to fetch me several times at the end of my flying day at White Waltham, with orders to bring me back from Debden early enough to fly the next morning. He was a dear man, but a hopeless navigator. After he had got us lost a couple of times, on April 28 and 29, I firmly took over the navigation.

My ATA training continued and so did my romance. Humphrey and I decided to get married, even though we had known each other for less than a month. On the night of 2 May, he was coming to my flat on the corner of Tite Street and Chelsea Embankment in order to arrange all the final details, but he didn't turn up. I rang Debden but couldn't get through to him, nor to one of the controllers, Bill Ross, who was a great friend of his. I thought that Humphrey must have been flying and put down somewhere, hoping he would be back by morning. The next day, as soon as I reached White Waltham, I tried again, but to no avail.

My job for that day was another cross-country in a Tiger Moth which was to take me to Hatfield, North Weald and – hurray! – Debden. I was to land only at Hatfield. Everyone knew by now that I knew my way around Debden, so I didn't dare land there.

Reaching Debden, I circled, but I couldn't see Humphrey's blue-nosed Spitfire anywhere. When I got back to White Waltham later, I rang again from the call-box outside the Mess. I was then passed from one person to another until, after some long time, I was put on to the Station Commander, Group Captain Johnnie Peel. It was he who had the unenviable task of telling me that Humphrey had been killed the previous day.

This was the first time that someone who really meant something to me was no longer around. I couldn't stop crying, but I didn't want other people to see me, so I stayed in that 'phone-box. Finally, the one-armed pilot, Corrie, who was hanging around outside waiting to use the 'phone, rapped on the glass, which brought me to my senses. Then he saw I was crying so he put his one arm around my shoulders and tried to comfort me.

I went into the Common Room and the CO called me to the hatch that went through to his office. He looked at me strangely, I suppose because my eyes were red. He told me to fly a Hart. He was obviously very busy and I was a pain in the neck to him anyway, so instead of the usual ceremonial, he just slapped a pair of ATA wings on the ledge and said, 'Here, Miss Barnato, are your wings. But, Miss Barnato, because you have your wings it does not necessarily mean you can fly', and slammed the hatch shut.

The next day was my leave day. I went to Humphrey's funeral. Nobody told me what had happened and I don't believe I asked. I just thought he had been shot down. Dead is dead without any unnecessary trimmings or explanations. The day after the funeral I was given another cross-country, this time in a Hart, with Debden once more one of my turning points. I began to wonder whether my CO was giving me Debden as a turning point once more to test me, to see if I could be trusted not to land there. I was alright until I got above Debden airfield, then I howled so loudly that it was a good thing no-one else was with me.

The wind changed by the time I got back to White Waltham and we were landing towards the east. I put the Hart down at the end furthest away from the control tower and hangars, then tried to turn cross-wind to taxi in. The Hart and Hind series had been developed by Hawkers to cover a large field of RAF requirements, coming into service in 1930. The Hart was a big biplane with a Kestrel engine, but it had no brakes and just a tail skid rather than tail wheel. The wind that day was so strong that I couldn't taxi across the aerodrome, and all the Hart did, no matter how much I tried, was to go round and round in circles, each circle taking me further and further away from where I wanted to go. No-one was going to come out to help me by putting a hand on the wing (She's a cadet, let her find out!). Finally I burst into tears again, but this time through frustration.

I put her into wind, switched off, then trudged back around the edge of the aerodrome, lugging my heavy parachute with me. When I got to the tarmac, all the other pilots waiting there burst out laughing. I didn't join in. My sense of humour was lying beside Humphrey in his grave.

It was over two years before I found out what had happened to the man I had planned to marry. I had known him less than a month before he was taken from me. I'd met him on 6 April and he was killed on 2 May. On 16 December 1944, I had to land at dusk in a Mosquito XXX (*NT241* 'G') at Chilbolton, between Andover and Winchester. I was trying to get to No. 456 Squadron at RAF Ford on the south coast, and was determined to get there as I had a date with Tony Bartley, but I ran into a lot of snow near the coast which was impenetrable, so after several tries I went back to Chilbolton, where I was stuck for the night.

When I finally got back to my base the next day, one of the Air Service Training engineers told me, 'A young fellow came in early, before the snow, in a Spitfire, to have something done to it. He was looking for you, waited a bit before he found out from Ops that you had put down somewhere, then went off by himself for dinner.' The young fellow was Tony – now a squadron leader, DFC and bar, and so on.

'Oh, yes,' I replied, 'and do you know he is one of the best aerobatic pilots on Spits in the RAF?'

'I don't know about that,' said the engineer, 'but wasn't he the fellow who got another pilot let off from a court-martial for taking a WAAF up on his lap from Biggin Hill?' The pal had been Gordon Brettell, who had flown with a WAAF on his lap in order to take her to a dance. Tony testified in Gordon's defence, having got the famous Spitfire test pilot, Jeffrey Quill, and Joe Smith, Supermarine's chief designer, to write that, in itself, the act of taking up a second person in a Spitfire did not put the aircraft in danger. This was supported by figures, calculations of centre of gravity and so on. When Tony was asked how he could prove it, he said because he had done it himself! Brettell got off, but was later taken prisoner over Brest and died at the hands of the Gestapo following his recapture after 'The Great Escape' from Stalag Luft III in 1944, when 50 escaping officers were shot.

I then remembered one lovely sunny day in April 1942 when Humphrey and Tony had been sitting around at Debden at 'Readiness', waiting for a call to 'Scramble', and laughing and joking about how Tony had managed to get Gordon out of the court-martial. They said that they had also once flown together in one Spitfire when their light two-seater aircraft had broken down and they needed to get to London urgently – for a party. They had been very severely reprimanded by the CO at Hendon, where they landed, nearly being given a court-martial for endangering His Majesty's aircraft, but in the end the CO let them off.

'Well,' the engineer went on, 'those friends of yours got away with it, but that little escapade had an unfortunate sequel.' I listened in grim silence, remembering. 'His squadron commander, a chap named Gilbert, was killed shortly afterwards in the same way, doing that very thing. But it wasn't a tiny WAAF he took up, but a big heavy controller. I suppose they couldn't get the stick back. Anyway, they were both killed. What a waste.'

Not only that, thought I. It was only now that I found out the truth about Humphrey's demise.

Humphrey had everything that made up a good fighter pilot – dash! flair! try anything! great bravery in taking risks! The whole squadron was under pressure at that time after suffering many losses, so they were given 48 hours off. During that time, perhaps because of those very qualities allied to the irresponsibility of youth, those things caught him out.

A few days later I rang Tony, who confirmed the story. He also said it had been Bill Ross with Humphrey in the Spitfire, which was why I had been unable to speak to him either. Tony then added, 'By the way, it was Humphrey's idea to keep you at Debden all the time when you first arrived in your Magister. The ground crew were all sworn to secrecy. We took all the plugs out!'

✦ *Chapter 6* ✦

Life with the Ferry Pilots

DOUGLAS 'POPPA' FAIRWEATHER was a legend in his own lifetime. There was no-one (and there were some, I'll tell you) who could, and did, fly so well in such terrible weather or nil visibility. He was a burly, jovial man, a lovable character with piercing 'navigator's eyes'. He must have had a natural homing instinct or inbuilt personal radar. Some people called him Captain Foulweather. I suppose because of his name he felt it incumbent upon himself to prove he wasn't just a fair-weather flyer.

One of the rules of ATA was that we had to carry maps with us. That made sense, as we didn't have any radio. Poppa Fairweather always carried a map. I'll tell you about it.

On 19 September 1942, I arrived up at Prestwick in a Miles Master Mark I (*N7509*) and was prepared to take the night train south as I had no return flying job. Those freezing, darkened, uncomfortable journeys I mentioned earlier.

I was bemoaning my fate while awaiting transport to the railway station when Poppa Fairweather landed and came into the Mess. He put a fatherly hand on my arm and said, 'There, there; you come back with me.' I had only just stopped talking on the tie-line to the CO of the Training Pool at White Waltham, who had given me orders to get down by train. 'I can't go with you unless you ask Captain Pickup first,' I said. 'Don't worry your little head,' he replied, picking up the 'phone. In next to no time, I heard his organizing ability in full swing.

'I've got an Oxford trip from here to Belfast, and an Anson from there to White Waltham. I'll get her to Waltham in the morning long before she could possibly get down from Paddington after her night train journey; and she'll be fit to fly and not tired out.'

So it was arranged. We flew out over the Irish Sea and when we landed at Belfast, tried to get rooms for the night but only found one in a nearby hotel. 'OK, OK,' said Poppa, 'you take it and I'll sleep on the mat outside.' This seemed unfair as he'd got to do the early morning flying, so it was my turn to leap into action. I rang up some friends in the 12th Lancers who were stationed nearby and in no time at all everything had been fixed up. Poppa and I went out to dinner with Charles Banbury and his pals (whom I had last seen in 1940 in the Café Godebert in Amiens before it was bombed flat), together with Pam and Mike Spurling, who offered to let me stay with them overnight. Poppa therefore could have the hotel room instead of the floor outside the door.

Came the dawn. I went to say goodbye to my hosts, only to find Pam alone in bed, Mike having already left for duty. She half awoke and I saw her put out her hand to the empty pillow, before realizing he had gone. I thanked her for having me to stay, while thinking that I was missing out on something: I wasn't married but it seemed there was a lot in this love business, so I'd better start looking around again.

Meeting at the airfield, Poppa and I took off in the Anson in thick fog. I couldn't see a thing but I suppose Poppa Fairweather could. As we climbed up in the mist from Belfast, Poppa took from his pocket a crumpled 2 inch x 3 inch map of the British Isles, quite obviously torn from nothing larger than the back of a pocket diary! He smoothed it out, then stuck it up in front of him. 'Rules is rules,' said he with a wink. That map was hardly an aid to navigation, but a map it certainly was.

He next pulled out a silver cigarette case – the sort with gold-coloured elastic to hold the cigarettes in place on both sides of the hinged lids. He puffed contentedly away as we droned out over the Irish Sea on a roughly south-easterly course. When he got to the end of the first cigarette he lit another from the stub of the first, which he then very carefully stowed under the golden elastic. He smoked continually in this way, until nearly all his cigarettes were gone – all except those stubs. From time to time he would flip open the case and count the stubs, as he took out a new cigarette to light it with the near-used stub between his lips. As can be imagined, his uniform jacket and trousers were soon covered in grey ash.

All the time we headed towards England, and then, I suppose, over the unseen land, cloud and mist obscuring all sight of the ground. After a long time, he removed the latest stub from his mouth and hid it away again, then I noticed we had started to descend. He let go of the stick, brushed the ash off the front of his capacious jacket with both hands, squashed his chin down into his neck, hauled back the stick and announced – 'White Waltham!'

Whilst we taxied in, I sat amazed. He didn't wear a wrist-watch, so I asked him how he knew we were there. 'Well, Diana,' he said, 'you see, it takes seven minutes to smoke each one of those cigarettes and I had smoked 23, so I knew how long we had been flying in this thing [2 hours 40 minutes according to my log-book entry]. Quite easy, but don't tell them I've been smoking.' He then slid open the side window in order to help clear the air, and the grey haze inside merged with the yellow fog outside.

Near the end of the war, Poppa was put onto flying the ambulance aircraft, which was a converted Avro Anson. He was flying north with a nurse in attendance to collect an urgent ambulance case when he disappeared. Later, some bits of the Anson were washed up near Morecambe Bay in terrible weather. We all grieved for them and said it wasn't the weather that got him – something else must have happened or he just ran out of cigarettes.

A.T.A. Accident Report:
Anson *4875*. Missing between White Waltham and Prestwick 3rd April, 1944. Capt D. K. Fairweather and SO Sister E. Kershaw. The aircraft disappeared on an ambulance flight from White Waltham to Prestwick. There was insufficient evidence to establish the cause but it was considered likely, however, that the aircraft was lost in the Irish Sea in bad weather.

Nothing here on earth, weatherwise, could keep Poppa on the ground. I suppose he may be flying about somewhere Up There, happy and unconcerned . . . or has St Peter fashioned some specially designed wings for him, with a built-in ball and chain to keep him safely on his cloud? Margaret may well be sitting beside him.

Margaret was Poppa's wife, also a pilot in ATA – a flight captain. She was to die in the same year Poppa was lost. Her brother was Lord Runciman, later an air attaché in Tehran, who had commanded No. 607 County of Durham Squadron of the Royal Auxiliary Air Force between 1936 and 1939. On 4 August 1944 she collected a Mr Kendrick from Heston to take him to Hawarden, and was then to take her sister Kitty on to Prestwick. Kitty was not a pilot but an ATA personnel officer who had some labour relations problems to sort out in Scotland. It was the very first time, and unhappily the only time, that the two sisters had ever flown together.

Near the wiggles of the River Dee the engine of their Proctor spluttered, the fuel gauge on one side reading low, so Margaret changed tanks. The engine did not pick up so she changed tanks back again, whereupon the engine stopped. She made a forced landing in a ridge and furrow field but the aircraft went up on its nose. Kitty was thrown out and badly injured while Mr Kendrick luckily only suffered a broken thumb. Margaret was killed because her glasses broke and some glass went through her eyes into her brain.

So two delightful Fairweathers had lost their lives flying with the ATA.

A.T.A. Accident Report:
Proctor III *LZ801*, near Wrexham, 4.8.44 at 14.50. Flight Captain the Hon. Mrs Margaret Fairweather killed. Flight Captain the Hon. Kitty Farrer and L. N. Kendrick injured. Crashed in field after complete engine failure. Technical investigation showed vent pipe of port petrol tank was completely blocked causing tank to collapse. In the circumstances the petrol gauge is likely to have indicated an incorrect reading, leading the pilot to suppose that the tank still contained fuel when in fact it was dry. The pilot is held not responsible

for this accident. Fitter was to blame for not picking up blockage on
D.I. [Daily Inspection] schedule.*

Finally completing my training, I became a fully operational ATA pilot
– fully, that is, within the guidelines of the organization. I couldn't, of
course, fly any old aeroplane, being restricted at first to single-engined
types, later twins. I was given the rank of Third Officer, which meant I
was limited to flying those single-engined aircraft. First and second
officers were those who had converted to twin or even multi-engined
machines. Ranks above those were mainly of command, eg flight captain,
captain, commander, etc.

White Waltham, it will be remembered, was where I had trained and
where ATA's headquarters were. Other ferry pools were set up when
things really began to expand. For some time, for example, I was to
operate from Hamble, down near Southampton. The first 14 pools (there
wasn't an 11th or a 13th) of an eventual 22 were:

No. 1 White Waltham	No. 8 Sydenham, Belfast
No. 2 Whitchurch, Bristol	No. 9 Aston Down, nr Stroud
No. 3 Hawarden, nr Chester	No. 10 Lossiemouth, Scotland
No. 4 Prestwick, Ayrshire	No. 12 Cosford, nr Wolverhampton
No. 5 Luton, later Thame	No. 14 Ringway, Manchester
No. 6 Ratcliffe, Leicester	No. 15 Hamble, Southampton
No. 7 Sherburn-in-Elmet, Leeds	No. 16 Kirkbride, Solway Firth

Light or training aircraft were one thing, but the types many early ATA
cadet pilots dreamed of, quite naturally, were the Hurricane and then
the Spitfire fighter types. Both fighters had more than proved themselves
in the skies over England, and were still taking the war to the enemy,
either in sweeps over France, or by low-level attacks on shipping or ground
targets along the enemy coast. Every ATA pilot longed for the day they
might fly one of these machines, and not only the men, but me too.

There was nearly always a Hurricane in the skies around White
Waltham because, as I have said, in the last part of the ATA early training,
pilots had to fly one of the school Hurricanes for three hours of circuits
and bumps. If they missed hitting the church at the end of the runway
on take-off, and didn't bounce high enough to break up on landing, then
they were passed on to the Training Pool, where after several deliveries
– and their first Spitfire flight – plus a lot of taxying other people around
for their collections or deliveries, they were posted to one of the ferry
pools that were by then in existence all over the British Isles.

I was so envious of those pilots on the course in front of me who had
already had a go at the Hurricane. I thought it was the epitome of all
my training. I longed to get my first single-seater aircraft noted down

---

* The tank air vents had in fact been doped over, just as in a Mustang I was to fly later in the
war which gave me similar problems – of which more later.

in my flying log-book. I was going to fly it alone, and without having had any dual with an instructor beforehand, unlike all the other types I had flown.

Having carefully read all the handling notes, learning them off by heart, while questioning every pilot who would talk to me about their own experiences, I then asked some of my RAF pals. Alas, my Humphrey was dead and so was Claud, so I couldn't ask them. I wondered if I would get a bout of claustrophobia after take-off, with a cockpit hood that needed to be shut over one's head once airborne.

I needed that Hurricane to tell me that at last I was a fully fledged ATA ferry pilot. I didn't realize how far I still had to go, but then, on 26 April 1942, it was my turn in one of the well-maintained but well-used school aircraft.

Everyone had said, 'Open up slowly, Diana, so that it doesn't swing, and once its tail's up and it's on its main wheels, you'll see forward a bit better.' Keep her straight, they continued, but as the retractable undercarriage lever was so well worn on the school machine, they told me I shouldn't have the trouble that I might experience later on with a new one straight out of the Hawker factory.

One could develop a swing on take-off on almost anything if one opened up too fast with a powerful engine and didn't use enough rudder. One could do it with a Hurricane, too, especially in a cross-wind. Even the CO of No. 1 Ferry Pool, Commander Frankie Francis (Francis Francis), did it! He was taking off in a Hurricane through the balloon barrage that surrounded the Hawker factory aerodrome at Langley. One or two of the balloons were, or should have been, taken down at the exit end of the runway to make a safe corridor for pilots, but Frankie swung and hit a cable. He collected a long and heavy piece of hawser which wrapped itself around his wing at the armpit end. In spite of the extra weight and hazard, he did a circuit around to the coming-in end of the balloon corridor, to land well enough.

Now all I had to do was to miss the church steeple. I stood cross-wind by the control box, got the green light, so turned into wind; I opened up and in no time bounced off the White Waltham furrow bumps – airborne! Exhilaration! . . . wheels up, ease back to climbing revs and boost, then cruising – ditto – then finally trim out . . .

I was well round the circuit at 1,000 feet before I remembered to close the hood. By then it was time to open it again for my first Hurricane approach and landing, so forget it! I did five circuits and bumps that day (1 hour 5 minutes) and, Oh! what fun I had. Now the sun shone in my eyes and on me. I was about to start delivering to our brave RAF fighter boys, or more likely, to take fighters only to various MUs (maintenance units) where radios, guns and other special equipment were fitted.

I completed my three-hour stint in the next couple of days, then shot a line to any of the other less fortunate course colleagues who had yet to get their hands, feet and bottoms on the Hurricane. Life was grand. Just the Spitfire to come.

In the event, I was kept waiting until 31 October before I was given the chance to fly a Spitfire. By then I had already flown 17 different types of aircraft and had 'amassed' a total of 342 flying hours. Now was the time to take extra care!

It was always said that pilots became over-confident know-alls at around 300 hours, but I had that ever-present vision of that burnt man who had tried to warn me off flying just as I was about to fly my first solo at Brooklands in 1937. I had progressed so gently up the flying ladder, through the well-organized schooling, into the 'training pool', and had delivered countless Hurricanes plus other single-engined types, so another new type didn't bother me at all. My first Spitfire didn't seem all that special when it happened, unlike my very first Hurricane. Inexperienced pilots were usually given their first Spitfire 'off a runway onto a runway on a nice day'. They were even kinder to me: the sun was shining too. I was given my Spit to take off from right outside the door at White Waltham, where I knew every bump and dip; one might even say I knew every blade of grass of that airfield by now. Perhaps it was so 'Whitey' and Co., the Operations officers, could look out of the Ops room window in order to see what a hash I might make of it.

Even better, it was a PR Spitfire IV (*BR425*). PR stood for Photographic Reconnaissance, so these aircraft did not have the extra weight of heavy guns, cannons or armour plate on them as they had to be able to reach the highest possible ceiling. It was their pilot's job to bring back pictures, not to engage in combat. Their speed and agility being their main defence against Luftwaffe fighters. They were also delightful to look at because their all-over camouflage against the sky was a pretty shade of azure blue (some were even darker), and Oh! they were beautiful to fly. So light, so manoeuvrable. Much better than the armoured ones.

It was love at first sight. We 'both' did a daisy-cutter of a landing at the other end of the flight, at Colerne, in Wiltshire. Colerne housed an MU as well as a night fighter squadron. This was No. 218 MU, which also worked with a BOAC repair facility which had moved onto the airfield in 1941. The night fighter unit was 264 Squadron, which had Mosquito aircraft, suitably painted black.

As it had taken me 40 minutes to fly there, I must have played about on the way, but no-one would have blamed me for those extra few minutes of familiarization, not to mention pure pleasure, in that, my very first Supermarine Spitfire.

Purely as a matter of interest, the 17 types I'd flown up until my first Spit sortie were: Fairchild Argus, Lysander, Master I & II, Magister, Tiger Moth, Hornet Moth, Avro Tutor, Proctor, Swordfish, Gloster Gladiator, Harvard, Hart/Hind, Puss Moth, Miles Whitney Straight, Vega Gull, Hurricane* and Wicko Warferry. In addition to these, I had by then also flown as a passenger in at least one Airspeed Oxford, Avro Anson, A-W Whitley, DH Dominie, Douglas Boston III and Short Stirling.

---

* *I had also flown a Sea Hurricane, whose only differences were instrument readings in knots and an arrester hook for use when landing on a carrier. The ATA did not deliver onto them.*

During my wartime career with ATA I delivered 260 Spitfires, from the light Mark I with the wooden propeller, right through to the heavier Mark XIV and F21 with the large Griffon engine. The types in between varied little from the flying point of view. They all flew beautifully, with the Spit characteristic of it feeling as if it was part of you. The Mark I was really light on the controls, the Mark V gave a fluttering feeling in flight, while the Mark IX had become more stable. All the PR Marks were lighter to fly, as already mentioned, while the Mark XII, with its clipped wing-tips, had a plainer and more solid feeling.

I didn't like the sound of the Griffon engine – not at all as comforting or glorious as the Merlin. By the time the Spit XIVs were being turned out, although most of the flying characteristics were still there, they had become much heavier because of the even more powerful engine. The airframe had to be made much longer in the nose to accommodate the larger engine, and therefore more care had to be taken when taxying or landing as they were quite nose-heavy as well. On all Spitfire run-ups, two airmen had to lie across the tail elevators so that the aircraft didn't tip onto its nose. As you taxied about, you had to move the rudder to turn the nose from side to side, in order to be able to see that you weren't about to hit something – or someone.

The Mark XIVs developed torque on take-off because of the extra power, so quite a bit of opposite rudder was needed so a swing didn't develop, and the XXI wallowed a bit on final approach at slow speed. However, I'm pleased to say I didn't break any of the 260 different Spitfires I delivered, whatever Mark they happened to be.

On one particular murky afternoon in October 1942, I was suddenly given a P.1.W. – Priority One. Wait – Lysander II (*L4781*). P.1.W. meant that the pilot had to get the delivery done with the utmost urgency and that any number of little sorties in the right direction could be flown, if the weather was too bad to go the whole way in one hop. It also implied that the pilot had to start at dawn if needs be, hang about all day or for several days if necessary (forget lunch), even if faced with an impossible met. report.

After playing 'grandmothers' footsteps' with the weather, plus an extra landing en route, I finally managed to arrive at my destination just before dusk. I was waved towards a group of soldiers with parachutists' 'wings' upon their uniforms. A smart-looking Major came up to my cockpit to ask if I would mind taxying the Lysander up to the petrol pumps to save time.

Having done so – I was always very obliging – I got out of the aircraft and the Major got in. Into the passenger seat climbed a tough-looking little man with a blacked-up face. The Major too was busily smearing more black stuff on his own face as the Lysander was being refuelled. There was a tremendous feeling of tension, anxiety and urgency – maybe even fear – around that group of soldiers, as well as a smell of cold sweat.

I went back to the Major, who was by now strapped in. He was the senior officer, so I asked him to sign my delivery chit. He said, 'I am glad you got here. In ten minutes we would have had to abort this trip.' Only then did it dawn on me that they were going to fly this Lysander out of England on some clandestine operation, whilst all I had to do was to take a train back to London.

On 24 May 1967, long after the war had ended, I was lucky enough to be given a seat in the crypt of St Paul's Cathedral on the occasion of the Service of Dedication to commemorate the Jubilee of the Order of the British Empire (holders of any degree of the Order had balloted for seats). The Queen was also seated in the crypt, along with other members of the Royal Family and various Bishops and other dignatories.

A man was sitting one chair away from me, but kept peering at me throughout the service. I was wearing a pretty silk dress with a little yellow straw hat, so I imagined he just fancied the get-up. Each time I glanced in his direction, he caught and held my eyes, with a half-smile on his lips. Suddenly it came to me. I remembered that he was the man with the blackened face who had climbed into the back seat of my Lysander to be dropped out over the Continent somewhere. Obviously he had survived!

After the service we walked out together. 'I knew as soon as you came in, that you were that ferry pilot who brought us our Lysander,' he said. I had to admit it had taken longer for me to recognize him. After all, the last time I had seen him, on that dreary evening, he was well 'camouflaged'.

I presume that during the long time those brave men had to wait for me to bring in their aeroplane, the antennae of his senses were at their highest susceptibility, as proved by his excellent memory. It was just before a terrifying mission when the Lysander was to land him in France.

He came to have lunch with me at River House, but even then, so long afterwards, he never told me what had occurred that night or subsequently.

I had only been out of the ATA Training Pool for a few weeks and been officially posted to No. 1 Ferry Pool when, on 8 December 1942, I was given a Master II (*DL486*) to take from Reading to St Athan, an MU in Wales. I don't remember now how I got across from St Athan to Llandow after the flight, but it was already late in the afternoon when I collected a Spitfire Vc, registration number *EE743*, which I had to deliver to RAF Hornchurch, the famous fighter station just north of the Thames in Essex. It was my 13th Spitfire.

It was a cold winter day. I arrived north of London as daylight was fading into a murky mist. I carefully flew round the London balloon barrage before heading for Hornchurch, but by then a sea fog had rolled in. There wasn't a hope of getting under it to land, so I headed north towards North Weald. Here I found that only the tips of the nearby radio masts were sticking out of the mist and fog, while all the time it was getting darker and darker. I was really caught out.

Looking at my map, I saw the red dot of an aerodrome named Broxbourne about six or seven miles away, but when I got to where it should be, I couldn't see a thing. Of course, I was looking for a proper aerodrome, not a grass patch! By now it was too late to go anywhere else, and behind me I could see the fog still rolling inland, so I took the Spit up and down the River Lee, over glasshouses and the railway, keeping very low to make sure I was in the right place where Broxbourne *had* to be. Suddenly a red-doped Proctor stood out through the gloom and mist. It was parked on a little concrete apron between some buildings which, I cleverly worked out, must be something to do with the airfield. Hurray!

However, as I was thanking my guardian angel, I noticed that the airfield was very small, so I took the longest run I could and skimmed in to land over some greenhouses. Horrors! – it wasn't going to be long enough! I shoved the throttle open and went round again, out over some high telephone wires beside a small road. It had got rather dark by now, so I flew very low and slow, with flaps down, easing once more over the greenhouses, and this time managed to touch down right at the near hedge (flying time 1 hour 10 minutes). I squeezed on a bit of brake, getting away with my arrival, and did not run into the hedge at the opposite end of the landing field

As I taxied in, I was vaguely aware of something following me. Outside the buildings, which now materialized into a hangar as I got closer, was a large crowd of people. (Works out, and day has ended, thought I.) A man detached himself from the crowd, came over and stood by the wing as I climbed out. 'We've never had a Spitfire in here before,' he remarked, adding, 'Glad you saw the man on the tractor!'

At that moment, whatever had been behind me clanked up and parked beside me in the shadows. It was a very old tractor.

I didn't want to admit that in the gloom I hadn't seen it cutting the grass on the landing patch, so merely said that I hoped I hadn't frightened the fellow. The man by the wing smiled at me and said, 'Oh no. He's deaf anyway, but he must have seen you going round again for him!'

It didn't seem quite the right moment to enlighten either of them as to how near I had come to possibly decapitating the poor driver. I just took up a heroic stance, knowing there are times when it is far better to keep quiet and wear a tiny halo.

Without much more ado, and being only just north of the outer reaches of the Underground's Central Line, I took the tube into London, meeting up with a number of pilot friends, some of whom had been former members of 601 Squadron. I was mindful that on the morrow I should have to get myself and my Spitfire off that tiny field and on to Hornchurch. We finished up at the '400' Club in Leicester Square, a fashionable night-club in those days. During the course of the evening I was told by all my experts the best tricks to use in order to get a Spitfire out of a tight place.

The next morning there was no wind to speak of, so I would be able to use the so-called longest run for take-off, although with no wind, there would be no extra lift to help me. Now, as I have already said, when a Spitfire was run up to test its engine, there had to be two men lying across the tail to keep the aircraft from nosing over. It was always a nasty, cold, noisy job for them, and once in a while pilots had been known to forget they were there and get airborne before their helpers could dive clear.

This time, the RAF ground crew were well briefed! We talked about the problem before starting up, agreeing that I would have four of them on the tail, run up the engine as much as I dared against the brakes, and at the precise second I nodded my head (as one hand would be on the throttle, the other on the stick and brake lever) they would then fall off – and fast.

We put the tail almost into the hedge because every inch counted. Everything worked to plan. The telephone wires on the exit end survived as I roared out of the airfield, then headed for nearby Hornchurch.

Air Transport Auxiliary pilots were given that intensive flying training, so, as I had only just come out of the school, I was flying very carefully and accurately (still with some help from my burnt pilot!). I don't think that later on in my slap-happy ATA career I could have got a Spitfire in, let alone out of Broxbourne.

Dear little aerodrome! I am glad it was there when I needed it. If it hadn't been, I wouldn't be – if you get my meaning.

◆ Chapter 7 ◆

Anyway, I'm Still Around

MY 22ND SPITFIRE was a Mark IX (*BS148*) from Hanworth to Cosford. By now I thought I was an experienced pilot, there is no doubt about that, and equally no doubt that I wasn't!

I had the feeling that I was still being wet-nursed a bit by 'someone', for I was continually being given Spitfires off a runway, onto a runway and not off and onto rough grass airfields, not to mention fine days too. When the weather was really bad, the Operations Officer would say, 'Sorry, nothing doing at the moment; go away and mug up on some met. or something.'

But then, on 20 January 1943, it dawned a lovely clear, bright day with a cloudless blue sky. I could see for miles, which suited me, as my navigation was of the map-and-squint-out variety. So I found myself in the Spitfire IX – a truly front-line fighter, and the envy of all the squadrons still struggling along with the Mark Vc – heading north-west above the Cotswolds along my chosen route, with the red line on my map unfolding like a ribbon. I knew I wasn't going to run into any balloon cables and would easily clear any hills en route if I kept at 1,150 feet. The highest hills I had noted were 1,050, so I added another 100 feet for safety. As usual, I was playing a game of checking the spot heights on the map against my altimeter as I skimmed along, just in case some day I needed to creep low under cloud, before I needed to drop down into the Evesham Valley, south-east of Worcester.

I was wearing my very best uniform jacket and skirt. I had been on leave, having got back to White Waltham a bit late, and had hardly had time to collect my delivery chits, check out the route, met., etc, and grab my maps and parachute before the taxi-Anson load was called. The Anson was to take the pilots to the collecting centre where our delivery aircraft were waiting. There had been no time to change into my trousers and flying overalls.

The previous night I had been taken out in London by some of my RAF pilot friends, and, as usual, we had ended up in the '400' Club. It

was all flying chat, of course, and two of the fighter pilots were Max
Aitken and Billy Clyde, both of whom had been in 601 Squadron during
the Battle of Britain. Max Aitken, whom I'd met before the war and
skied with, was the son of Lord Beaverbrook, our wartime Minister of
Aircraft Production; he held the DSO, DFC, Czech War Cross and had
just been awarded the Air Efficiency Award. He had fought valiantly
and had just finished a tour commanding No. 68 Night-fighter
Squadron based at Coltishall. He was about to go overseas, and when
I next heard from him he was in the Eastern Mediterranean. Billy, who
had skied for Britain before the war, then gone off to live in Mexico, had
also fought with Max in 1940, won the DFC and was now a squadron
leader.

As we talked, Max and Billy were absolutely horrified to discover that
ATA ferry pilots were expected, indeed able, to fly with no radio, in
every sort of aeroplane in all kinds of weather, even though they had not
been shown how to blind-fly – or at least I hadn't! ATA decided that
their recruits, such as I, would not be taught to fly on instruments – for
as we must stay in sight of the ground, we should be alright. By the same
token, if by chance we should come into contact with enemy aircraft
flying over Britain, we would normally be low enough for the ground
defences not only to recognize us, but to engage and shoot down any
enemy marauders that might be around. People in authority do come
up with some wonderful theories, don't they?

Sometimes we did several different deliveries in different types of
aircraft in a day, so we would have had to carry about with us a whole bag
of crystals for the radios, wasting a good deal of time tuning them in,
then testing them, before we could take off. The few radio channels then
in use were needed by the RAF, so any extra transmissions by us might
have been picked up by the enemy's radio monitoring service. Most new
aircraft were not fitted with radios until they had been delivered to MUs.

It was also thought that if ATA pilots went into, or above, cloud with
short-range aircraft, they might not have the fuel to be able to go to an
alternative airfield should the weather close in at their destination. I
think the powers-that-be made a hash of that decision and I am certain
more ATA pilots would have survived had blind-flying been a requirement
of training. If nothing else, we would have grown far fewer grey hairs
above our worried brows.

Soon I found myself admitting to my friends that not only could I not
blind-fly, but that I had absolutely no idea of how some of the blind-
flying instruments worked. On hearing this, Little Max (so called by
some of us to distinguish him from his famous father) and Billy proceeded
to draw a lot of diagrams on the night-club's pink linen tablecloth while
giving me instructions about what they meant, plus a lecture on what
to do if I got into cloud:

'Straighten up first,' advised Max, 'and *think*. You usually go into
cloud sideways anyway, if you're trying to avoid it.'
'Watch your safety height, so climb up high enough,' added Billy,

'and get back on your original course, then turn slowly round onto your reciprocal. Keep that turn ever so shallow. Not more than a Rate One turn.'

'Leave your throttle setting where it was when you went in,' said Max, 'then let down in as shallow a dive as you can.'

'Don't worry about your speed building up if it's a fighter,' chipped in Billy, 'just be sure of your gyro heading. Above all, decide before you start to descend about your safety break-off height.'

'If you get to your break-off height and you are still in cloud,' said Max, drawing once more on the tablecloth, 'then forget it. Get up again high – and quick; then bale out!'

I was being hit from both sides by this barrage of useful information, some of which I suppose was going into my thick brain. All pilots knew it but I didn't. Little did I think how lucky I had been to be told all this by these two experienced fighter boys, that night.

Max's clear instructions to 'if in doubt, bale out', struck a chord. The ATA told us that trained ferry pilots were worth more to the war effort than an aircraft, so that in a bad situation, we were to save ourselves if we could and forget the aeroplane.

Meantime, I was still enjoying my Spit IX flight towards Cosford in lovely sunny weather, the beautiful Cotswolds beneath me, all sweetness and light, God was in his heaven, all's right with the . . .

Suddenly – literally suddenly – I was in cloud! There had been no fronts forecast on the weather maps, and although the Met. reporting in those days was a bit haphazard to say the least, they wouldn't have missed a whole front! Well, would they?

At first I supposed that I had merely flown into a patch of cloud whilst I was playing my spot heights game, so I did what Max and Billy had told me: straightened out, got back onto my course and *thought*! I didn't seem to climb up, but when I glanced at the altimeter it was at 6,000 feet, with thick cloud still outside.

I was faced with two alternatives: bale out or try to turn round, then let down towards lower ground behind me where I knew the sun had been shining. But I couldn't bale out for I was wearing a skirt! (Remember I hadn't had time to change into my slacks.) The wartime black stockings were a bit short too, leaving off just above my fat knees, so my wartime panties, being made out of silk from old parachutes, didn't come down to meet the stockings, leaving a large gap of ME in between. The parachute harness chafed the insides of my legs anyhow, so I thought that not only will it hurt when I bale out and the 'chute jerks me to a halt in mid-air, but it will really look so silly floating down in a hitched-up and very tight navy serge uniform skirt. We were very modest in those days.

So my second alternative came into play. I had passed Little Rissington under my starboard wing on the way up, which was 750 feet above sea level, and hopefully still in the sunshine. I decided to turn round and put down there in order to check the Met. before flying on.

The turn seemed to take ages but eventually the reciprocal course turned up on the gyro and the compass caught it up, so my let-down began – ever so gently. I had decided that as Little Rissington was 750 feet, I would give myself a break-off height of 800 feet. Madness (now I can tell you) to allow just 50 feet clearance from the deck, but I didn't know any better, did I?!

The descent, although fairly shallow, was obviously in a series of scallops. I couldn't keep the descent needle in the right place, which meant that the little aeroplane symbol on the artificial horizon instrument kept zooming down into the wrong place, as well as going sideways. But the direction was OK, so I thought, 'Any moment now I'll break cloud.' But I didn't. Seconds later I was at my chosen 800 feet break-off height. So that's it! Poor little Spitfire, that could be the end of you, or me. I'll have to go up again and do some more *thinking* about baling out. Oh, if only I wasn't wearing a skirt!

I didn't feel a bit frightened, at least I didn't think I was – if I had time to think about it at all. The altimeter jerked alarmingly to 600 feet and at that very moment I came out of cloud at tree-top height. The trees flashed by, with cloud sitting on the topmost branches and rain simply pelting down. As I crabbed in and out of the stuff beside the trees, I caught a glimpse of an aircraft on a bit of grass. 'Aha,' I thought, 'Little Rissington . . .' But it wasn't.

It was a tiny grass aerodrome partly surrounded by those trees I had nearly crashed into. I kept flying in and out of cloud as I tightened my turn to keep near my little grass bolt-hole. But worse was to come. As I looked more carefully, I could see it was all covered in water, looking more like a pond than an airfield. We had had a lot of snow which had recently melted, and this, added to the deluge of rain now cascading down, was fast making the place into a swamp.

With a Spitfire, if one landed in large puddles, the water tended to come up and smash the flaps, or perhaps break just one, causing you to swing. Also, because Spits (and some other fighters) were nose-heavy, they could easily flip right over on such a landing. Only three days before, a Hurricane had done just that with an extremely tall ATA pilot (First Officer Alan Coleman) in charge. He had been strapped upside down in the cockpit with the hood open (always open for take-offs and landings) and had drowned in the middle of an aerodrome in just a few inches of water.

I was thinking of all this. Anyway, I was going to have to put down there, no matter what, because I wasn't going to be able to go anywhere else.

I landed – 'splosh'. Loads of muddy water came up all over me (cockpit hood open, remember?) I skidded through the puddles, somehow stopped safely, then gingerly taxied over to what I assumed to be the dispersal area, parking beside an Airspeed Oxford. Rain was still teeming down. A very tall RAF man came out of a Nissen hut with a camouflaged rain cape held aloft over his head. As he came towards the Spitfire, I got out of the cockpit, stepped onto the wing – where my knees collapsed! I didn't think I'd been frightened but . . .

I had no intention of letting this fellow know how I felt, so in my now kneeling position, I quickly pretended to be leaning over and scrabbling around in the cockpit for my maps. He came alongside, gallantly held the cape over me, then, looking up at the cloud-covered treetops and back at me, said, 'I say, Miss, you must be good on instruments!' When I whispered that I couldn't blind-fly, he threw his head back and roared with laughter. You see, he thought I was making a joke of it, being modest, not shooting a line, and so on . . . Then he added, through his giggles, 'And I am the Link Trainer Instructor here', which made it my turn to think he was trying to be funny.

I didn't like to ask where I was, as I hoped he'd think I knew, but as my knees had started to work again, we went into the hut. There on a notice board was a large notice saying 'Royal Air Force, Windrush. Navigation and Blind Flying Establishment. Altitude 560 feet.' (Windrush was between Oxford and Cheltenham.) Would you believe it! – with all my problems I had to land up at a place for blind-flying instruction! Even the name Windrush seemed good to me. Quite appropriate for that weather!

I told him I had been caught out in cloud up in the hills to the north-west, then had tried to go back to Little Rissington. He went a bit pale, I thought, and said, 'Oh no, Miss. You've passed it. We are its satellite. It's four miles over there,' pointing over my shoulder. 'They've got no trees to keep this muck off the deck, and they're 200 feet higher up than us, so they'd be more than right in it by now.' My guardian angel had been with me, obviously.

I rang through to Ops at White Waltham to say where I was, but was put directly through to my CO, Commander Neville Whitehurst OBE. Rather curtly, I thought, he said, 'Stay there!', then, after a pause, added quietly, 'I'm glad you got down safely.' He went on to say that it wasn't merely a weather front, but that it had been a day when the dewpoint (which is the moisture content of the air) was unusually high for this part of the world, meaning that with a very slight variation of temperature, the whole of the middle of England had suddenly condensed into cloud. Every pilot of the Training Pool had been caught out by the weather, and had had to put down somewhere. Several aircraft had been broken, and two of us had been killed.

My knees began to go again, but the RAF man arrived with a mug of steaming tea. Whilst there, an officer, although he said he didn't believe I needed it, gave me my very first hour of Link Trainer instruction. As soon as I was put into the Link, the instructor quickly found out what I had told the airman, that I really couldn't blind-fly.

Fifty years later there was a sequel to this story. In August 1992 I had a letter from an Albert Yarwood, who had seen my story of the landing at Windrush in one of Laddie Lucas' books – *Out of the Blue* (Hutchinson, 1985). Lo and behold, Albert was that airman who came out to me with the cape over his head! One reason he had been so interested in my instrument flying was that he was an instrument fitter.

He told me that when I landed he had been about to go on leave, and had on his best blue, which was why he was so anxious to protect himself from the weather with the gas cape when he came to me. In the event, he muddied up his uniform trousers so much picketing down the Spit that he had to delay his departure. Sorry, Albert. He also said that he was the only one on duty as everyone else had gone off for lunch. In his letter he asked me to reply and confirm it all, as his friends would never believe him. I was glad to do it, and to talk to him on the telephone after so many years.

There was nowhere for me to stay at RAF Windrush, so I telephoned some friends who told me to try to come over. However, they had no petrol for their car, the tractor was in use, and the trap-pony was lame. There was no transport on the aerodrome either, so I was left with no alternative but to trudge the four miles – still in the downpour – while wearing my RAF issue, over-large flying boots.

I arrived and rang the doorbell, to be greeted and let in by a woman who took one look at my drenched and bedraggled state and said, 'Wait!' in a voice rather like the one I use when the dog comes in from the garden with muddy paws. In next to no time she was back again, holding out a lovely white bathrobe and some pink fluffy slippers. There was already a large pool of water on the hall carpet.

'Give me your uniform,' she commanded, then added, 'These are Madam's, but she won't mind.' Just inside the front door I wriggled out of my soaked jacket and skirt and put on the bathrobe, still warm from the linen cupboard, then she led me upstairs. She ran a bath for me, put in some bath salts, and said, 'The Master's round the farm, but he'll be back soon,' closing the door as she went away.

What luxury! I lolled back in the bath, my teeth stopping their chattering, while playing with the bathplug chain with my toes against the overflow vent. Thinking over what I had been through, the overflow and chain became the artificial horizon, while the steam acted as the clouds.

It occurred to me that if the Oxford had not been parked just where it had been, outside the Link Trainer building, I would have missed seeing it and Windrush altogether. I wasn't heading for that little airfield – it wasn't even marked on my map, so I didn't know it was there. Yet it had turned up dead on my treetops cloud-break, exactly when it was needed. And I couldn't blind-fly – but I did!

Even now, when I think of that day, my teeth begin to chatter. Strange things happened to make me still be here. *Someone* was looking after me.

I hope the ink came out of that tablecloth at the '400' Club!

◇ ◇ ◇

It was curious, but after having had the wind-up (a lovely description, I always think, used generously by those intrepid aviators in the First

World War) on one flight, it definitely slowed down my bad-weather flying ability, so for a short time I was extra cautious.

The day afterwards, having trudged back to RAF Windrush, though in improved weather, I took off in my Spitfire IX in order to complete the trip to Cosford. I was using the gyro which I had set by the compass. By the time I got south of Birmingham and Rugby, the compass needle was swinging alarmingly. I reset the gyro from time to time to correct its precessing, but the compass was obviously not very accurate, so I had to try to catch the middle setting of the compass needle's swings.

There was a thick haze about. Slant visibility was lousy but straight down wasn't bad. I flew over an aerodrome, so thought it prudent to check exactly where I had got to before I ran into the balloon barrages around some of the cities of the Midlands. I wanted to fly past them, of course, not get lost and fly into them, so I landed to check for certain (I had learnt my lesson about balloon cables very early in my training Magister, near Gloucester).

The airfield I landed at was Honily. Having got the runway heading, I set my gyro by that when I was overhead once more, then flew on, disregarding the faulty compass, to my destination.

Having landed, I 'snagged' the compass on my snag-sheet, explaining to the mechanic, who said he would get the compass swung. Then he added, 'I expect you've got a magnet in your boots, Miss!'

Whether I landed at Honily really to check, or because I was still suffering from fright, I can't now recall.

Cardiff was not the best of aerodromes to fly to or from. The approach, with your back to the Bristol Channel, was over a very high dyke, so it couldn't be a low arrival. At the other end, just to be helpful, was a balloon barrage. There was just enough room to do a steep left-hand turn after take-off in order to fly away from them, but if you were trying to land, and had to go round again, then your mind had to be made up pretty early on, otherwise you were in amongst the cables. All very dicey, but Cardiff deliveries were always good practice for short landings, although one needed to be wide awake.

On 9 February, after taking a Hurricane IIC (*KX695*) into Cardiff, I was with a load of other pilots being collected by an Anson. In fact it was a second Anson, as the first had gone U/S. It was flown in by George Parnell, tall, lean and walrus-moustached. He had a shambling walk and puffed his cheeks out when he talked. I never saw him wearing a side-cap, always preferring his wide-topped ATA dress hat which always seemed over-large – but then, so too were his brains.

He was a clever man, for amongst other things, he had invented a circular slide rule 3½ inches square. It was the best aid to navigation and easily operated with one hand. It did calculations of drift, conversions of mph to knots, miles to kilometres, metres to feet, gallons to litres, kilos to pounds – in fact, anything a pilot or navigator needed, as well as time, speed and distance calculations. It was so simple that even I could work it. In fact it was my most valued accessory. It also had a map scale to go with the various flying maps then in use.

Another feature of Cardiff was the sea-birds. On this day there was, as usual, a positive snowstorm of seagulls all over the take-off run. Generally they got out of the way when they heard the noise of aero-engines, but this time two of them weren't quite quick enough. I was up the front end of the Anson next to Parnell as we became airborne. All at once there was a mighty bang as the perspex windscreen shattered between us, followed by a judder from behind. I thought someone had shot at us.

It was too late for Parnell to land again, so with a sudden heave of the stick, plus a kick on the rudder, he turned sharply to avoid the fast-approaching balloons. Then there was another noise and shudder, this time on the wing on my side.

When I'd got my ideas in perspective, I looked around to see some of my colleagues plucking white feathers from their navy blue uniforms, while a very large but very dead sea-bird was impinged on the crash axe that hung at the far end behind and between the last seats. The axe was badly dented into an arc, looking more like a boomerang – some force, eh?

It was extremely cold without the front window, but George got us back down alright, then we inspected the damage. The large gull had gone right between all of us! – right down the aisle, narrowly missing everyone, which was pretty lucky (thank you again, guardian angel). It had been stopped from going through the rear bulkhead, and maybe out the tail, by the opportune placing of the axe. Had it done so, it could well have seriously damaged the operation of the elevators or tail-plane.

The wing came in for the worst. In spite of the slow 90 mph take-off and climb speed of the Anson, the second, rather smaller, seagull was embedded 9 inches into the main spar. Glad it wasn't me! Those birds looked much larger dead than alive, I can tell you.

Parnell came in for some teasing, mostly by way of relief. 'Were you clear for take-off?' or 'You'll fly into a nice white loaded cloud next!' to 'Fix a scarecrow on the front next time' and 'Look at my best uniform, Parnell', to which last remark he replied quietly, 'You should be happy you are able to!'

The very next day, the 10th, I was down in that part of the world again. A heavy band of nasty weather was lying north to south across England, rolling back slowly towards the east. A few pilots had put down to wait until it cleared before trying to get further eastwards to their various destinations.

I had flown a Hurricane IIC (*KX759*) from Langley to Cardiff in lovely weather, but had had to put down at Whitchurch later because of the visibility. Here I found some other ATA pilots also waiting to be collected and flown back to White Waltham.

In the late afternoon, the transport Anson arrived as usual, this time piloted by the famous and dearly loved record-breaker, Jim Mollison, the widower of Amy Johnson, who had been killed in 1941 flying with ATA. Jim had already collected several pilots from here and there, plus another bunch from Hullavington, which made us 12 in number including Jim.

The payload of the Anson was 1,987 lb, but in the main we were a skinny, hungry-looking bunch of men and women that day, and as the aircraft was no longer fully topped up with petrol, I don't suppose we were much overloaded, even though our 11 parachutes added a further 440 lb. However, it was all a bit of a squash in the back.

Jim said he thought that by the time we got back to White Waltham the front would have cleared there, so we felt glad that we were in no danger of being stuck out overnight. Jim was 37 then, having been an RAF pilot in the early 1920s, serving in Waziristan at one stage. His record-breaking solo flight from Australia to England had taken place in the summer of 1931, followed the next March by his flight to Cape Town, and by other record-breaking flights across the Atlantic in 1932 and 1933, one with his wife Amy. He had a lot of flying experience.

I sat beside Jim in the co-pilot's seat. We went over Reading, flying along just under cloud-base with the sun behind us, shining on a black line of frontal weather ahead. Passing over the railway yards, I saw a spume of smoke coming up from them. I thought it was probably some train letting off steam. Suddenly, from the mass of cloud in front of us, out popped an aircraft, just like a cork from a bottle – going like stink. Not only that, it was coming straight at *us*.

At first, I thought it was a Mosquito, because at that time, the Mossie was just coming out of the Leavesden and Hatfield factories, so I imagined it was some thick ATA pilot flying in the muck who had still got his head down on instruments but who hadn't realized he had cleared the weather. But then, against the dark cloud, I saw tracer coming out at us from what appeared to be the gunner of the silvered aircraft. I then noticed the huge black cross on the fuselage and swastika on the tail-plane. An Me 110!

Jim saw it all too. 'Jeese!' he yelled, 'it's a Jerry!' He yanked the Anson up into the overcast to hide as the German flashed past, very close, on our port side, its guns still blazing. We were swallowed up in the cloud for a while, then Jim let down onto White Waltham. After we'd switched off, we heard the air-raid sirens wailing, and everyone was scurrying around with their tin hats on. As we all clambered out of the Anson, everyone asked us, 'Did you see the Jerry?' Rather proudly, we said, as we shrugged our shoulders, and with our noses in the air, with half-lowered eye-lids, 'Oh yes, of course we did! It shot at us too!!'

We looked the Anson over but we couldn't find a bullet-hole anywhere. Rotten shot, we all agreed; how could he have missed us? Perhaps the sun was in his eyes. Thinking back, it was the one time when we should have been delighted to have been disappointed. Later on we heard that the German aircraft had been one of a series of those flying hit-and-run raiders. Our British radar was pretty moderate in those days, so the enemy, in poor weather, was able to fly across to Britain, come out in the clear for as short a time as possible, do some low-level bombing attacks, then head for home in the same weather. The smoke I had seen coming up from the Reading railway yards was the result of the German aircraft's bombs from its first pass. We seem to have been right on its line – and in its way – for its second run, so it had a pot at us as it went by.

What that German gunner didn't know was that it would have been a triumph and a very good bag for his squadron had he, by chance, shot down 12 highly trained ferry pilots all at once, when he was only after a railway line.

'Come on,' said Jim, 'it's time for tea,' adding as we walked towards the canteen, 'You know, Diana, by tomorrow they'll all be saying that I shot it down!' True enough, a couple of weeks later the press wrote up the tale with such lurid detail that it made me realize that my guardian angel himself, whom I have been telling you about, must have been flying alongside us and that Anson-load of pilots.

The only other times I got shot at was by our own side. Natural hazards, I suppose, but disconcerting. We used to take Hurricanes regularly from Langley to Cardiff and I don't know what the ack-ack boys were up to with their aircraft recognition, but frequently when I was flying across the Bristol Channel at between 1,500 and 2,000 feet, there would be a shudder by the aircraft as little blackberry-shaped puffs of dark smoke suddenly appeared, very close, all round it. They were fired from the coast behind.

At first I didn't know what they were, but then it dawned on me. I thought it must be just one of the ordinary, everyday problems of a ferry pilot. I usually had my tail to the coast by then, so just kept on going towards Wales, hoping to get out of range. I suppose it was very difficult, in poor visibility, to decide, with a finger on the trigger, so to speak, whether it was one of theirs or one of ours. But then I was in a single-seater, and single-seat enemy fighters would not normally have come that far. Twin-engined aircraft yes, but a lone fighter? I did notice the Welsh side never had a go at me – perhaps their eyesight or aircraft recognition was better.

It did not occur to me to say anything to anyone. They hadn't got me yet. In the back of my mind I could not believe that people weren't able to tell a Hurricane from, say, a Messerschmitt 109 or Focke Wulf 190, and hoped they were just practising with blanks. But one day, a notice appeared on No. 1 Pool's board, requesting any pilots who thought they'd been shot at over the Bristol Channel to report to the CO. Perhaps one of the high-ups had got a burst. Anyway, there was quite a long queue.

Among some of the incidents which occurred to other women pilots was one concerning another Diana. I was sitting in the sun on the wall outside

Ops at White Waltham when a Hawker Typhoon roared over the aerodrome very low and very, very fast. The noise certainly shattered my peace. It went past a couple of times. 'Whitey', the Ops Officer, poked his head out of the window with his field-glasses, saying, 'That's Wamsey, with the last one out from Langley this morning.'*

Wamsey was First Officer Diana Ramsey, a dainty girl with an upturned nose and a short upper lip. She kept her pretty light brown hair off her face with a narrow navy blue velvet ribbon that matched her uniform. We all of us affectionately called her Wamsey, teasing her for not being able to pronounce her 'R's properly.

Suddenly the roar of the noisy Sabre engine went dead. The Typhoon was still going round the circuit very fast indeed, even without its power on. Wamsey came round on finals and flew across the aerodrome, trying to lose speed in a series of humps like a dover sole or flat fish along the bottom of the sea. Approach speed over the hedge in a Typhoon should be 100 mph but she was way over that. Any forced landing without an engine would have been difficult enough, but at such a high speed it couldn't come off. She pulled up to miss the church at the western end and went on out of sight.

We found out later that her throttle and boost controls had jammed at fully open during take-off, giving her over 400 mph plus severe engine overheat. She had to switch off to try a landing or bale out, being unable to go back to Langley because of the balloon barrage and shortness of the landing run. Anyway, we all favoured the idea of our own blood cart and crash wagons' well-practised efficiency.

Doc Whitehurst, CO of No. 1 Ferry Pool, came running out of the ATA building. 'Come with me, Diana, if you like,' he said. I popped into his car beside him and drove off. We parked as near as we could to the place where he had seen the Typhoon disappear, and walked over a couple of grass fields. There were some cuts in the soft ground where the still-milling propeller had hit as Wamsey still tried to get the aeroplane to land on its belly (she was going too fast to lower the undercarriage).

Next, we saw two large oak trees she had flown between, knocking off a sizeable branch and a part of a wing. We hurried on past some cattle to a large ditch at the boundary of a wood. We dreaded what we might find next as we came upon a tunnel of broken saplings in front of us. We crawled along, passing another wing on the way, then came out into a circle of flattened and broken trees which looked as if a couple of dinosaurs had had a fight in there.

On the other side of the clearing, against some larger trees, reared up what was left of the Tiffie. No wings, no propeller, just a crunched fuselage and the engine, pointing towards the sky. Diana Ramsey was astride the engine, reaching up as high as she could to try and rescue her hair ribbon that somehow had got blown off and caught high up in the trees when her flying helmet ripped off in the final crash.

* *The factory near Slough, where we collected Typhoons for delivery.*

There was a nasty smell of very hot engine and fuel was everywhere. Doc, fearing it would ignite any moment, shouted, 'Come down, quickly; come down!' We tunnelled our way back to the ditch, Wamsey seemingly completely unperturbed by her good luck in surviving such a horrendous smash-up. When we reached the ditch, however, she stopped and turned white. 'I can't go on! I can't go on!' she cried as she spotted the cattle Doc and I had passed earlier. 'I'm frightened of cows.'

• Chapter 8 •

All in a Day's Work

WE WERE SUPPOSED to deliver aircraft in one piece, without overstressing the engine or airframe. Consequently, ATA pilots were naturally not taught how to aerobat, merely instructed how to get out of a spin, should we have the misfortune to get into one in the first place.

One day I was flying another light, pale-blue PR Spitfire, this time from RAF Benson in Oxfordshire. It was a day when the sky too was a lovely shade of blue, so, feeling very good about things in general, I thought it was about time to see if I could at least do a roll.

It was a very very hot day, and the Spitfire had been standing in the sun for some time, so it was a bit like being in a cucumber frame once I got under the hood. I was wearing my navy blue flying overalls, with only my shirt and undies beneath. The Spit was one of the first with a round, bubble-type canopy. I guess it had at last been found possible to bend perspex around corners while still retaining sufficient strength. The hood was a triumph, as you could put your face near to the curved sides in order to peer forward. This allowed you to see a bit more in front, over that large engine cowling, as well as behind, now that the perspex bowed outwards.

At about 5,000 feet, while keeping the nose on my chosen delivery course, I put the ailerons over on one side, then the other, but couldn't quite summon up enough courage at first to turn the thing right over. At last it happened, but I promptly got stuck upside down! In this attitude, while wondering what to do next, from out of my top overall pocket fell my beautifully engraved, round, silver powder compact. It wheeled round and round the bubble canopy like a drunken sailor on a wall of death, opened, then sent all the face powder over absolutely everything.

When I found myself right way up again, the inside of the canopy was like a frosted lavatory window. I smeared a clear view but it made an awful mess. I was very hot and sticky anyway, and brushing my overalls made the stuff fly up again, sticking to my face and neck. It was simply amazing how much powder there seemed to be. It rapidly spread over the whole inside of the cockpit, instruments, windscreen, knobs and switches – just everywhere! To add to my discomfort, as I righted the aeroplane, that dear little powder compact dropped down into the fuselage beneath the control wires under my feet. It was just sitting there, shining up at me. There was no immediate danger of it jamming anything but I couldn't reach it to make certain.

When I arrived at my destination, I landed, then taxied in to park beside the Watch office. As I switched off, a very tall and extremely handsome RAF flight lieutenant came striding out of the door with a jaunty step, a charming smile, and a purposeful approach. He was beside the Spitfire before I had time to get out, hopping onto the wing to meet me.

However, one glance was enough. His expression changed as his mouth dropped open in sheer disbelief! 'I was told,' he gasped, 'that a very very pretty girl was bringing us a new aircraft. All I can see is some ghastly clown!' He jumped down from the wing like a maggot from a bait tin, turned on his heels, then fled away to a parked car, got in, clanked the gears and was gone. It might have been the start of a beautiful friendship, even a romance. My appearance soon changed that.

I gave myself a personal memo: Be quite sure, Diana, before doing your next clever bit of aerobatics, that the top pocket buttons of your flying overalls are done up.

◇ ◇ ◇

I had first left White Waltham in May 1942 for a few weeks' trial posting at No. 15 Ferry Pool, Hamble, by the Solent, just down from Southampton, but in June 1943 I was posted there permanently. There were only eight other pilots, one being Honor Salmon, or, to give her her full title, First Officer Mrs Honor Isobel Pomeroy Salmon. She was a warm, smiling, friendly person with light brown hair and blue-grey eyes. I was still a very new pilot but she was extremely kind, extending a motherly friendship towards me.

She had lived with her parents on the high ridge near Marlborough, so I suppose she knew that area well. One day, shortly after my arrival, Honor got caught out by bad weather, crashed in an Oxford into the hills very close to her home and was killed. It was supposed that she had chosen that route because she knew the area, thinking she could winkle her way between the hills and up valleys in that nasty weather.

Our CO at Hamble, Margot Gore, called us together over the tannoy to tell us the dreadful news. I was devastated, not only at her sudden death, but because, of all the other pilots, it was Honor who had really helped me to get used to being in and flying from a new and, indeed, an all-women's ferry pool.

Some time later, Margot told us that Honor's parents had specially asked that her possessions at Hamble be shared out between all of us, so we were asked to choose something from her locker, which, as it happened, was right next to mine. Somehow, when it was opened, her tragic death really struck home to me; I didn't want anything of hers. But someone said, 'Oh, Diana, you're about the same size', handing me one of Honor's most beautiful pale-blue shirts. It was made from a lovely soft wool, yet looked enough like our ordinary-issue shirts to be able to be worn with our ATA uniform. As clothes were rationed and could only be bought with coupons, I accepted it.

When I got back to my digs, I tried it on, whereupon I promptly burst into tears. It fitted me perfectly but I could never bring myself to wear it. Nearly 50 years later I still have it. Although I sometimes take it out of the cupboard, I have never been able to put it on again. But I remember with pride the woman who wore it. In my heart she has never died.

After that, when someone had an accident or was killed, I scarcely talked about it at all. To have dwelt on such things as I have just done would have been hopeless for my morale. Anyway, I had all those marvellous aeroplanes on which concentration was necessary. The accident reports, if relevant to any fault in that particular type, would be promulgated in due course. Getting bumped off, for whatever reason, was one of the normal hazards of the life. It could happen any time, like stubbing your toe or getting grit in your eye.

All the women ferry pilots at Hamble loved to fly, no matter what! One wintry day I was back early, sitting cosily in the Hamble Mess, when I heard the sound of a Merlin engine, very low overhead. It was a filthy cold, sleeting afternoon. Shortly afterwards in came 'Jackie' Moggridge, a very small, dark-haired South African pilot, and a very good one too. She came running to me, her eyebrows and eyelashes covered in snow and frost. 'Do you know,' she gasped, 'it was so bad I was map-reading on my approach!'

Another day she brought in a Spitfire to Hamble again. Margot saw her in silhouette as she climbed down from the cockpit and nearly had a fit. She hadn't noticed before, and called out, 'Jackie, you're pregnant!' Jackie was seven months gone at the time and hadn't said anything about it as she didn't want to be stopped from flying.

Another pilot from overseas was Margot Duhalde, who came all the way from Chile to help in the war effort. She was always affectionately known as 'Chile' because of the shoulder flash on her uniform. She had done a lot of flying, some of which had been with the Chilean Air Force.

I had first met her at White Waltham. When she arrived, the head boys told her she couldn't possibly be a ferry pilot as she didn't speak English, so would be unable to understand the schooling or read the handling notes. Chile was an extremely pretty, dark girl, with tiny, beautiful hands. She was told to try to learn the language. To that end she was allowed to stay at White Waltham, working with the engineers in the huge open-sided hangar – and this was in the winter of 1941–42.

While she was thus engaged, I was warmly ensconced in the various classrooms, learning navigation, meteorology, and what made propellers go round, whilst poor Chile was freezing outside. She used to come in at the end of the day absolutely covered in oil and grease with her dark hair matted, while her lovely little hands were icy cold and black. She was determined to fly for England, and she stuck it out for several months. She learnt very little 'proper' English but the engineers thought it was very funny to teach her swear words, at which, without knowing, she became an apt pupil.

She was eventually posted to Hamble and was an efficient and much-liked pilot who had an excellent record. She survived right through until ATA was disbanded. She is now back in Chile and is still flying. In 1989, on the 50th anniversary of the founding of ATA, she was presented with her wartime medals at RAF Lyneham by HRH Prince Michael of Kent.

Among other nationalities engaged in ATA work, and one of the more unusual, was Prince Suprabhat Chirasakti of Siam, the brother of Prince Birabongse, whom I'd met at Brooklands and who raced E.R.A. cars before the war. His famous cars were called 'Romulus' and 'Remus', and another was named 'Hanuman', the name of an important Siamese monkey god. Both brothers were nephews of Rama VII Prajadhipok, King of Siam. They lived not far from White Waltham.

Prince Suprabhat was a neat, small, smiling, twinkly-eyed, quiet young man. After his training he was posted to Kirkbride, near Carlisle. We called that ferry pool the 'Naughty Boys' Pool', for it was a tough place to fly from. Most of the very tough, experienced pilots were sent there. I can't think why little Chirasakti was – there was nothing tough or naughty to be seen in 'Chira's' make-up, and it was especially unkind for him as some of his family lived near White Waltham.

Kirkbride really was a hard pool to be in. The weather could be exceptionally bad on the routes they had to cover, one of which was the Dumfries Valley, up or down, to and from Prestwick.

It was important to save petrol. Seamen in naval convoys were dying in those early days bringing fuel across the Atlantic, so even in bad weather, instead of flying the longer route around the coast west of the valley, some people still flew up the valley. The wide entrance lured you into it even when very low cloud was sitting on the tops of the mountains, but the valley got narrower and narrower until there was no room to turn around. In poor visibility and heavy cloud cover it wasn't so easy to get up through the overcast, which we were not supposed to do anyway, and safely let down somewhere else away from that mountainous region. Many people got caught out and flew into the sides of the valley. Soon after his posting, so did the little prince from Siam. He must have found the far end blocked by low cloud, couldn't get out and hit the side of the valley.

Accident Report. 12 September 1942. Hurricane *JS346*.
Prince Chirasakti.
Near Langholm 11.30 hours; aircraft flew into hill, the pilot having persisted too far into hilly country in bad weather contrary to orders . . .

Keen type, pressed on too long. He shouldn't have been sent there so early in his flying career. I shed a tear. I never flew up the Dumfries Valley but always round the western edge of the hills by the Irish Sea. Longer, but less dangerous.

Another personality was Ed Heering, a Yank. He held the rank of second lieutenant in the US Army Air Corps but was persuaded to come over to fly for England with the ATA. This was long before Pearl Harbor. He was sent by ship with a batch of ten other pilots.

Ed was a tall, lean, softly spoken, blue-eyed, fair-haired 21-year-old. The other pilots were tough fellows and their ship had a rough time coming over. Their convoy was intercepted by German U-boats and two ships were sunk.

The new American pilots, who flew as mercenaries on contracts, being paid more than their English counterparts, were posted to No. 2 Ferry Pool at Whitchurch near Bristol, where Ed checked out on a Fairey Battle on 12 August 1940. Shortly after their arrival, the tough ones – not Ed – behaved with unseemly indignity after a flight to Hawarden. They set off Verey signal pistols (with the colours of the day) and got very drunk at Blossoms Hotel, Chester.

ATA was in its infancy. The Commodore, Pops d'Erlanger, who was pushing ATA all the way to fashion it into the superb organization it eventually became, heard about the fracas and was horrified at the exploits which reflected badly on the whole of the new organization. He recalled the pilots to White Waltham, lectured them, then shipped the whole lot back to the USA – including Ed, who with his quiet nature could never have been embroiled in such goings on.

When Ed arrived back at Halifax, the Air Attaché to the US, who had been responsible for talking him into going over in the first place, could not understand why the pleasant American Army Air officer had also been sent home. Ed shrugged his shoulders – he didn't know either. Tarred with the same brush, he supposed. The Air Attaché got the tie-lines red hot to Pop d'Erlanger, who acquiesced: Ed could return. But by then Ed didn't want to go. He'd had enough of rotten and dangerous sailing experiences, nor did he fancy England in the cold winter. He said, 'No – not again.' The Air Attaché persevered, and Ed returned to England on another fearsome trip.

Pops called Ed to his HQ office, saying, 'I shall be keeping an eye on you, Heering,' and posted him further north than before, to No. 4 Ferry Pool at Prestwick, then even further north, to Lossiemouth, where with several other ATA pilots he was attached to No. 46 MU and RAF Repair Unit, there being no ATA ferry pool.

After a while, Ed was told to report back to White Waltham to see Pops. Ed couldn't work out on the journey south what he might have done wrong this time. Back in the CO's office, Pops began, 'Yes, Heering, I have been watching your progress.' Ed quaked. Pops then went on in a favourable vein. He told Ed to go back to Lossie, where there was now to be a proper ferry pool instead of the pilots' attachments. Ed was to design all the buildings – the Mess, Ops room, meteorology, maps and signals, medical section, locker rooms – the lot. The RAF would construct it, Ed would oversee it and report to Pops when it had been completed.

It was ready in three months. When he reported back, Pops said, 'Well done, Heering, now go back and command it!' So Ed became a commander of a ferry pool when he had only just turned 22, and a Yank at that. His pool was happy and well run. His pilots' ratio of accidents to delivery numbers was minimal, all of which reflected down from the top.

In the autumn of 1942, Ed was given 30 days' leave to go home to America to get married. His return voyage was on the *Queen Mary*, which was being used as a troop-ship. At 14:10 local time, a day out (away) from Greenock, the British escorting cruiser *Curaçao* cut across the *Queen Mary*'s bows during a zigzag anti-U-boat manoeuvre. The *Queen Mary* struck the cruiser amidships, cutting it in two. It exploded and sank with 472 casualties.

The *Queen Mary* wasn't permitted to stop to pick up anyone because of her vulnerability, and with so many more people on board. She proceeded at 15 knots instead of 28 as her bow was stoved in and the front compartment filled with water. This was yet another horrendous trip for Ed who didn't have much luck with his Atlantic crossings . . . or did he? He survived, unlike thousands of others.

Once back in England, Ed stayed on for the rest of the war, doing a sterling job.

Every male pool commander was made an OBE at the end of the war, while the two female commanders rated only MBEs. Captain Ed Heering didn't get anything at all – the only pool commander who was not honoured.

After the war, Ed joined World Airways, becoming their chief pilot. He went back and forth over the Atlantic with passengers and freight, flying into Gatwick several times a month. Later he became personal pilot to Edward Joseph Daly, the owner of World Airways, flying him worldwide in a Boeing three-engined 727 or Convair twin-engined Metropolitan 440.

After 50 years, Ed finally retired on 15 January 1988, having flown 34,000 hours (3.88 years) while at the controls of 135 different types of aircraft.

Pool commanders such as our Margot Gore, at Hamble, could not possibly fly every day. It didn't mix with their administrative duties. They could not run the risk of being stuck out somewhere for the night, maybe even a few days, if the weather clamped. It must have been extremely frustrating for Margot not to fly whilst sending off her pilots to deliver such a variety of beautiful aeroplanes. She also had overall responsibility if any of her pilots broke an aircraft or their necks.

When she could do so, she flew. With apparent ease she brought in huge four-engined B24 Liberators and B17 Flying Fortresses onto the tiny little Hamble field, skimming about two feet over the Air Service Training hangar that was in the way, and then, after a dainty landing, only needing half the strip before she stopped. An extrememly skilled and accurate effort every time.

Margot opened the hatch one afternoon in summer. 'There are four Spitfire Mark XIVs to move from Eastleigh to Witney,' she said to me. 'You can do them all with a personal taxi [a Fairchild].' Sounded lovely to me.

It was a beautiful sunny day with no weather problems. I took off and as always headed six miles north of the top of the Hamble River, then to a hill – height 423 feet – from which I set my course, having thus avoided the Southampton balloons. Margot told me Witney was a small humpy-bumpy grass aerodrome, and to be extremely careful taxying as these new XIVs were very, very nose-heavy. She added that she was sending me as I was good at Spits, but to watch out all the same.

Fancy four lovely Spitfire XIVs in one afternoon! Tiny little short flights, sunshine everywhere, with a Fairchild following me back and forth between the take-offs and deliveries, then taking me home for a late tea afterwards. The Spits all started first go, no wasted time. We didn't nose over after landing on the hillocks. Life for a ferry pilot was good sometimes.

I thought I was near the peak of my flying efficiency. By 1943 I could handle any aircraft up to 'Class IV plus'. So far, I hadn't broken anything. I had flown through the most dreadful weather, but still kept to the ATA rules, effectively staying within sight of the ground, even though, at times, one could hardly see it. Even so, I could still not blind-fly – yet – for any length of time. Of course I had used instruments in poor visibility, or fogs, if only to stay right way up. Now and then I felt brave as I darted in one side of a fluffy cloud and out the other, thinking myself very daring.

One day I was given a Spitfire to fly from Eastleigh to Cosford. I headed up from the south in my nice Spit, passing over Worcester in the sunshine, my route to Cosford taking me up the Severn Valley, leaving Kidderminster on my starboard, so that the line of the Birmingham balloons was safely out on my right-hand side. I got over the tree-covered high ground which lies on the right of the Severn River, then, nearing Kidderminster, the cloud, which had been non-existent behind me, came right down to treetops so I couldn't get through. It was maddening and I had instant visions of my trip in January when I had ended up at Windrush.

I was so close to Cosford and wanted to get home to Hamble that evening, as I was due to go on my day's leave. I decided to go over the top. This was the first time I had consciously broken ATA rules. If I couldn't make Cosford, I would fly back to the clear weather behind me around Worcester, but thought maybe I should get lucky and find a gap in the clouds to come down through to Cosford. I didn't think it could be suddenly all that thick everywhere. Perhaps the clouds were only local, caused by temperatures over the forests, which had mingled with the smoke of Birmingham drifting out. How we can deceive ourselves.

I climbed up and up, but the clouds were higher than I had expected – I came out at 12,000 feet. I had no oxygen to switch on and realized that it was silly to have flown so high without it. I had carefully checked my watch, and on DR (Dead Reckoning navigation) knew where Cosford should be. At the precise second I had calculated, the white clouds 'greyed', and I thought I saw a tiny gap. Anyway, the clouds were thinner there. I dived for the gap, standing the Spit on its nose. What a stupid act!

Speed built up alarmingly as the cloud closed over me. I watched the altimeter but kept on going straight down. I was afraid of overflying Cosford in that heavy cloud by easing out of my vertical descent too soon. Suddenly I broke cloud with enough height to come out of the hurtling downward plunge. Cloud base was about 400 feet and I was right in the circuit of Cosford. It was a tremendous feeling, for not only was my elementary navigation spot-on, but my reasoning about it being in the clear where there were no trees had also turned out to be correct.

Back at Hamble that evening, when I was booking in my delivery chits at Operations, a tall, fair, Danish pilot named Vera Strodl beckoned me aside. She too had taken off from Eastleigh for Cosford, at practically the same time as I had done, also running into exactly the same lump of weather south of Cosford.

She looked at me suspiciously. 'The others didn't get there. Did you go over the top, Diana?' 'Mmm,' I nodded, putting a finger to my lips. She raised her blond eyebrows. 'Sh! Sh!' she whispered, 'So did I!' We conspirators silently crept into the Mess for tea.

◇   ◇   ◇

Sometimes small things went wrong with the things we flew. On 28 May I had a Mustang I (*AG642*) to take from Kidlington, near Oxford, down to St Athan, in South Wales, just along from Barry. There was a petrol tank in each wing of the Mustang. I started up on the left-hand tank.

With the engine running, I checked that it could also run off the right-hand tank, then switched back to the other before getting airborne and heading west. Near my destination I checked the fuel, being mystified to see that the tank I had been using showed only five gallons on the gauge. This had to be wrong as I had only been in the air for 35 minutes.

I changed tanks, whereupon the Allison engine promptly stopped! The fresh tank was now also showing empty, even though I had not used it, and it had been full when I took off. The enforced engine silence was shattering. Changing back to the other tank, I was mighty relieved when it picked up again. I made a straight run into St Athan, hoping that no-one else would take offence if they were in the circuit.

The Allison died again just as I got to the runway intersection. I got out and discovered petrol oozing from both tanks. I tried to push the Mustang onto the taxiway but it was far too heavy. Nobody came to help me, so I walked a very long, windy way to the Watch office where someone muttered something about female pilots cluttering up their runway. Our taxi-Anson had already arrived to collect me and take me to Brize Norton for my next job – a Spitfire VC tropical (*EF686*) with its big chin filter, which I was due to fly up to High Ercall in Shropshire, not far from The Wrekin. Several other ATA pilots were in the Anson, and fast getting annoyed at being kept waiting. Delay was always a nuisance, for often it meant being stuck out overnight if you couldn't complete the various deliveries by nightfall.

The Station Engineer Officer came rushing up, so I gave him my snag-sheet, telling him what had happened. As we taxied out in the Anson, a tractor was already towing in my Mustang. I was very unpopular with everyone at St Athan that day.

A few days afterwards I was told that the air vents of both tanks had been doped over, creating a vacuum. In consequence, the petrol was syphoning itself out en route. It was the same problem which led to the death of Margaret Fairweather over a year later. An error by some ground mechanic had nearly put paid to me, but I learned the lesson and from then on always checked that the air vents were open. Thank goodness my guardian angel was still working well!

In addition to that sort of superior snag we also had inferior snags. Amongst these were those little things that went wrong, such as the air speed indicator going unserviceable (U/S). That could be awkward on approach and landing. Sometimes the hydraulics went U/S, which prompted emergency undercarriage and flap lowering, not to mention the possibility of having no brakes.

These sorts of things were commonplace, but luckily not quite everyday occurrences. As we became more experienced, and used to all our main types of aeroplanes, we knew that we could generally overcome these little difficulties, so we were never unduly worried. After all, except for our leave days we had been flying every day for all the war years, so small mechanical failures such as having no brakes did not bring us up short, so to speak.

But a bad snag, if combined with bad weather, sometimes did.

There were some pilots whom things happened to that were definitely not their fault at all. Audrey Sale-Barker, whom we called Wendy, who skied for England before the war and who married Lord Selkirk, the Duke of Hamilton's brother, after the war, was sitting stationary in an aeroplane at White Waltham when some clot came along and taxied straight into her, nearly demolishing her and both aircraft.

Then there were other pilots who had a record of a trail of broken aeroplanes, where 'things happening to them' that were not their fault were compounded and exacerbated by their subsequent actions.

Such a one was Frankie Francis, the CO of No. 1 Pool before Doc Whitehurst took over. One day he was flying a twin-engined bomber along the east coast when he ran into a severe electrical storm with lots of thunder and lightning. He thought that he had been struck and that one wing was on fire. He stopped the engine that side, trimmed against its lack of power, then with great difficulty climbed out of the small cockpit window. If he had not been a lightly built, lithe little man, he could not have got out, but he did, so safely parachuted down.

The accident investigation people decided later on that there had been no fire at all on Frankie's aircraft. They concluded that the electrical charge in the storm had produced conditions known as 'St Elmo's Fire', which is caused by static discharge. No doubt Frankie's wing looked like the Christmas pudding alight after an over-dousing with too much brandy, but it seems he baled out of a perfectly good aeroplane. Bad luck Frankie!

On another occasion, Frankie was in a twin-engined Mosquito in the circuit at Hatfield, the de Havilland factory airfield where they were built, when one of the electrical feathering propellers feathered itself. Instead of immediately doing a correct single-engined approach and landing, he pressed the button and the engine unfeathered itself. When it seemed to be purring along nicely, Frankie decided to land, but when he was on finals, and at under single-engined safety speed, the same engine suddenly refeathered again. With only one engine, Frankie stalled and crashed onto the edge of the grass runway.

The Mossie was one of the first bonded metal and wood aircraft, and Frankie's ended up looking a bit like a dog's dinner. It was a proper write-off. There was scarcely a bit left that was larger than a matchstick but Frankie stepped out of the mess with just a tiny cut on his forehead plus a bruised hand.

So a lot of things happened to Frankie – but then, not only did he have the awesome responsibility of running No. 1 Pool, he also flew a lot of aeroplanes.

◇   ◇   ◇

While I was daily 'dicing with death', some of my father's friends had moved down from London to live at Ridgemead, 'to escape the bombs'. They gave their ration books to the cook, but food was already very short, so every Friday evening early in the war, on his way home from his work in London, my father stopped at a fish shop in Harrington Road, South Kensington, to buy up all their unsold fish and left-overs. Fish was unrationed. Strangely enough, this usually included the more expensive things such as lobsters, turbot and prawns! And then there were always chitterlings (soft cod's roes), of which my father was very fond.

A huge wooden crate would be loaded into the boot of his Bentley, which he drove once a week for this express purpose. There was still a petrol pump at his garage at Ridgemead with a huge supply of fuel which I never got my hands on, or he just saved up his coupons for his weekly jaunt. For the rest of the week he drove a small pre-war Lancia. I don't think the Lancia had enough space for the fish crate, except on the passenger seat. The Bentley was used only on Fridays. My father explained, 'The smell's behind instead of beside!'

Petrol was also rationed, of course. Although black market petrol coupons were to be found, they did not fit my limited purse nor my principles. Going to London by train kept my self-imposed halo nice and shiny.

I could save up enough petrol to drive to Ridgemead now and then from Hamble but not all the way to London where, in the day time, I rode a smart white bicycle. I was collected from River House, Chelsea, in the evenings by my admirers in their cars, using their petrol. My mother had converted River House into five flats, one being free for me to use, of which more later.

During the day my bike and I got along fine, as there were hardly any cars on the roads. On one occasion I skidded and fell off in greasy and oily Berkeley Street, right in front of admirer Bobby Sweeny, the famous pre-war British Amateur Champion golfer and Walker Cup player with a +3 handicap, who, to my chagrin, was escorting another girl.

Bobby was extremely good-looking, and had been to Oxford. An American from California, younger brother of Charles, who had been the mastermind behind the American Eagle squadrons earlier in the war, Bobby had become adjutant of the Eagles. Later he became a pilot himself, flew with RAF Coastal Command and won the DFC for attacking and sinking U-boats in the Atlantic. Bobby and Charles, captain of the Oxford golf team, often came down to Ridgemead to play golf with my father.

In London there was the blackout and air-raids, which made driving difficult and unattractive. Not a chink of light was allowed to be shown from windows or doors. All cars had black metal hoods on their headlamps which only allowed a tiny slit of light to show through. Knowing the route helped and good eyesight was paramount. There was no street lighting either – nothing to help the German bombers.

British fighter pilots had great success shooting down enemy aircraft in the night sky once airborne radar had been perfected. The Beaufighter was fixed up with this early radar. The RAF didn't want the Germans to know about it, naturally. John Cunningham, later Group Captain, with DSO and two bars, DFC and bar, and a test pilot for de Havilland, who did all the testing on the Comet, had a good record of kills. He had wonderful vision. Years later, when I was a co-guest on Alan and Lois Butler's yacht (Alan was head of de Havilland at Hatfield, and Lois I have written about already), John always saw land or other ships long before I could do so. I'll tell you another story about John in a later chapter.

On my London leave days I always changed into a long evening dress before being taken out to dinner, usually ending up in a night-club such as the '400' or the Orchid Room. I spent so much time in smoky night-clubs that it is a wonder it did not shorten my life. I never thought flying would.

In the early hours of dawn I would change back into my uniform at River House for my next assignment. There were two taxi-driver brothers, Bert and Ozzie Jenkins. They ranked at Hyde Park Corner and I had a weekly arrangement with them to get me to the 04.20 train from Waterloo to the railway station at Eastleigh, by Southampton, where I used to leave my car so that I could drive back to Hamble. They never let me down. Whatever the bombing situation, whether or not the shrapnel was raining down or the sirens going, or the reassuring noise of our anti-aircraft guns, one or other of the brothers would be sitting outside River

House in his taxi, wearing his tin hat, when I came tripping out at 4 in the morning. The two men looked rather alike. In the dark I could only tell which one it was by the greeting. Bert would say, 'Good morning my little butterfly!', whilst Ozzie would regale me during the drive to the station with details of the places the bombs had fallen during the night.

I would curl up in the train under my thick flying coat for a couple of hours' nap. Arriving at Eastleigh, I just had time to drive fast to the cottage to tidy up and have breakfast. I had no breakfast if the train was late, maybe delayed by air-raids, before going to Hamble to fly all day. I never felt tired . . . I pine for my youthful energy.

Gold, the butler, had been with my father for many years. He started as a footman in the Grosvenor Square flat. He later went into the RAF too, becoming batman to Air Chief Marshal Sir Arthur 'Bomber' Harris, C in C of Bomber Command. I think Air Chief Marshal Sir Wilfred Freeman, a good friend of my father's, arranged that. Gold stayed with Harris for the rest of the war, doing exactly the same job wearing RAF uniform instead of my father's livery.

The long table at Ridgemead was always superbly laid by Gold, with a row of five of my father's Brooklands' trophies along the middle: a first prize, a very large cup in the centre, flanked by two slightly smaller second prize cups, while next to them two even smaller third prize cups.

One cold evening, I arrived at the start of a weekend, when there was going to be a dinner party for 20. The bathrooms were very modern, with coloured baths lying from corner to corner in their large sunken squares. They looked lovely but they were too shallow to get one's shoulders covered with hot water. Added to that, in wartime Britain you were only supposed to use 4 inches of water in order to conserve supplies of fuel. A piece of insulating tape had been stuck onto each bath in order to remind the user.

There was no heating of any kind in those bathrooms and I had been lying sideways to try to get warm while the water had been slopping away down the overflow hole. Suddenly, Gold banged on the door – 'Miss Diana, Miss Diana, your bathwater is overflowing all over my table!' How could it be? I wondered, there was no water visible on the floor.

But bathwater had come through the ceiling, landing up on one end of the beautifully arranged long table. Every centre piece, napkins, linen and silver had to be dried or changed. The guests had assembled so dinner had to be delayed whilst Gold reset the whole thing. It was one of those rare times my father scolded me, but he took it back the next day when it was found that the overflow pipe had cracked in the frost. I had not exceeded the 4 inch rule . . !

I can only remember being scolded by my father once before, when I had not yet joined ATA, nor had the accident happened with Bobby Loewenstein's point-to-pointer. After Red Cross hospital work I had

Above left *Grandfather Barney Barnato.*

Above right *Gra Falk, my maternal American grandmother, and me (on the right!).*

Pictures from a remarkable life

Right *My sister Virginia and me at Brooklands, Easter Monday, 1928 (I'm on the left). How I hated that grey wool dress made out of knitted stuff like combinations.*

Above *Our rabbits in flower pots, Elsworthy Road garden; they became hand-muffs!*

Below left *Virginia (left) and me with Dugan of Deloraine, first prize winner at Regents Park and District Dog Society Show. Then he got run over.*

Below right *My father Woolf Barnato (in white) and Bernard Rubin, first at Le Mans, 1928.*

The next year he won it with Henry Birkin (right) – the first Speed Six win. My father did the hat trick in 1930.

My father dropped this bottle of champagne over Gatwick to inaugurate the new civic aerodrome there on 4 April 1931.

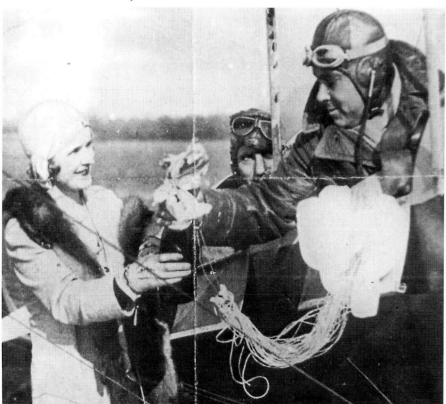

Left *Leaving Honolulu, 1934: Virginia, stepfather Richard, Mama and me. Note the shrapnel wound scar on his forehead, received whilst flying with the RFC in the First World War.*

Far left *In my débutante coming-out dress, 1936.* (Norman Parkinson)

Left *At Brooklands in 1938, whilst learning to fly. Note hangar and fuel pumps.*

Above *My first Bentley (CXF 114), a 21st birthday present from my father.*

Right *Looking terribly serious in my Red Cross outfit, 1939–41.*

My father's house, Ridgemead, its white walls camouflaged because of the war.

My friend Dick Fairey helped me get into ATA. He lost both legs after spending four days in an open boat after his ship was torpedoed in the Atlantic.

Constaki Cawadias, a friend of Virginia's, who was in MI9 in Greece.

The Gestapo found this photo of Virginia in Con's Athens house. The picture then appeared in a Wanted poster, but she was in Hollywood. (Norman Parkinson)

Left *Claud Strickland, RAF fighter pilot and close friend. He was later killed in action while flying with 615 Squadron.*

Below *Hatfield 1940: the first eight women pilots accepted to fly with ATA.*

Bottom *The first women ATA pilots, left to right: Joan Hughes, Margaret Cunnison, Henrietta Stapleton-Bretherton (CO's secretary), Mona Freidlander, Gabrielle Patterson, Rosemary Rees, Lois Butler, Marion Wilberforce, Pauline Gower (CO) and Margaret Fairweather (who was later killed).*

Right *Margaret Fairweather (left), Mona Freidlander and Joan Hughes.*

Below right *Ronnie Malcolm (how he fitted into a Spit I don't know), Captain Douglas Fairweather (who judged distances by smoking cigarettes), Jim Kempster and Harry Ellis, summer 1941.*

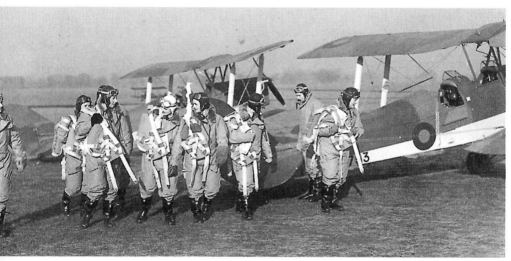

Above left *Humphrey Gilbert DFC. In less than a month I'd met him, fallen in love, become engaged, and lost him when he was killed in a crash shortly before we were to be married.*

Above right *Me in full ATA war-paint, 1942.*

Below *Humphrey Gilbert, CO of 65 Squadron (far right), with Tony Bartley DFC (centre) and Flying Officer Bill Davies. Tony often visited Ridgemead and is still a friend. Note dog in cockpit.*

Above left *Another fighter pilot visitor was Bob Tuck DSO DFC. The plaster on his forehead was due to an injury received when he was shot down in June 1941.*

Above right *Another friend at Ridgemead, who played golf with my father – the British amateur golf champion Bobby Sweeny, who served with the Eagle Squadron and later with RAF Coastal Command.*

Below *My father nearly in full war-paint; he went on to become a Wing Commander. Note Ridgemead's camouflaged walls and his newest Bentley Mk V.*

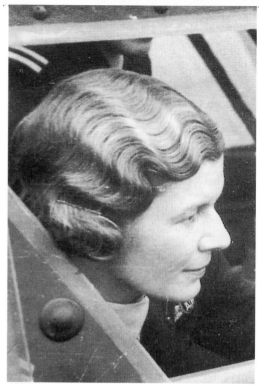

Above left *Commodore Gerard d'Erlanger CBE, founder of ATA (right), with Lord Beaverbrook.*

Above right *Senior Commander Pauline Gower MBE in an Oxford.*

Below *Some more of the ladies: (left to right) Lettice Curtis, Jenny Broad, Wendy Sale-Barker, Gaby Patterson and Pauline Gower.*

Above *A visit by Mrs Eleanor Roosevelt, White Waltham, 1942. Left to right: Opal Anderson (USA), DB, Edith Stearns (USA), Kay van Doozer (USA), Pauline Gower, Mrs Roosevelt.*

Below *Two of my father's friends and frequent visitors to Ridgemead: Air Commodore Bill Paine (left) and Chief of the Air Staff Sir Wilfred Freeman KCB DSO MC.*

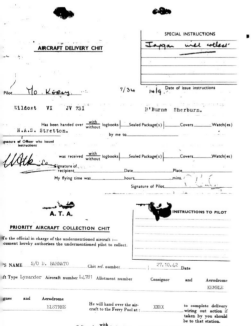

Above *Taxi-Anson at White Waltham, September 1942. The woman pilot is Ann Wood (USA), although she appears camera-shy. Our parachutes weighed 40 lb. (Flight)*

Left *Our aircraft chits: (top) one of Third Officer Ruth Kerly's chits for a Grumman Wildcat, and (bottom) my P.1.W. chit to fly a Lysander to Elstree.*

Above right *Getting my hands on a Hurricane was a huge step forward (the Spitfire soon followed). (IWM)*

Right *Ian Fenwick did these cartoons of us at Hamble in 1943; he was later killed in Italy. The first one refers to the 2/6d fine if one taxied in with flaps down, the other highlights our main drink – hot orangeade!*

"Got caught with your flaps down, so to speak?"

WITH THE A.T.A. ANY HOUR
BETWEEN 0900 AND 1600 —

The Spitfire was a delight to fly – and I delivered 260 of them.

The girls of No. 15 Ferry Pool, Hamble, in 1944. Diana on the tail, Chile in the cockpit (left), and Margot Gore is by the white dot below the hood.

And some of the chaps . . . (left to right) George Parnell (my pilot when we hit two seagulls), Harry Guest, Walton, Henry Stringer and Ron Elliott.

Hamble. Left to right, back row: Maureen Dunlop (Argentina), Roberta Leveaux (USA), Doreen Illsley, Rosemary Banister, Kay van Doozer (USA), Emily Chapin (USA), Mary Wilkins; third row: Vera Strodl (Denmark), Betty Hayman, Grace Stevenson (USA), Jackie Sorour (South Africa), Margaret Duhalde (Chile), DB, Dora Lang (killed); second row: Anna Leska (Poland), Rosemary Rees, Margot Gore (CO), Philippa Bennett, Veronica Volkertz; front: Anne Walker, Taniya Whittall (killed), Mardi Gething (Australia).

Above left *'At Home' at Hamble. Seated at the back, Veronica Volkersz; left front, Doreen Illsley, Anna Leska's back, Dora Lang (killed in a Mossie), and Ethel (standing); right, Maureen Dunlop and Margot 'Chile' Duhalde.*

Left *DB in taxi-Anson. An Me 110 nearly got us near Reading in one of these on 10 February 1943.*

Above *Max Aitken, fighter pilot son of Lord Beaverbrook, on a pre-war skiing trip. Following an evening of blind-flying chat at the '400' Club, his lesson helped save my life the next day.*

Above right *Another successful fighter pilot, Laddie Lucas, who played golf with my father on visits to Ridgemead.*

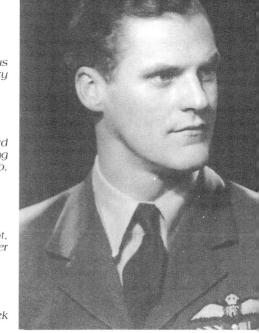

Right *My husband Wing Commander Derek Walker DFC.*

Far top left *Our wedding day, 10 May 1944.*

Above left *A Grumman Avenger like the one I flew on 27 June 1944, but mine had the supercharger linked up the wrong way round!*

Left *Cutting the cake – note model of Typhoon on the top. Derek had been flying Typhoons when I first met him.*

Above *I took 'Splinters' Smallwood's Spitfire to Brussels in October 1944 . . .*

Above right *. . . and the day after I'd brought it back, Paddy Dunn flew it and the engine blew up on take-off! Both men were to reach high rank, of Air Chief Marshal and Air Marshal respectively.*

Right *The cocoa. I could put 40 1-lb tins in my parachute bag and smuggle them to Brussels.*

Top left *A Spitfire XXI. I first flew this type on 1 February 1945 – my 241st Spitfire flight.*

Middle left *A Mitchell bomber: mine caught fire on the way to Hawarden, on 11 May 1945. (RAF Museum)*

Left *Shawbury, 13 June 1945. We took a couple of ATC cadets who used to assist ATA pilots (left) in this Anson. Elizabeth May and I are the two females.*

Above *The Hawker Typhoon. The bottom fell out of my world – literally – when flying a 'Tiffie' on 30 April 1945, but I got it down.*

Right *And I nearly wrapped a Warwick V round a windsock a week later.*

Above left *Leonard Thornhill. He and I so nearly crashed head-on into an Avro Lancaster on 21 July 1945. Poor Len, he died as this book was almost finished (October 1993).*

Above *Captain Cuthbert Orde wanted to draw Derek, but he had to settle for painting me when Derek refused. In 1945 the picture was in the portrait painters' exhibition in London and now it hangs in my dining room.*

Left *I didn't always wear uniform: DBW at River House, 1945.*

Above right *The Mustang in which Derek was killed on 15 November 1945.*

Right *ATA came to an end in November 1945. Later there was the laying-up of the ATA flag at the church near White Waltham. Left to right: Ron Elliott, Eric 'John' Crowder, Ann Wood (USA), DBW, Faith Bennett, Jim Quaife, Dick Martens and H.C. Mason.*

In 1946 came the unveiling and dedication of the ATA Memorial Plaque in the crypt of St Paul's Cathedral by Lord Beaverbrook. Left to right: 'Whitey' White (Ops White Waltham), Ron Elliott, Faith Bennett, DBW, Lord Beaverbrook, Jim Quaife. Commodore d'Erlanger stands behind the canon.

With Whitney Straight and his daughter Camilla in front of his Percival Proctor.

Above left *Joan, my second stepmother; my father sent me as envoy to ask her to marry him.*

Above right *In the cockpit of a Tiger Moth after the war, at Woodley, near Reading.*

Below *With Freydis Sharland, also a WJAC pilot and former ATA pilot. We are standing in front of the first 'Grey Dove' (a Fairchild Argus).*

Left *Princess Marina, Duchess of Kent, christening 'Grey Dove' at Hendon, 17 July 1948. Note its wrinkled cowling following the fire a few days earlier.*

Below left *'Grey Dove' II – G-AMRF.*

Bottom left *Lord Brabazon of Tara christening 'Grey Dove' II.*

Right *With Jaki (dog no.3) at the controls of 'Grey Dove' II.*

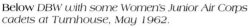

Below *DBW with some Women's Junior Air Corps cadets at Turnhouse, May 1962.*

Above *With Lord Brabazon again, this time receiving the Jean Lennox Bird Trophy at the Royal Aero Club, May 1963.*

Below left *After the women's Speed Record Flight – 1,262 mph – on 26 August 1963, Squadron Leader Ken Goodwin and I pose for the cameras. And behind is the Lightning which I flew – XM996, a Mark T4.*

Below right *The fastest woman in the world – DBW in full jet gear.*

Above left *After receiving the MBE in 1965 – in the same list as the Beatles!*

Above right *Taking Lord Shackleton for a ride when he was Air Minister. WJAC summer camp, Hurn, near Bournemouth, 1965.*

Below left *On 14 June 1965 I finished third in the Air Race for Women Flyers, organized at Shoreham by the Royal Aero Club. I flew 'Grey Dove' IV – an Auster Alpine.*

Below right *Diana Barnato Walker MBE, with 'Grey Dove' IV. (Frank Meads)*

Master of Foxhounds, Old Surrey and Burstow, outside Horne Grange on Yum-Yum. Jack Champion BEM, the longest-serving huntsman in the UK, is riding Kilkenny.

Uncle Jim Joel with his Grand National winner Maori Venture in 1987. He was the kindest, sweetest and funniest member of the family.

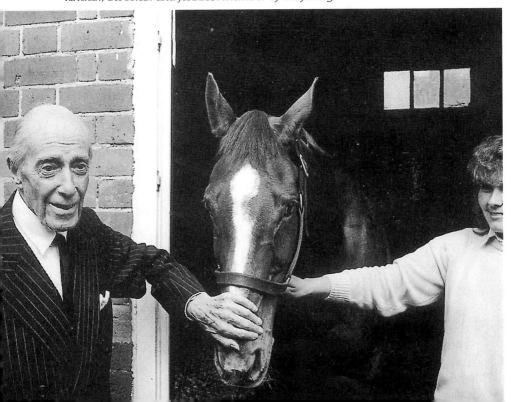

been out to dinner every night in one week, mostly up to London to the Café de Paris, a popular restaurant in Leicester Square where 'everybody' went to dine and dance to 'Snakehips' Johnson's marvellous band. Girls dressed up in beautiful long dresses, not their war work uniforms or, in my case, my Red Cross costume. The Café de Paris was in a basement, two floors down, so despite the London blitz it felt safe from bombs.

Claud Strickland, on leave, came to collect me from Ridgemead. I went into the bar to say goodnight to my father. He was alone – rare – for he usually had friends round. He said gruffly, 'Diana! You treat this house like a hotel!' (True.) 'You stay in for once.' With a bad grace I acquiesced. My father, Claud and I had a delightful dinner together, then heard from somebody who rang up that the Café de Paris had just been bombed, the band-leader, 'Snakehips' Johnson killed with many other people, while others had received terrible injuries in such a confined space. By pure chance a bomb had entered through a ventilation shaft and gone down to the basement before exploding.

If my father had not put his foot down over my behaviour, I would most certainly have been there too. My guardian angel at work again?

The weekend at Ridgemead turned out to be terrible. The very next evening after the bath episode, I got back again in time for dinner. No matter where I was sitting at the table, as the daughter of the house I was always served last. The 'guests' naturally took precedence, even though many of them were there all the time.

The main course was turbot in a yellow sauce made out of dried eggs, superbly camouflaged by the mountainous and ever-perspiring cook, Mrs Stacey. When the dish was finally proffered to me by Gold, there were only the scrapings left, plus a tiny little bit of the tail. I started to eat it but it tasted of disinfectant. Gold came round with the vegetables, so I complained to him. 'This tastes of disinfectant! Please tell Mrs Stacey!' There was a sudden, nasty lull in the various conversations about the table. After all, food was food, even with Lysol added.

Gold looked at me, then said quietly, but politely, 'You be me, Miss Diana!' Everyone heard and all roared with laughter.

The next morning was a leave day, so I went down to the stables. The old groom, Ide, who stood about 4 foot 6 inches tall with shoulders like a boxer, was a superb horseman who had survived the trenches in the First World War. 'Too small to be hit, Miss!' he would say. Later he'd been a jockey, and had held a trainer's licence in France.

He greeted me with a touch of his battered trilby, then beckoned me over behind the stables to the brick-walled manure dump. It was quite empty of manure but teeming with rabbits. Mostly they were wild rabbits, but here and there was the odd multi-coloured one. There must have been about 80 or so altogether. 'Goodness me, Ide, what are all these doing here?' 'Well, Miss Diana, I don't know what to do with them. It's getting very hard to feed them.' I should think so, I thought, with no corn ration. 'And I can't stop them breeding, can I!'

I asked why they weren't being used up, telling him that we'd eaten rabbit stew a few days before. 'Did you really, Miss? Well, they didn't come from here. Please will you tell the Captain?' he beseeched.

It turned out that Mrs Stacey was ordering rabbits from the poulterer in the village while ignoring Ide's lot, which had originally started with only four for the big house. But you know what rabbits are. My father told me that the secretary had not remarked on the bills, so I should go and confront Mrs Stacey with the news of the 80 rabbits waiting to be eaten up, and that my father wanted some of them used.

I crept through the double doors of the servery into the kitchen. The enormous Mrs Stacey smoothed her pure white starched apron over her capacious bosom, drew herself to her full height, then towering above me, said, 'Well, Miss Diana, the staff won't eat tame rabbit!'

I retreated back to my father who laughed, saying, 'I suppose she gets a rake-off from the butcher on the other ones, but go back and say that if the rabbits aren't used now and then, she may go on an extended holiday.' Taking a leaf out of Gold's book, I very nearly said, 'Daddy, you be me!', but my nerve failed me.

For the next week we were served a continuous supply of rabbit – stewed, casseroled (with dumplings), braised (with apple), plain roasted (with herbs), broiled (in a red wine sauce) – you name it . . . This went on for over a week, one excellent rabbit dish after another. By the end of it I longed for turbot – even with Lysol . . !

Our Mrs Stacey had won, as well as proving a point. By then, the front of the house didn't like tame rabbit either!

In September 1943 I returned from Hamble to White Waltham for a month while I converted onto Class IV aeroplanes – heavy twins. Flying my first heavy twin didn't seem exciting at all. We did dual in the school with an instructor before going solo. In general I found the weather always seemed to be better in twins – I suppose because the visibility out of them was so much better than in the majority of single-seaters with their noses in the way.

In the school we flew the Pegasus-engined Wellington, fondly nicknamed the 'Wimpy' after the character in the Popeye cartoons. Later Wellingtons had Merlin Xs and XIs, or twin Wasps or Hercules VI, XVI, or XVII engines. Like a fluttering bird of prey, the Wellington was slow to settle onto its final flight path let-down. Because of their geodetic construction, the wings always waved about at you, especially in rough weather conditions.

Oh yes, I made mistakes! We had to do the ATA cockpit checks before starting up. Test everything was the rule: but, if I hadn't . . .

I was in the cockpit of a Wimpy, swivelling my neck left to right and back again, trying not to part my hair in the overhead fuel exchange switches, when I saw a neat little switch on the control panel. Unmarked!

Automatically I pushed it down. Oh dear! It was a new jettison switch for petrol.

There was a flood of fuel onto the tarmac and the waiting-to-see-me-off ground crew were soaked. The Wellington had to be shifted from that hardstanding to a dry one because of the fire risk. No tractor could be used in case of sparks, so we all had to push it. Some push!

I was not popular with the ground crew. After the delay and subsequent refuelling, I thought how far I could have driven in my wartime Opel car with the petrol I'd jettisoned. What a waste! For once our little blue book of handling notes had not been updated in time to include the new petrol elimination switch. Could have been a Diana eliminator switch if I'd tried it in the air.

I will also mention here the Class V tricycle aircraft category. There were not too many tricycle twin-engined aircraft: the Albemarle, Boston, Havoc and Mitchell were some that I flew. In the fighter field there was the American P39 Aircobra and the P38 twin-engined Lightning. For the uninitiated, this meant that they had a nose wheel rather than a tail wheel, so three-pointer landings were out. One landed on the two main wheels, then gently dropped the nose wheel onto the runway. We learnt on the Armstrong Whitworth Albemarle, an aircraft designed as a reconnaissance bomber but used as a glider tug or special transport aeroplane. It had two Bristol Hercules engines.

The Albemarle was not considered a very successful aircraft and was nicknamed 'Beaverbrook's Flying Brick', because he had ordered them. As Lord Beaverbrook was head of the Ministry of Aircraft Production, produce them he did. He got results by red tape cutting and ideas. We and the RAF wouldn't have had so many aircraft to fly without him. England owes him a lot.

In those days, we waited cross-wind, facing the control box before getting the green light to turn into wind for take-off. In the school we were warned never to stand cross-wind in an Albemarle with the pilot's little cockpit window open, or we'd get gassed by the carbon monoxide, or at best, get a hefty headache.

Having completed the Class IV conversion course by mid-October, it was back to Hamble as a first officer, able now to include heavy twins and then tricycles in my flying repertoire.

• Chapter 9 •

Then Along Came Derek

HERE IS ANOTHER tale of a pilot's ineptitude, as well as an example of not being able to get what was wanted – in this case some cushions. Because of that, I nearly ended my existence and might have broken a decent aeroplane.

On 17 October 1943 I had my first Hampden, serial number *P5309*. It was a torpedo bomber version, the Hampden no longer being a front-line bomber aircraft, had been relegated to carrying torpedos on anti-shipping strikes. Once more my destination was Cosford, having to collect the twin-engined Hampden from 415 Canadian Squadron, based at RAF Thorney Island, Hampshire. Thorney Island was, in fact, almost an island that jutted out from the south of England, just to the east of Portsmouth. No sooner had one taken off than one was out over the sea.

The Hampden was pretty easy to fly, but it was made for long-legged pilots, so people my size couldn't reach the rudder bar. Several American aircraft presented the same problem; maybe they built Yanks taller, but most English aircraft were more accommodating for smaller folk. Be that as it may, I needed some cushions to put behind my back, otherwise the rudder pedals were out of reach. However, the flight crew, as well as the driver of the car which took me out to the dispersal point, were, for once, most unaccommodating. They simply said there weren't any, so that was that! Maybe they didn't understand my problem, or I didn't put myself over properly, but in any case no-one was going to go all the way back to the Mess or crew room – a long way it seemed – just to acquire cushions for a stupid little lady pilot. Perhaps they imagined I just fancied a bit of extra comfort?

I wasn't getting anywhere with them, so, unwisely as it turned out, I thought I could manage without. I rolled up my parachute bag and my jacket, putting them, plus the aircraft journey log-books, on the seat behind my back. This made quite a good wedge in the small of my back, which pushed me far enough forward so that I could reach the rudder pedals to their full travel.

The throttle levers on a Hampden were on the left-hand side, mounted on a block. They were much longer than most throttles and stuck up in the air. On a twin, the practice was to leave the throttle tension nuts quite loose, so that one or other of the throttles could be easily moved a bit more or a bit less, to stop a swing of any kind developing on take-off.

It was a bright sunny day, the runway in use being the one heading to the south, toward the sea. The next bit of land to the west was Hayling Island, while Portsmouth came next. There was a large hangar with a big orange windsock on top of it on the right-hand side of the aerodrome. The windsock was jutting out quite a bit, as the wind gusted off the shiny sea. The runway was not quite into wind, but near enough, although I wasn't helped by having the sun in my eyes.

A Hampden had the feel of a surge of power on take-off which was strange to find in such an, even then, old-fashioned-looking aircraft. I opened up, my hand going out over the top of the throttle block in a large arc to full boost, then we were airborne. At that moment, the top half of me, which had nothing behind it, was pushed backwards by the 'G' force of the acceleration, and my finger-tips slipped back off and out of reach of the throttles. The throttle tension nuts were loose, as I mentioned, and the right-hand throttle lever didn't hold at full throttle but started to slip back. I was powerless at that moment to reach it anymore in order to push it open again.

Having now left the ground, I had no option but to stay with it and hope I could get my body forward before disaster befell me. As I watched events as in slow motion, the Hampden, with the left-hand engine at full boost while the right-hand motor was reducing power, began to swing to the right – towards the hangar . . !

My tummy muscles were screaming as I tried desperately to lean forward against the force of the take-off speed and get my hand back onto the throttle levers again. Added to all this, the control column then jerked out of my right hand as my shoulders continued back. It was only because the aircraft had been trimmed for take-off which kept the thing pointing skyward.

Try as I could, it was impossible to reach the throttles with my fingers, so it seemed inevitable that the Hampden and me were going to fly straight into the hangar! Somehow I wriggled into a hump, brought up my left leg being able then to kick the right throttle forward. The right-hand engine roared back into full power, the swing was halted, and I saw the windsock veer past, just inches underneath me. It had worked . . . phew!

No-one except a tiny, agile, dwarf-like person should have been able to get a foot up so quickly from the rudder bar to the throttle block in such a relatively confined cockpit. However, fear is a great motivator, and the desire to go on living, fuelled by adrenalin, works wonders.

I suppose the windsock on top of that hangar must have changed direction as I went past. Back on the ground, the men who had seen me off were probably wondering why I was showing off. Perhaps, they thought, I was having a fit of pique for not being given a cushion or two. Or perhaps they were merely thinking, 'Woman pilot'!

I didn't care what they were thinking. I was still alive and that guardian angel was continuing to be helpul.

I had a lovely flight on 12 December 1943 from Portsmouth to Cosford in an Oxford (*NM290*). Before I left Hamble, Margot told me that Cosford would give me a job back. She didn't say what sort of aircraft it would be, but that Cosford would issue the delivery chit as the aircraft had been on their books for a few days 'as it had been unserviceable, but was now OK'.

The chit handed to me at Cosford was for a Blenheim IV, serial number *V6527*, for Stoney Cross, ten miles west of Southampton. It was marked 'N.E.A.', which meant, 'Not Essentially Airworthy', or fit for one flight only. We pilots called it 'Not Exactly Airworthy'!

It always slightly aggravated me that I might get bumped off flying something like that, especially when, in this case, the aircraft was going on to a bombing range as a target to be broken up anyway. I just hoped it wouldn't break up with me in it.

The Blenheim was quite a nice twin to fly, but its single-engine safety speed (115–120 mph) was above its final approach of 90 mph, which meant that if one engine packed up on finals, and you were under safety speed (which you had to be if you were flying it according to the maker's specifications), then you simply went in – bang! This, you will remember, is exactly what happened to my friend Bobby Loewenstein. Of course, if you were coming in on a 'Barnato Bomb Approach', which was Derek's name for my way of pulling both engines right back, then gliding in from a great height (Derek was my future husband; you'll meet him shortly), in this way with no power needed on finals, you wouldn't drop a wing and stall in, if an engine suddenly stopped on you.

Derek, who was a very experienced pilot, naturally disapproved of my 'BBA', even though I explained that I couldn't be caught out on finals as I was above single-engine safety speed, so didn't need any engine power to drag me in.

A problem with any Blenheim was that it had a poor cockpit layout. Its Mercury engines had two-pitch propellers, so you had to change to fine pitch on finals. There were four knobs just behind the pilot's left elbow. Two of these were painted green, being the pitch change, while two others, painted red, were exactly underneath them. These were idle cut-outs for stopping the engines. You couldn't just reach back for the knobs, you had to turn round and look, so as to be sure you were pulling the right ones. Pulling the knobs out was also tricky from that angle, because when you turned round to look, it was difficult to keep the aircraft from turning round as well. It was for me, anyway.

When I first caught sight of *V6527*, it looked a very sorry mess indeed, but although the ground crew at Cosford assured me that it had passed its DI (Daily Inspection), I checked that it was signed out. I did a very thorough walk-round, noting evidence of old leaks from the starboard engine, plus sundry patches on the fuselage and tail-plane. I couldn't be certain but I thought the port undercarriage oleo-leg was listing a bit. The wings did not look quite parallel to the ground, but it could have been the angle of the concrete standing at dispersal.

Still, it was a lovely day, and the ground crew were most helpful. The starboard engine took quite a time to start, then when it finally got going, clouds and clouds of smoke came out of it. I felt a little more confident after run-up, so I signalled 'chocks away'. As I did so, I thought I saw expressions of relief on the ground crew's faces at the imminent departure of their problem N.E.A. But perhaps I was a trifle paranoid?

On the way south, all sorts of little things began to happen. The starboard revs suddenly went down to zero on the rev-counter, but as the engine was churning away happily in spite of its earlier smoking, I decided that it was only an unserviceable rev-counter. It didn't matter, as I could easily tune the engine by ear from the other one.

Next, the port engine oil pressure gauge fluctuated alarmingly, then also went down to zero. That worried me no end, so much so that I throttled back until I saw that its oil temperature gauge was keeping at normal. So I decided that it was the oil pressure gauge which was at fault.

It was difficult to keep the engines tuned up to each other because there was a lot of uneven play in the throttle controls, for in spite of loosening the tension holding screws, the throttles kept jamming, so I kept one hand on the throttles, jiggling them throughout the rest of the flight. But the thing that really worried me most of all was the fumes in the cockpit.

It was an extremely slow aircraft. Its ATA cruise speed should have been 180 mph, but it wasn't. I had wasted a lot of time on the ground at Cosford with my very careful external checks and run-ups, and 12 December was nearly the shortest day of the year, so the daylight was now starting to go. The ATA were not supposed to fly at night, being instructed to land 20 minutes before dusk. I obviously wasn't going to reach my destination before darkness set in, so decided to put down en route at Membury, situated on the hills between Lambourne and Hungerford (flying time 50 minutes).

My decrepit Blenheim and I were waved to a hardstanding by an American airman. He looked a little startled when he saw a girl (gal!) in the cockpit. Then, unlike Bobby Loewenstein, I couldn't stop the starboard engine. Its idle cut-out red knob didn't work – that was U/S too! In the end I just yanked the throttle of that engine back with a jerk, which stopped it quite easily. I suppose it was so oiled up.

I explained to the airman that my aircraft had been signed out for one flight only, but that if he would do a DI in the morning, I would take it on. He looked somewhat dubious.

I was driven in a smart American jeep to the Watch office, where I rang Margot to say where I was down before being taken to the CO in the Officers' Mess. I was given the usual delicious American dinner of unrationed food: tinned pork chops, sweet corn, sweet potatoes followed by lashings of ice-cream. This seemed to be the ritual laid on for starving

British pilots when they dumped themselves on the Yanks – or maybe I was lucky?

When I got down to the Watch office the following morning, I was told that their CO had said that 'no-one could fly that messed-up dog's dinner again'! I explained that ATA were their own Captains, making their own decisions as to what, when and where they flew. I was taken to the CO again who tried to dissuade me as he '. . . didn't want his runways blocked by my forthcoming prang!', nor did he '. . . want the responsibility of my imminent demise'.

In the end I rang Margot ('What, another woman?' said the CO). She confirmed the ATA rules, assuring the American CO that her ATA pilots, such as I, were fully competent to judge a situation. The man finally shrugged his shoulders, saying that he had been going to ask for a ride, but when he had gone down to have a look at the Blenheim, not to say the ground crew's report, he had changed his mind. As far as he was concerned, he was entirely against the flight, but as he was apparently overruled, it seemed he had no responsibility in the matter, even though it was 'his' airfield.

The Blenheim was not in the same place where I had left it. As the Americans were not trained to work on Blenheims, an RAF ground crew had been specially brought in to do the DI on the aircraft, and they reported that the right-hand oleo-leg had gone down in the night, but that they had jacked it up and refilled it with hydraulic oil. I noticed that they had wound a lot of thick black insulating tape around the leaking joint. They suggested that perhaps I could fly the short distance with the wheels down in case the tape jammed up the retracting mechanism. They also said they had moved the aircraft away from its overnight standing because the port engine had leaked a lot of petrol onto the ground, but they had found the leak, fixing that too. I began to wonder if the American CO wasn't right after all.

Both engines started up first go, and the flight to Stoney Cross, apart from the small snags, was not exactly uneventful. The wheels went up – and came down, but I lost my port engine on the landing run (flight time 40 minutes). On my aircraft snag-sheet, I wrote:

1. Petrol leak from port engine;
2. Oil leak from starboard engine;
3. Starboard rev-counter U/S;
4. Port oil pressure gauge U/S;
5. Uneven play in throttles, plus jamming;
6. Starboard idle cut-out U/S;
7. Fumes in cockpit;
8. Leak in starboard oleo-leg;
9. Engine quit when throttled back in flight.

I got fond of nursing that little Blenheim. It was its last flight, so I didn't really need a snag-sheet at all – nobody was going to fix anything that was wrong anymore. But it felt good to let at least someone know what an ATA pilot could fly and deliver.

However, the American CO might have been proved right . . .

Food was very scarce during the latter years of the war, but there was a farm near Hamble, so early in the year I 'ordered', and paid for, a turkey, to be collected just before Christmas. I practically put a label around its neck, for I often visited the bird, spending a good deal of my spare time with it. After all, it was something of a rarity.

It didn't seem to grow very fast on its wartime rations, as animal feed was rationed just as much as everyone else's. On Christmas Eve 1943, the farmer spoilt my turkey's Yuletide by wringing its neck, and I went to collect it on my way to the aerodrome. It was handed over, feathers and all.

I was one of the lucky pilots to be getting Christmas Day off, for the CO and the Operations Officer knew I was going home. Having delivered a couple of Fairey Barracudas (a Fleet Air Arm three-seater torpedo and dive-bomber), I was given a Spitfire VIII (*LV675*) from Eastleigh to in transit at White Waltham.

At Eastleigh, the usual ground crew giggled when I climbed into the Spit, wedging the rather scrawny turkey down in the gap behind the throttle and boost levers. One of the ground crew jumped onto the wing to help me with my straps, then produced a tiny bit of mistletoe from behind his back, holding it above me. 'Aha, we've got you at last,' he laughed, while one of the others said very cornily, 'Ho, ho, two birds in one cockpit, but only one's got feathers!' One after another they proceeded to give me a smacking Christmas kiss. It was under the mistletoe, I was strapped in, hardly able to move at all because of the turkey taking up most of the spare room, so I didn't have much of an option.

But they were a good bunch of lads. They teased me and told me I was blushing. One of them said, 'Airmen don't kiss officers, but here goes.' I was slightly embarrassed at all their pretence of love and affection.

When I ran up the aircraft to test the engine, there was a huge mag. drop that wouldn't clear even on a second run-up. So I switched off, asking them to change the plugs. I didn't feel quite so guilty asking them to burn their fingers on my behalf because that made it quits for my blushes.

On arrival at White Waltham I was told there were too many aircraft there for safety over the festivities in case of German raids, so would I mind dispersing mine to Smith's Lawn, situated in Windsor Park? That suited me a treat. Smith's Lawn wasn't used for polo in those days, it was an RAF training establishment. There were a lot of Tiger Moths on it, as well as some Wellingtons and Spitfires. The advantage to me was that it was very close to my father's house, so after landing and chocking up, I walked home through Windsor Park to Ridgemead, humping my 'chute over my shoulder, with my map bag in one hand, whilst dragging the turkey behind me with the other. An awkward lot of luggage.

I showed the turkey to my father, who thanked me and gave me a big hug. He told me to take it through to Mrs Stacey. 'Humph,' she said, jabbing my turkey with her fat thumb, 'and who do you think is going to pluck it so late on Christmas Eve?' My tummy's anticipation promptly stopped. All that nurturing and interest since it was a baby turkey, and now maybe the dogs would get it instead of me.

I remember a similar incident with Mrs Stacey, although the outcome was far different. Another ATA pilot, Leo Partridge, had got hold of a brand-new Opel car that had been 'caught off a German convoy near Liverpool'. 'Rather like falling off the back of a lorry . . ,' my father had said, who borrowed it from Leo for his girlfriend Vera. She was learning to drive so wasn't going to be let loose on his Bentley or his Lancia.

The Opel's clutch was so fierce that she didn't get on very well, so Leo got the car back again. He sold it to an American ATA pilot who soon found out its faults and swopped it with me for one of my gold watches – that didn't go either! The American said something to the effect that '. . . if he kept the Opel any longer he wouldn't go either!' Something about the vibration. So my Bentley was put away for the duration, while the Opel became my aerodrome car.

One day when I was driving it back from Hamble, having saved up my petrol coupons, a very small, creamy coloured chicken shot out from the side of the road and ran slap into the back wheel of the Opel. I didn't know where it had come from, there being no houses nearby, nor was there anyone about. I didn't want someone else to squash it, so I backed beside the feathery mass, scooped it up onto the floor beside me, then continued on my way to Ridgemead. I did wonder what might happen if the chicken woke up.

Reaching home, I gave the bird to Mrs Stacey, who, as usual, failed to appreciate my offering. 'Hmph! Very skinny; not much of a bird!' Nevertheless, it turned up for dinner deliciously cooked with mushrooms and rice. I told my father of its demise. He was furious, almost choking. 'Dishonest!' he cried. 'That is stealing! You should have taken it back to its owners.' He put down his knife and fork, refusing to eat any more of it . . . I did.

The next day the vibration in the Opel was much worse, and while going down the drive there was a sudden crunch as the back axle came apart. It was made in two pieces, and lay with the joint just under the middle of the flimsy back seat. It was quite lucky that no-one was sitting there or their flying, not to mention social, career might have ended. The American pilot knew a thing or two more about engineering than I did. I had a wreck but at least he had a gold watch which he could have repaired.

My father was pleased, grinning as he said, 'There you are, that's because you were a thief! Judgement of Solomon!'

◇   ◇   ◇

As well as house guests, we had some famous fighter pilots visiting Ridgemead. Tony Bartley I've already spoken of; others included Duggie

Bader, our famous legless pilot, before he was shot down in August 1941. All these people played golf with my father. Then there was Bob Tuck, before he too was taken prisoner early in 1942.

Bob Tuck, or Stanford Tuck, turned up one day with Ronnie Jarvis, a pre-war dancing partner of mine. Ronnie was the nephew of Isaac Wolfson, of Great Universal Stores. He and Bob had been on an exchange exercise with the Navy, seeing what it was like being attacked by German fighters when you could only chug along at a few knots instead of zooming away out of danger or shooting back.

Ronnie had joined up as a sergeant pilot but was later commissioned. He shot down a German or two but he didn't last long, being in turn shot down. Laddie Lucas was another RAF pilot who was also a superb golfer who played against my father. He had a splendid record on Malta and, having returned to England, was on the staff at Fighter Command under Sholto Douglas, who was then C in C. I have kept in touch with Laddie ever since, even contributing little snippets for some of his marvellous books.

Paul Richey I met again. He was now a squadron leader. Max Aitken I have mentioned already. He and some of the other men who had flown with the famous 601 Squadron in the first year of the war, I'd also known in their pre-war Auxiliary Airforce days.

A really great friend of my father's was Air Commodore Bill Paine. He had flown in the First World War and was Air Correspondent for the *Daily Telegraph*. In the second war he had a job with the Ministry of Aviation, so he and my father used to drive to London together. Bill lived at Ridgemead and, before I was married, shared a suite and bathroom with me. I had the large double room while Bill had the small single. Most unfair really, as he was always there and I only happened in now and again.

One day in the spring of 1943, I arrived at Ridgemead and wandered into the garden, down to the overheated, open air swimming pool. The coal locker was in a brick-covered square place, almost open to the elements, so steam used to rise even on the hottest days from both the boiler house and pool. Swimming in such luxury was, of course, delightful, even in mid-winter. As I approached, I saw Bill, that large, impressive, stern RAF Air Commodore, with my father, both in uniform, doing – guess what?

As far as I could see, they were playing 'ducks and drakes' with flattish stones, throwing and bouncing them out over the swimming pool. When I turned up they both looked rather sheepish and stopped. They told me to dive in and collect all the stones from the bottom of the pool, which I did. When the subsequent bombing of the German dams by the famous 617 Dambuster Squadron in May became known, I realized that they had been practising the then very secret theory of the bouncing bomb, not just being two middle-aged men playing kids' games.

◇   ◇   ◇

In 1944 I was sharing a cottage at Hamble with two other ATA pilots,

Anne Walker and Faith Bennett. Anne was in love with Group Captain W. G. G. Duncan-Smith DSO DFC, a highly experienced fighter pilot who would later be even more successful in North Africa and Italy. 'Smithy' we nicknamed him. In his book, *Spitfire into Battle*, Smithy mentions me. I quote:

> I had a shock one dismal afternoon when a Beaufighter crept in to land while the airfield was closed due to severe bad weather. The intrepid pilot turned out to be Diana Barnato, a pilot in the Air Transport Auxiliary. Looking very beautiful [but probably not feeling it. DB] in her immaculate uniform, she ran a comb through her hair before climbing out of the aircraft to tell me she was short of fuel and had had a very rough flight through thunderstorms. Not the least put out by the weather or the fact that she had made an emergency landing, her only concern was not to be a nuisance or disturb anyone. I discovered later she had flown a considerable distance and that her Beaufighter had not been equipped with any radio or navigational aids, while she carried out the flight with only her map and the aircraft's compass. They were an exceptional group of pilots in the ATA and Diana was one of the very best.

What kind things charming Smithy said about me. And I remember that day too! It was nasty weather for flying. After the tall radio masts near to North Weald turned up *beside* me, it was time to put down and wait until the weather improved.

Faith Bennett, meantime, was a girlfriend of Sholto Douglas, or to give him his full title at that time, Air Marshal Sir (William) Sholto Douglas KCB MC DFC, later Marshal of the Royal Air Force, Lord Douglas of Kirtleside GCB, Commander in Chief, RAF Fighter Command, 1941–42. In early 1944 he was C in C of Coastal Command. You will never guess in what way I knew him in those mid-war years.

The cottage had a spare bedroom, and as one or two of us frequently got stuck out due either to bad weather or unserviceable aircraft – or both – there was plenty of room for extra guests and the cottage was usually full up with our various friends. By then I had met Derek Walker about whom I shall say more later, who was also a friend of Smithy and of Anne. Several times I asked them to invite him over from Tangmere, where he was based, so he wouldn't guess that it was I who had fallen for him.

The rules of the cottage were simple. Whoever arrived home first after the flying day had to light the boiler so the rest of us could get a hot bath as soon as we came in. After all, although I could fly all sorts of complicated aeroplanes, I hardly knew how to strike a match, let alone lay and light a boiler fire. At Ridgemead I even used to ring for Gold, perhaps disturbing him from his afternoon nap, to light any fire that might be needed. How Gold must have disliked the upstart daughter of his beloved employer for interrupting him for such a trivial chore. He never showed it, except the once, in the matter of the Lysol in the turbot.

After sorting out the boiler, the first one in the cottage was then supposed to lay the table for dinner. Often the latter didn't happen, as we were usually taken out to 'The Bugle' at Hamble, or the 'Polygon' in Southampton, or a dark little dive called the 'Clausentium Club', an eating haunt with a scratchy gramophone playing in the background.

It was very gratifying some days, when returning tired out from flying, to see Sholto's large staff car with his furled standard on the radiator, plus a glum-looking driver, sitting outside the cottage. The driver usually had a long wait. Sholto always managed to get off work earlier than any of us could, so arrived first. He was also very domesticated, so it meant that the bathwater would be ready and the table laid! To find this very important man, whose underlings thought him something God-like, in his braces and shirt-sleeves, placing knives and forks on the table, was quite a sight.

After the war, when Sholto was with British European Airways, he offered me a job to be the first woman pilot with them. I did not accept because I was not brave enough or tough enough to be an 'Aunt Sally'.

As mentioned, Derek Walker was a friend of Smithy and Anne, and, as I said, I got them to invite him to the cottage, so I was pleased that he took an interest in me before too long. I had first met him at Tangmere when I flew in a replacement Typhoon for his squadron. He happened to be in the Watch Office when I checked in to get my 'chit' signed. He thanked me for delivering the aeroplane in one piece, adding, 'They get broke later on anyway.' I didn't know which way to take that. Our friendship grew and later he used to come along to my father's house.

Derek was now a Wing Commander with a DFC, having spent the early war years flying in the Middle East and Greece. He had joined the RAF in 1937 and the following year was flying with 142 Bomber Squadron, but shortly afterwards he was posted to Iraq where he served with 84 Bomber Squadron. By 1940 he was a Flying Officer with No. 30 Squadron in Egypt. In November he led four Blenheims out to Greece where the Squadron was heavily engaged with the Italians.

I remember Derek telling a funny story about when he was based in Shaibah, Iraq. The Officers' Mess wanted some fresh eggs so he flew off in his Blenheim and 'acquired' some chickens. He put them in a basket behind the seat in the navigator's compartment, above the bomb bay, but they got loose during the flight, fluttering and squawking around the cockpit. Things were getting a bit dicey as Derek could not ward them off, or catch them while flying at the same time. Taking desperate measures, he put the Blenheim into a steep dive, and as he pulled up sharply, all the chickens finished up in the back of the aircraft.

He and another pilot shot down a Cant Z.1007 in February 1941, but then came the retreat from Greece and by April he was operating over Crete. There is the famous story which appeared in the book *Wings over Olympus* by Tommy Wisdom, the war correspondent, when Derek took Wisdom on a recce sortie looking for stray soldiers on the southern beaches of Crete as the island was being taken by the Germans. They had a fight with a Messerschmitt 110 which limped away damaged. On another occasion, he told me, he attacked an enemy destroyer and put a bomb down its chimney stack. He wouldn't tell me about it at first, but then, late one night, when he was slightly high, he finally said, 'Ha! Bloody lucky pot shot. Straight down the jacksie.' This I took to mean that one of his bombs had targeted right down the ship's funnel. I laughed, even though there must have been a tremendous loss of life.

When he was in Greece, he helped to evacuate the Greek Royal Family. He showed me some photos of himself with some of the Royal Guards – those Evzones, dressed in traditional costume. It was bad enough for them to climb into Derek's Blenheim wearing their short, frilly skirts, but even more undignified having to put on a flying helmet over their red felt, long-tasselled caps. Derek had said, 'Glad the RAF don't dress up like that, in ballet skirts and with pompons on our shoes.'

Back once more in Egypt, the Squadron reformed at Amriya with Hurricanes before moving into the Western Desert. In August, Derek was given command of No. 260 Squadron of the Desert Air Force, also flying Hurricanes. He led his men from various landing grounds in the Desert, but on 13 December 1941 he was wounded in the left shoulder and right ankle. He and another pilot shot down a Messerschmitt 109 near Tobruk that morning, but in a second sortie that afternoon, escorting Blenheims attacking the Martuba Road east of Tmini, they got into another fight with 109s, and Derek was hit, but managed to get back home.

Recovering from his wounds, he was put in command of 261 Squadron in January 1942, then 127 Squadron in February. He remained with this unit until June, having a detachment on Cyprus (Nicosia).

Returning to England, he took a fighter leaders' course at Charmy Down, then a refresher course at No. 52 OTU, then, having converted to Typhoons, became a supernumerary with 175 Squadron until given command of 182 Typhoon Squadron in August 1943, flying from New Romsey. By late 1943 he was a Wing Leader in No. 16 Typhoon Wing, being in charge of No. 124 Airfield, and about to start his fourth tour of operational flying. It was while with 182 Squadron that he received his DFC. The citation read:

Acting Wing Commander Derek Ronald Walker RAFO, 182 Squadron RAF. This officer has completed two tours of operational duty, throughout which he has displayed exceptional keenness and a fine fighting spirit. He took part in the campaigns in Greece, Crete and the Western Desert, where he was wounded. Wing Commander Walker has led his squadron and Wing on many bombing attacks and fighter sweeps and has displayed great gallantry. He has destroyed at least four enemy aircraft in air combat and others on the ground. He has also destroyed or damaged much enemy transport and sunk one destroyer. At all times Wing Commander Walker has set a fine example of courage, determination and devotion to duty.

Derek was 28 when I met him. He had a blue-eyed, twinkling gaze, and the habit of throwing his head back into a proud commanding stance, then dropping his eyes. He was forever scanning the skies for aircraft. He walked with a jaunty, swashbuckling, springy step, with a drop of each shoulder. A jutting chin, curly brown hair, lean figure and beautiful, sensitive hands.

He was as brave as they made 'em – a leader of men. He had the ability to raise a laugh and could lift people up out of any desperate situation or mood. He could raise morale and spirit, call it what you will. He gave out the ability to continue difficult tasks to all who crossed his path. A good mixer too. Everyone liked him.

It was something of a whirlwind romance but our love was very deep and very real. I was sitting in the study at Ridgemead one day in a large green armchair. Derek came in and sat on the arm, saying something like he 'absolutely couldn't live without me'. This was obviously an important statement, so I played for time by not saying anything. He then said, 'Shall I ask "Babe"?' He and Derek got on very well together. I said, 'We'd better.' Funny sort of proposal, no bended knee or anything.

Many of my admirers had, by then, been killed in the war, so I thought I should hook him quick, in case one or the other of us got bumped off whilst flying.

We arranged to marry on 6 May 1944 at the church of St Judes, Englefield Green. After the date had been fixed I realized that it would be two years to the day since one of the saddest days of my life. I had gone to Saffron Walden, near Debden, for Humphrey Gilbert's funeral. I suppose I should have persuaded Derek to change the date, but then I thought the happy wedding day would exorcise any remaining heartache about the death of the pilot of the blue-nosed Spitfire.

Derek was best man to Squadron Leader Mike Ingle-Finch DFC AFC and Pam, the day before our wedding. He had been a Battle of Britain pilot, then a test pilot, and then commanded 175 Typhoon Squadron to which Derek had briefly been attached. We all went to the West Country together for our honeymoons. We only had a few days' leave.

Derek's best man was Wing Commander R. T. 'Dave' Davidson DFC, a Canadian. Dave had, like Derek, seen considerable action. They had both served in 30 Squadron in the Middle East and Greece and then the Western Desert. He had then seen action over Ceylon in 1942 and then, back in England, had flown Typhoons and became a Wing Leader in the same Group as Derek, he commanding 124 Wing, Derek 125 Wing, within 16 Group. Dave was among the very few fighter pilots to have shot down German, Italian, Japanese and French aircraft.

The reception was held at Ridgemead, during which several of Derek's pals fell into the lily-pond in the garden, while some of mine overbalanced into the swimming pool. One lily-ponder was Squadron Leader Mike Read, who had commanded 182 Squadron after Derek. I have a photograph of him fished out and laid out on the floor.

Two days after the wedding, Dave Davidson failed to return from a sortie over France. Fortunately he survived a bale-out, evaded capture and, after spending some months with the Resistance, managed to get home. He brought with him much valuable information about V.1 rocket bomb sites, as well as some horrendous stories of German atrocities he had witnessed. He received the French Croix de Guerre as well an an American Air Medal and remained in the RCAF until 1967. Sadly, he died in 1976.

A short time before the wedding, Bert Jenkins, my faithful taxi-man in London, called at River House with an old cardboard box containing 12 beautiful dark green Bristol sherry glasses. I asked him to come in so that we could toast each other's future well-being. Several other people were there. My mother arrived unexpectedly and everyone chatted away happily.

Bert then left and my mother said, 'What an utterly charming man; who is he?' I told her he was a taxi-driver from Hyde Park Corner. She became quite stuffy, saying, 'Really, Diana, fancy having a taxi-man in your drawing room.' She was right, he was charming. He was also reliable. I think of him often and I still use the green glasses.

◆ *Chapter 10* ◆

Invasion Year

MARRIAGE DIDN'T STOP my flying. It didn't stop Derek either. After our honeymoon, which was only those few days at Totnes in the West Country, it was back to the daily grind for both of us. Derek was now based at RAF Millfield, where there was a Typhoon Fighter Leaders School and SLAIS – Special Low Attack Instructor School, but flying about in his personal aeroplane and liaising with 2nd Tactical Air Force units. Everyone knew that the invasion of Europe must be getting near, but we had no idea it would be one month to the day after our wedding. D-Day for us had been 6 May; D-Day for Europe was 6 June 1944.

Derek and I were sometimes able to get away together and stay at my father's house. One day he was jumpy as hell but I didn't know why; the Invasion was Imminent! There was a terrific gale blowing and he never slept a wink. He kept getting up and going to the window to check the storm-force winds and look at the sky. All night heavy aircraft, some towing gliders, were droning southwards overhead. Then they all came back again. It was the invasion, delayed for 24 hours. Derek was on tenterhooks, as the weather had been terrible for days. Unlike me, he knew that the troops who would 'hit the beaches' were already packed in their boats awaiting General Dwight Eisenhower's signal to 'GO'.

Derek left at the crack of dawn to go back on duty with 2nd TAF, while I went to my ferry pool. My only job, of all things on that most exciting and historic of days, was to doddle along the south coast with a piffling little A.O.P. Auster V (*NJ616*) Army spotter plane, from Hamble to 126 Wing at Tangmere, to replace theirs which had been blown over by the gales.

Later that evening I flew a FAA Albacore from Hamble to Eastleigh. Whilst I was tootling along the coast, I saw tanks still moving on the roads, going to be loaded onto ships in the ports. Bailey bridge sections were also being towed out to the ships.

Hundreds of tanks, trucks, bren-gun carriers, jeeps and equipment,

not to mention thousands of soldiers, had been parked and billeted in
the woods and surrounding countryside around Southampton, Hamble
and Gosport. I saw all the boats going out; ships seemed to stretch as
far as the eye could see across the Channel. I also made out the huge
'Pluto' (Pipeline under the Ocean) 'cotton-reels' holding up the oil
pipeline, bobbing about in the rough sea, as well as some of the Mulberry
pre-fabricated harbour being floated out towards France. The Allied
planning people had decided against taking an enemy-held port: Dieppe
in August 1942 had learnt them that lesson. This time they were taking
their own harbour with them.

This was it! The invasion – to push back the enemy into their own
country. So many people I knew were in those tanks, those ships and
those bombers and fighters that once again were droning high overhead.
I wondered how many friends I would ever see again.

The ATA women at Hamble had watched the build-up, and now the
invasion was on. With it came the constant noise of bombers, fighters
and fighter-bombers, all heading to and from the beach-head where
history was being made.

Derek rang me later that night. Although I didn't say on the telephone
what jobs I had done that day, especially as it was only an Auster and
an Albacore, I mentioned vaguely that I had been in the air, flying along
the south coast. Because security consciousness was drummed into all of
us, not least by the poster 'Careless talk costs Lives', I did not tell him
what I had watched. He just said, 'I suppose you got in the way.'

The Spitfires and Typhoons were attacking targets along the French
coast every day, as they had been doing for weeks, as well as gun
positions, radar stations and the tiny construction sites which we later
came to know as V.1 rocket-launching sites. These had begun to spring
up like mushrooms in the first half of 1944. They were well defended
with masses of light anti-aircraft guns, so were pretty dangerous things
to go for. Just six days after the invasion began, the rocket bombs began
to be fired towards England: we ferry pilots were to see any number in
the air. As D-Day approached, and afterwards, the wastage in aircraft
was amazing, especially among the Typhoon squadrons, who now added
Army support sorties to their list of operational duties.

ATA was kept on its toes. With the present size of the RAF and its
various commands, the flow of new or repaired aeroplanes was constant.
Being at Hamble, I was always taking fighters into airfields or from MUs,
as the southern part of England was just a huge collection of fighter
aerodromes, all of which had been poised for the big day. When it came,
RAF and USAAF fighters and fighter-bombers simply swamped the sky
in order to protect this, the biggest invasion fleet and operation the world
had ever known.

Later on, our airfield at Hamble, being right on the south coast, was
designated a 'prang-patch', along with others, for any RAF, FAA or US
aircraft coming back in trouble from the war front in Normandy, just
80 miles or so across the Channel. There was great faith in the ability
of the crash crew and blood-tub (ambulance) to lever anyone out of

trouble should it occur. Several aircraft did make emergency landings at our base.

Late one afternoon in July, the alarm bells went off. We women all hurried out to see an invasion-striped Spitfire in the circuit, but it wasn't one of our deliveries. The crash and ambulance men threw down their playing cards to rush off to start up their wagons, expecting an imminent disaster, but the aircraft made a beautiful landing, then taxied up to the Mess. Out climbed my Derek. I tried to look nonchalant.

'Don't go anywhere near my 'plane,' he said, 'I'm afraid there's a terrible smell in the cockpit!' We wondered, oh dear, something awful has happened. Something dead in there perhaps?

Now the war had been on for a long time and food rationing was drastic. People weren't starving but we were hungry. Derek went back to the Spitfire, fished out a large circular parcel and brought it over to us. He had been over to Caen in Normandy and had brought back a huge Camembert cheese. No such cheese had been seen in England since the fall of France in 1940. We all fell upon it and as we munched away, Derek said, 'Diana, darling, this is something I liberated especially for you.' Derek, you were unique.

One day I was over the south of England, ferrying a Mustang to an aerodrome on the coast. It was a really lovely day, so I was singing a waltz to myself as I flew along. I kept dead on course but, as I sang, dipped the wings of the Mustang, first to the left, then to the right, in time with the tune. The Mustang, as we pilots say, was 'absolutely part of you', being most light and responsive on the ailerons like the Spitfire.

My day had not begun well. When I was starting up, the chin-strap on my flying helmet came adrift, so, knowing it might well blow off as I took off down the runway, or later, upon landing, when the hood would be open, I had put on the only thing I had to hand, which happened to be a red – bright red – woollen pixie-hood! It tied under my chin with a bow, while on top of it I put my RAF flying goggles. With it in situ my hair cascaded out of the edges as well as down at the back.

The pixie-hood wasn't going to keep out the engine noise like my flying helmet would have done, so I put in wax ear-plugs as well. The effect, when singing to myself, was a cross between being under the sea and singing in the bath.

So there I was, oblivious of everything except the beauty of the day and the glorious response of the controls, with an orchestra of my own making. A marauding Messerschmitt or Focke Wulf 190 could easily have picked me off. How lucky we were to have our fighter supremacy or this could often have happened to us.

Suddenly I was aware of a shadow overhead. Looking up, I saw the underside of another aeroplane. Luckily it was not a German fighter, but a Spitfire. As I watched, a second Spitfire side-slipped in beside me, wing-tip to wing-tip, then a third came in on the other side. Naturally I stopped the waltzing and the opera business abruptly, keeping my Mustang very straight and level. Boxed in, I then had a fourth Spitfire zoom up from underneath me to take position dead ahead, while the fellow overhead dropped down, then back a bit, to a position just under my tail. Now, completely hemmed in by these four fighters, I could see they were Free French, having Cross of Lorraine markings on their engine cowlings – probably from No. 340 FF Squadron, which was operating patrols over the Channel from Merston, on the south coast, during this period.

We ATA people always flew alone, so no-one ever taught us to fly in formation, but those Free Frenchmen were very good. Then again, I was keeping the same height and course, not daring to move the stick more than a fraction lest I hit one of them, or they hit me. I was extremely anxious, as their formation was so tight on me.

They were obviously having great fun. The two on either side of me, I could see, were roaring with laughter. There was little doubt they knew I was a woman, what with my red pixie-hat and flowing hair. They pointed with glee at my hat, one putting one arm across his chest, the other arm out as far as his cockpit would allow, in the pretence of dancing a waltz, closing his eyes in make-believe bliss. Surely he hadn't heard me singing a waltz just a few moments earlier? For my part, I was wishing he would keep at least one hand on his controls. I was also terrified he would keep his eyes shut just that bit too long and bump into my wing-tip.

There was nothing I could do except go with them. And they kept right with me – right there. Perhaps, initially, they had thought I was in difficulties – or even drunk. But what were they thinking now when they saw a girl flying a Mustang in such an unconventional manner? Had I stolen it, perhaps? Meanwhile, I was praying they would leave me before I ran out of fuel, for instead of going to the south coast, I was having to fly inland. In the event, they made me go all the way to Kenley with them, and I only made my escape when they finally peeled off to land there.

I reflected on the sortie. Here was a prime example of an Anglo/American/French co-ordination and co-operation: an American Mustang with a half-English, half-American woman pilot, escorted by British Spitfires being flown by French pilots. Entente tri-cordiale.

I got to my destination just in time to catch the waiting taxi-Anson back to Hamble. When I handed in my delivery chits, Operations quizzed me about the extraordinary extra length of my flying time. My explanation was not believed, and even though it was a fine, clear day, I suppose they thought I had got lost. Well, I hadn't – I'd been out with the boys!

Our ATA training taught us to discover, notice and appreciate any faults in any aeroplane 'before' they happened – or certainly before something really dreadful happened. On 11 June I took a Wellington XIII (*MF575*) from Hawarden to Gosport and had a tiny emergency when the green lights, showing my undercarriage was down and locked, failed to work, but I landed safely.

On 27 June, just three weeks after the Normandy invasion, my CO at Hamble called me to Operations. 'Diana, your return job! I want you to be very careful and if you don't like it, don't take it. Go around it very carefully, run it up, test everything, then leave it if there is anything suspicious.' This sounded really great and I felt so pleased I was on duty.

She added that after my flight up to Hawarden in a Vultee Vengeance IV (*HB495*), an American single-engined, two-seat dive-bomber used by the RAF and Fleet Air Arm, the ferry pool there would fly me to Royal Naval Air Station, Burscough, north of Liverpool, where the RAF were sending in a special ground crew for an aircraft which two naval pilots had disliked. The first pilot had done a precautionary landing there, while the second had aborted his take-off because, he said, something was wrong, returning it to dispersal. Pretty good so far. I was really keen now!

I couldn't wait to get to Burscough. When I did, I found the aircraft in question was a gull-winged naval thing. In my memory I can see it now, with its elbow-bent wings, standing forlornly by a blister hangar with its ground crew, plus transport, in waiting. I looked around it as I spoke to the senior airman. He told me that they couldn't find anything at all wrong with it. Now, they and the other ATA pilot who had flown me over were all waiting on my 'whims'. Will she, won't she? – I could almost hear them thinking.

What was it? At first I thought it was a Corsair, a fighter used by the US Navy in the Pacific as well as by our Fleet Air Arm, but this was at least a two-seater, if not three, plus a rear gun turret, so obviously it wasn't the single-engined Corsair. Reading my delivery chit to check the aircraft number (*FN883*), I saw that it was a Grumman Avenger I, an American carrier torpedo bomber, used by both the American Navy and the FAA. It was a big aeroplane, weighing nearly 11,000 lb empty, 2,000 lb heavier than a Corsair. It had folding wings just like the Corsair in order for the aircraft carrier to stow more aircraft in its hangar deck. This made me make a mental note to keep my fingers crossed that the wings wouldn't fold up on me during flight or I would reach my terminal velocity pretty soon. Then what?

I walked round it again, doing more than my usual 'kick-the-tyres-and-see-the-pitot-head-cover-was-off' routine. The pitot-head tube stuck out somewhere in front of all aircraft, allowing airflow to enter the operating gauge of the air speed indicator as one flew along. The cover stopped dust, rain, frost and ice getting into the tube, spoiling the airspeed reading. If the cover was left on, the ASI didn't work at all. Dear Reader, it was very important to see that the cover with its easily seen red pennant had been removed.

I was very thorough, while keeping the ground crew waiting and anxious. I knew they would be keen to get rid of their 'Jonah' which had defeated other pilots, but which was also cluttering up an otherwise deserted aerodrome. I was also remembering that old Blenheim that everyone had been so keen for me to take away. At least I had got a good American dinner out of that flight. Would I be as lucky this time?

Everyone appeared a little bit more friendly when I climbed up into the cockpit. Was this a good sign, they wondered? The Avenger started up like a bird, running sweetly with no mag drops. According to the notes, an Avenger can only be run-up on the ground to a stated boost and revs, which were marked on the throttle and boost gauges, as well as on the levers. It could not be taken up to full throttle on the ground because it had only toe brakes, no parking brakes, so would fly forward off the chocks. Therefore, there was no way to check the two-speed supercharger, which could only be checked above those stated revs and boost. It was used only above a certain height, in order to give more power in the rarified air. If the blower was at the wrong setting and too much power was applied, the engine could blow up.

With great relief to everyone, I agreed to take it. Smiles all round. The take-off was dead into wind off the narrow naval runway. I decided to use no more power than I had used at run-up, hoping that would get me off the ground. Not using the higher settings for take-off and climb meant a much longer run as well as a slower rate of climb, but I had plenty of runway. I knew the engine was OK up to those power settings that I had tested.

I opened up very slowly, not to mention gently, taking off while watching the speeds and temperatures closely. When I had reached 5,000 feet, I throttled back to cruising revs and boost and flicked the switch over to check the supercharger, whereupon the revs and boost disappeared downwards. So, nearly, did the Avenger and I.

I put on a little more power to keep my altitude, then changed the switch over again, whereupon the rev-counter and boost gauges surged nearly off the clock while the double-row Wright Cyclone engine roared back at me with distinct disapproval. I tried again, with the same results.

Something, as the FAA pilots had reported earlier, definitely wasn't right. No wonder both those previous pilots had put it back on the ground. Luckily I was still mooning around over Burscough in order to force-land there if it came to it.

What was wrong was now obvious – even to me. The supercharger was linked up the wrong way round. Knowing this, I was able to fly all the way to Worthy Down, in Wiltshire, with the switch in its 'wrong' position (flying time an anxious 1 hour 15 minutes), but we didn't blow up. On my snag-sheet I wrote, 'Supercharger U/S. Linked up wrong way around.'

Margot Gore, my CO, called me to her office the following day, telling me the 'authorities' had taken the trouble to ring through to her to ask her to commend the pilot (me!) on finding the fault on their Avenger that had mystified the male sex. I grew at least an inch in stature after that interview, thinking to myself, 'There you are, you see, the ATA training must be better than the Navy's!'

◇   ◇   ◇

I got hold of another Navy plane a couple of days later, on 30 June. I was up at Speke, near Liverpool, having to fly a Blackburn Skua (*L2908*) down to Eastleigh. The Skua was not a new aeroplane, having been used by the Fleet Air Arm since before the war. It had been a two-seat single-engined carrier fighter and dive-bomber, but by 1944 had been relegated to training or target-tugs, so was pretty clapped out.

By this time I had passed once more into one of my 'know-it-all' periods, a time when over-confidence can make a lot of pilots come unstuck. Once again this delivery was marked as N.E.A. (fit for one flight only), so I should have treated it with special caution, but in my happy-go-lucky mood I didn't even take the trouble to read *all* the ferry pilots' handling notes. Perhaps I was still feeling blasé about my Avenger trip? All I did was have a quick glance at the fuel system notes, plus the relevant flying speeds.

The Skua was very nose-heavy. Some poor fellow had to lie across the tail even during taxying. Another very unpleasant and cold job. It was a simple, single-engined, old-fashioned-looking contraption with a Bristol Perseus XII engine. Apart from remembering to keep the stick hard back whilst taxying, I didn't think there could be much to know about it. The petrol was in three connecting tanks, so when the forward tank was half empty, it had to be switched off and kept in reserve for landing. A full forward tank made the aircraft even more inclined to nose-over on landing.

After take-off, the undercarriage came up and the red lights showed that it was locked up, but the undercarriage warning horn still blew! Quite a noise! 'N.E.A. again,' I groaned. I put the undercarriage up and down several times but still the horn blew, so I was condemned to fly the one-and-a-half-hour trip with this additional noise trying to deafen me.

I duly switched off the forward fuel tank when it became half empty, then when I reached the Eastleigh circuit, switched over to it again for the landing – whereupon the engine promptly cut. I quickly changed to the other tank, pumping like mad on the priming cock, to send petrol to the carburettor as well as the engine. I pulled hopefully at the cartridge starter, which luckily had another cartridge in it, and the engine leapt into life once more.

The wheels came down, the undercarriage green lights came on, but as the horn was still blaring, I pushed the emergency red knob to use the hand pump, just in case the wheels had not fully locked down. The wheels did not collapse on landing so I taxied in with the horn still creating its awful din. I wrote on the snag-sheet about the engine failure from the forward tank petrol starvation, as well as the horn problem.

The mechanic in charge looked over my shoulder, saying that there was a test button for the horn on the ASI switch on the floor, near the pilot's right foot. If I had pushed that once or twice, the horn might have unjammed. 'It was in the notes, Miss!' If I had taken the trouble to read all the handling notes, I wouldn't have gone to bed with a raging headache plus ringing in the ears.

It was an unpleasant flight. I didn't like the Skua at all, N.E.A. or not.

Large flying-boats were the only type of aircraft that women pilots were not allowed to fly. We were allowed to fly the Air-Sea Rescue single-engined amphibious Walrus and Sea Otters off land, but not off water. Margot Gore said the high-ups at ATA thought that if women pilots got stuck out for days with large flying-boats in some far northern place with the Navy or RAF crews, all sorts of antics might ensue. 'Nonsense,' she said, 'there are better places to choose.' Anyway, we got stuck out all over the British Isles, sometimes in other very strange places, with the opposite sex. Ample opportunity for desire to override discomfort on land, without getting sea-sick from the swell as well.

There were not many large flying-boats to deliver. I believe the head boys deserved those jobs for a few days' break from their onerous, responsible organizational duties.

I flew my first Walrus on 3 July 1944, a Walrus II (*HD877*) belonging to 277 Squadron at Shoreham, flying it to Wroughton. The Walrus was my least favourite aircraft. I would not have liked to have been killed in one: a most unglamorous end. Every Walrus I flew knew I didn't like it.

It was difficult to get into: either a climb and hoist up the outside of the cockpit, or a crawl along the inside of the hull, past anchors and cables. They were awash with paraphernalia that was murder for elbows, knees and finger-nails. After opening the throttle for take-off, nothing much seemed to happen at all, it just rolled along with everything clanking in the back. It didn't get airborne before the control column had biffed you in the bosom several times over the bumps. When you hauled back, nothing much happened either, until it felt like getting itself airborne. Then it wallowed and flew much more like a boat than an aircraft.

Then there was the undercarriage. It took a lot of elbow grease to pump it up. This made only two knots' difference in its dreary slow cruising speed of 83–88 knots, so we usually left it down. It climbed at 75 knots, approached to land at 65 knots and clanked onto the ground at 53 knots. Not much scope, with its speeds in no way critical to the pilot – provided the engine worked.

ATA handling notes said the rudder and elevator were very sensitive during take-off. Let me tell you, as far as I was concerned, nothing was sensitive about that clattering lump of so-called flying machine.

The Hamble girls cleared the factory at Cowes, Isle of Wight, and flew – if you can call it that – the Walruses to one of the various Fleet Air Arm stations or maintenance units.

My friend Anne Walker (with whom I shared the cottage) didn't like the Walrus either – who did? Except, of course, the people who were saved or collected from the sea by virtue of its amphibious characteristics.

Anne took off one day in a cross-wind, a hazardous performance with all that double wing. She swung, finishing up at the end of the take-off run in a haystack. She was knocked out and the whole caboosh, aircraft and haystack, went up in flames.

Fortunately for Anne, a baker's delivery boy was cycling along the lane just beside the aerodrome boundary. He pedalled frantically to the blaze, pulled Anne out of the conflagration, then rescued his bike plus a lot of burnt loaves of bread. Bread was rationed, but he offloaded some of the singed stuff. Anne brought it back for tea. We said that when we had extra guests to stay, she should do it again.

Philippa Bennett was a first-class pilot with a four-engined rating: very reliable, and really good. On a rare occasion, for her, she was given a Walrus, and meticulously pumped up the wheels en route. However, she forgot to pump them down again. She made a really beautiful, gentle landing, as she always did with everything, but on the two underwing floats.

The ground crew jacked up the Walrus and pumped down the wheels. The landing onto the smooth grass of Eastleigh aerodrome had been so good (unlike most of mine) that I believe the floats were not even dented. Just a touch of paint needed here and there.

A male pilot from another ferry pool was in a Walrus flying north towards the Wrekin in Shropshire. He was over the Severn River where it winds through a deep-sided culvert with forests on either side when he had a complete engine failure. He didn't have much choice but, rather than crash into the tops of the trees, he pointed into the narrow cleft and landed on the water. He threw out the anchor and waded ashore.

The accident report stated: '. . . the pilot is highly commended. After a complete engine failure he landed on a bend in the river. The aircraft was slightly damaged when the tide receded'. I believe the Severn is tidal up to Iron-Bridge, just south of the Wrekin.

In mentioning the Wrekin, which lies south of Wellington in Shropshire, I should tell you of our superstition in ATA. Whenever we were in the vicinity, we had to 'always tip our hat to the Wrekin, even if you couldn't see it'. It is 1,335 feet high, so we were often flying along below or beside it, as the top was often in cloud.

On 12 July I flew another Grumman Avenger Ic (*FN877*) from Worthy Down. I was supposed to deliver it to No. 852 Squadron, FAA, at Abbotsinch, where a FAA pilot would fly it onto an aircraft carrier sitting in the Clyde. However, the undercarriage failed to retract due to faulty locking mechanism, so I had to land again. After the problem was fixed I was off again, and made it on the second attempt.

Three days later, on the 15th, I got my first Douglas Boston IV (*BZ539*), to be flown from Prestwick to South Marston. The chit said P.1.W. – 'Priority 1. Wait'. It had been more than two years since I had flown as a passenger in Sas de Mier's Boston at Debden. Having arrived at Prestwick, I then had to wait for the aircraft to arrive from America. I hung about for several hours before it finally bounded in with its Atlantic Ferry Command pilot, who looked tired, crumpled and worn out – somewhat like his aircraft.

The cockpit was full of smoke ('no smoking allowed') and the stale smell of cigars. The cigar butts were everywhere, littering the floor. Whatever I touched had lumps of parked chewing-gum on it. I flew the pilot from Prestwick to Lyneham where he was dropped for his lift home, and then went on to South Merston – in all, two hours fifteen minutes flight time.

I was exceedingly busy during these two months, with 36 deliveries and four taxi-days in June, then 31 deliveries and another four taxi-days in July. Typhoon *EJ967* on 12 August gave me another undercarriage problem: this time it wouldn't retract due to an airlock, so once more I had to land and have it fixed before completing the delivery. On that occasion I brought back another Typhoon (*EK434*) for No. 84 GSU at Thruxton.

A Spitfire VIII (*MV414*) on 21 August was from the secret aerodrome at Chattis Hill, but again I had problems. Taking off, I had to land at Down Ampney with oil on the windscreen. Off again, heading for Cosford via the much-known route past Swindon towards Bristol to try to get up the Bristol Channel to the Severn rather than fly over the higher Chilterns in low cloud, I had to put down at Filton due to bad weather and more oil on the windscreen – not good in lousy weather. Next stop was finally Cosford, having made the journey in hops of 30, 35 and 30 minutes. I brought back a Spitfire IX to 83 GSU at Bognor – without a single mishap.

I got my first Sea Otter on the 27th – *JM916*. I gave an Air Training Corps cadet named Sharpe rides all day as he was to be my Hudson 'stooge' later with my last job. Poor lad, stuck down the back of the Sea Otter from Hamble to Cosford, bumping about in the dark of the hull with all those anchors, cables, etc, and noise. I don't expect he liked the Sea Otter after that. Then a taxi-trip to High Ercall in a Fairchild before taking Hudson *FK782* down to Gosport. August gave me another 31 deliveries and four taxi-days.

Another first that month was a Mosquito FB IV (*HR346*), from Hullavington to Colerne. I flew there with Anna Leska, our Polish pilot, then she got a lift with me and we both popped two more Mossies back again between Colerne and Hullavington.

It was rare for Ops to allow a pilot to be carried by another in a delivery aircraft, for if one aircraft went U/S then the programme was wrecked, but popping back and forward between Hullavington and Colerne hardly fitted into a getting-stuck-out category. It was near enough to our home base of Hamble and there were lots more Mossies to be shifted.

Much earlier, at White Waltham, 'Whitey', the No. 1 Pool's Ops Officer, nearly took a short cut whilst juggling with the day's flying programme. He could have allowed seven or eight pilots to fly between jobs in a delivery Liberator but at the last moment decided to send a taxi-Anson for them instead in case the Lib was U/S.

The large four-engined aircraft took off with a very experienced pilot at the controls and crashed into a hangar, then burnt. The pilot and his flight engineer were both killed. The accident report was inconclusive: either he hadn't removed the outside elevator clamps, or he forgot to unlock the controls, or the controls merely jammed, or was it sabotage? Good thing Whitey sent the taxi-Anson.

Being an Ops Officer was a very stressful job, full of constant decision-making. As the day went on, the programme was continually changing: someone stuck somewhere for weather or U/S aircraft, or even something broken . . . Usually the middle job went wrong . . . The Ops Officer had all the extra taxi link-ups to fix. The sign of a good Ops Officer was not only getting through the day's dish-out of aircraft to be moved, but, in spite of constant vicissitudes, getting the pilots home at the end of the day so they were there to be sent out for the next day's schedule.

• Chapter 11 •

Doodle-bugs and Things

THE INVASION OF Normandy could not have been mounted without the mastery of the air over southern England. There were no German aircraft to be seen in the skies overhead, but the menace of the V.1, or doodle-bug or buzz-bomb, as they were named, was here instead.

One must remember that most of southern England was one vast supply dump cum supply depot, full of men and equipment. If the Luftwaffe had been able to attack anywhere along that coast, the damage inflicted would have been tremendous. Soon after the invasion began, the danger from the V.1 flying bombs became very real, not only for London, but for this vast area of men and machines and, of course, for every civilian.

Earlier in the year, 'something' had exploded on the other side of the Hamble River from our cottage. No-one said it was a conventional bomb and everyone wondered what it had been. When queries were posed, lips were buttoned.

I frequently asked questions about all sorts of things of my father's various high-up friends, but did not expect to be faithfully answered. Even though England was, by then, a closed island, everyone was extremely security conscious. When important Royal Air Force or Fleet Air Arm officers asked me about the flying capabilities of some aircraft that I had flown and they had not, or where I had taken them, even I would not talk about it all.

Then these 'somethings' became widespread and started exploding all over the place, more and more in and around London. They did dreadful damage and they were very scary. So the first one near Hamble was a V.1, a jet-propelled flying bomb launched initially from near Douay, near the French coast.

Wing Commander Robert 'Dave' Davidson DFC, our recent best man, was, as mentioned before, shot down in his Typhoon on 8 May – two days after our wedding – but managed to evade capture and was picked up by the Resistance. One of the pieces of information he brought back was that over 15 per cent of the bombs blew up on the launch pad. But too many still got off and, despite guns and fighters, caused much death and destruction.

The doodle-bugs looked like enormous, cumbersome cigars with small square-cut wings, while the jet was mounted atop the rudder. These jet-propelled missiles with warheads flew quite low, at about 2,000 feet or so, and were timed to have their engine cut out over London or whatever other town or city at which they might be aimed – if the Germans got the range right. When the rocket died, the buzz-bomb simply nosed forward towards the ground, where it would explode.

Sometimes they didn't topple but glided silently after the fuel ran out. It was frightening and demoralizing to see them gliding, and to know that in a few seconds they would arrive and blow up something and someone. A true 'terror weapon'. When flying, they had their own very distinctive sound, as did every engine or aircraft.

I was in London on leave, and was having lunch with Irene Haig, one of the attractive daughters of the famous Earl Haig of First World War fame, in her Eaton Place flat. She later married Gavin, who became Lord Astor of Hever. A V.1 went burping past up the road, obviously about to cut out. I was terrified and dived under the table. Rene was completely calm and unperturbed. This was the first buzz-bomb I'd nearly met personally and I wasn't used to them as were the brave Londoners.

The very next morning I was lolling around in bed in River House when my second close-to buzz-bomb went gliding past the window of the third-floor flat. Tite Street isn't very wide and the bomb went between my house and the house opposite. The engine had already cut out as it came over the Thames and it swished past and exploded at the top of the street. I was glad it was time to get back to Hamble and the safety of flying.

When I was delivering aircraft to some of the forward fighter bases along the south coast, I would often see the V.1s coming in over the sea from the direction of France. Sometimes they would fly across in front of my aircraft.

I would also watch Spitfire XIVs and the Tempest boys – sometimes a Meteor jet – catch up with the buzz-bombs and, from an angle, shoot them down over open farmland before they could do tremendous damage to London. Sometimes, when we saw these buzz-bombs, we ATA women were flying Spitfire XIVs or Typhoons or Tempests ourselves – the aircraft with the speed to catch them – but it wasn't our job to shoot at anything.

In the beginning, some of the RAF aircraft were lost because they were faster than the V.1s, and if the bomb was shot at from behind, the chasing aircraft caught up and ran into the blast as the bomb exploded, sometimes with fatal results for the pilots. So a deflection shot was introduced.

I enjoyed watching a successful chase. There was our RAF fighter catching up the shiny tail of the V.1, and even in the sunlight the explosion was bright and impressive as it blew up or hit the ground. If it was flying near enough and low enough, my aircraft wobbled with the blast.

Some of the zanier RAF fighter pilots flew alongside the V.1s and tucked their wings under the buzz-bomb's wing and tipped it up. This upset the gyro guidance system and it would then plunge into the ground. This was also fun to watch from the air, but was discontinued after fatalities when the V.1s blew up the RAF fighters as well. Apparently, the German intelligence service got the word back that RAF pilots were doing this, and rigged up a trip-wire under the bombs' wings to counter this tipping manoeuvre.

I flew my first Tempest V at this time, while the buzz-bombs were coming over with alarming frequency. Being a fast fighter aeroplane, Tempests were urgently needed to combat the doodle-bugs. I flew Tempest *EJ712* from Aston Down to Newchurch, delivering it to 486 (New Zealand) Squadron which was based there.

There was also a Mustang (*AP260*) from Gatwick to Aston Down where I discovered the petrol cocks crossed – yes, another petrol problem – but I delivered it alright. Three days later, on 19 September, in bad weather, I took a Spitfire IX (*MA813*) up to Cosford, then a Walrus from there to Eastleigh.

On this sortie I was flying on the east side of Southampton balloon barrage above a smattering of low-lying sea fog. Of course, that Walrus didn't like me either, so its engine suddenly blacked out the view by spewing out a lot of oil all over the windscreen. Now a Walrus hardly flies anyhow, as I've previously mentioned, but without power it goes down mighty fast. I couldn't choose what to do or see where to point. It was a case of take a deep breath and shove the stick forward before the thing stalled.

Into the sea fog we went: mind the balloon cables didn't come into it. I thought we would hit the ground as the sea fog was right down. 'Ha, ha,' they'd say, 'broke her neck in a Walrus did she, ha, ha!' I blinked through an oily gap in the windscreen. I was out of cloud, a few feet above the nice smooth grass of Eastleigh aerodrome. Lovely place to find in front of me, to clank onto. The Walrus's idea, not mine. We'd also missed the balloons.

I haven't any good yarns about Sea Otters. It was a better version of the Walrus with a 'pusher' instead of a 'puller' engine mounted high up, but, begging the Fleet Air Arm's pardon for my loathing of their Walrus, they did have some slightly nicer aircraft. Amongst others, there were three Fairey built aeroplanes, the Fulmar, the Firefly and the Barracuda. If you managed to climb up the outside of the Barracuda to the high-up cockpit, you were monarch of all you surveyed, good visibility out of it. A nice hefty thing with plenty of room in the cockpit.

The only snag, apart from getting in and out, was that before putting the wheels down in the circuit, you had to open up the engine so you didn't drop out of the sky. Most aircraft had to be throttled back to lose speed before wheels could be put down, but not the Barracuda – that was original. It also landed and stayed landed. I would say it was unbounceable. I'd rather fly them than the Walrus any day.

I flew a Sea Otter (*JM951*) and a Barracuda (*MX634*) on 29 September – Hamble to Wroughton, Wroughton to Hawarden – then a

Wellington XVI (*NC609*) from Hawarden to St Athan, but, with sea fog over that base, had to put down next door at Moreton Valence, in Gloucestershire. The tail wheel of the Wimpy sheered whilst taxying in. Luckily I had been seen to do a beautiful daisy-cutter of a landing, so was not blamed. The subsequent accident report noted that a locking pin in the tail wheel fork was sheared, probably due to a previous heavy landing. I was not held responsible.

September had added 33 aircraft deliveries to my flying log-book, with six taxi-days, covering 14 different aircraft types. The busiest day had been the 16th, when I had flown a Spitfire XIII, a taxi-Fairchild, an Avenger, a Wellington and a Mustang. The Wellington was fun. *HF171* had to be taken from Gosport to Gatwick, when bang! crash! draught! – the cockpit emergency exit hatch blew open in flight. The Avenger I took from High Ercall to Worthy Down, not helped by the fact that the compass and gyro were both U/S. It didn't matter. It was a nice day and I was flying my old familiar route south.

The next day, 17 September, was the Battle of Britain anniversary service. We had the service in the evening at Hamble Parish Church and all the girls went along after flying had ended. The hymn we sang I stuck in my log-book; I don't know who wrote it:

Lord of all might, Thou God of Love,
Whose throne is in the heights above.
The wind thou holdest in thy hand,
The lightnings move at thy command.
Look down in mercy; hear our prayer
For those in peril in the air.

Their escort be: Their guardian strong,
As through the skies they speed along.
Through clouds and storms and trackless space,
Guide and uphold them with Thy grace.
Look down in mercy; hear our prayer
For those in peril in the air.

The solemn hours when they ascend,
Our home and freedom to defend.
Be Thou their armour in the fight,
Whose souls are precious in Thy sight.
Look down in mercy; hear our prayer
For those in peril in the air.

Thou art the Life of wingèd things,
The joy of every bird that sings;
The love that heeds the raven's call,
That stoops to mark the sparrow's fall,
Look down in mercy; hear our prayer
For those in peril in the air.

◇   ◇   ◇

I was hanging about in the Mess at Hamble on the misty afternoon of 29 October 1944 when Alison King, the Ops Officer, peered in round the door and said, 'Oh, Diana, if you're not doing anything, there's a Vengeance here for Gosport. Would you like to pop it over? We'll send a van to collect you.' Although it was a request, one never refused.

Gosport, a Fleet Air Arm Station, was only around the corner from Hamble, so I was delighted to be able to relieve my boredom. I went into the Maps, Met. & Signals rooms. The weather was foggy but, after all, it wasn't far to fly. Signals told me that there was some work going on at Gosport, so I had to be careful of any runway obstructions.

I had flown over there with something else just a few days earlier and had spotted a lot of 'plum-puddings', as my maternal grandfather always used to call road-works signs with red danger lanterns, so I was going to have a good look before landing anyway.

I strapped Vengeance *HB512* (a Mark II target-tug version of the aeroplane) to my backside, and was just about to start up when Alison herself came rushing out towards me. 'Diana!' she shouted, 'do you know it's only 400 yards?' 'Mmm, yes!' I replied casually, nodding, then started up. Alison, looking a bit nonplussed, shrugged her shoulders slightly before turning back towards the ATA hut. I did just wonder why she'd worried to tell me. After all, surely she knew that an old hand like me wouldn't ever go off, even for ten minutes, without first checking with Signals for anything unusual, which is why they had told me about the works and the runway length. I knew you could land very short with a Vengeance, so knew I'd have more than enough room.

When in the air, I found it really was very very poor visibility indeed. It was, in addition, already starting to get dark but, knowing that part of the coast much better than the back of my hand, I was able to creep around Hamble, fly very low along the coast, then into the circuit at Gosport. There, to my amazement, through the ever-increasing fog and darkness, I could just make out that there was absolutely nothing at all blocking any part of the runway. It was completely clear.

'They're all barmy,' thought I, as I brought the Vengeance into land, then taxied in. When I got back to Hamble, I gave my delivery chit to Alison, saying, 'You know, it wasn't only 400 yards, but the entire length of the runway was clear. What were you going on about?'

'Well,' said Alison, 'the latest Met. report came in after you'd left the Mess, showing that the weather was deteriorating, and it was already down to 400 yards in the fog there, and decreasing fast. I just wanted to warn you to stop you going. You wouldn't take any notice of what I said. It was the visibility, you goose, not the runway length!'

Obviously a breakdown in communications.

Among the 28 different nationalities who flew with ATA, some were from Poland, and, of those, several were women. One was the beautiful 'Vega' (Jadwiga) Pilsudska, the daughter of Marshal Pilsudski, while another was a slight, dark-eyed girl called Anna Leska, whom I have mentioned before. Both flew in Poland before the war began.

When the Germans occupied Poland they stationed armed guards around the aerodromes to prevent any attempts at escape. One night, Anna, with a friend of hers, crept onto an aerodrome at night and jumped into the nearest aircraft. Without being able to strike a light to check if there was any petrol in it, they started it up first go, then took off under the surprised noses of the unsuspecting soldiers. They just got to Rumania before they ran out of fuel.

They met up with Anna's father, who was in the Army, and some escaped Polish airmen. Anna was put in jail for a few days by the Rumanians, but when let out, after a series of vicissitudes made her way to France, then to England, where, after a session acting as interpreter for the Forces' Ministry at the Foreign Office, she was accepted to fly with ATA. She was eventually posted to Hamble and survived the war, which she wouldn't have done without her brave escape. She was a much-loved but fiery character. We all liked to be flown by her when she was the taxi-Anson pilot.

One day, Anna was landing a Typhoon onto Eastleigh while the balloons were down, so all directions were usable, when the test pilot Squadron Leader Michael Graham landed across wind, as he hadn't noticed the landing 'T' had been changed during his five-minute air test of a Spitfire. The two fighters met somewhere in the middle. Anna and Michael chewed up each other's aircraft on their landing runs, making a mess of both. It is said that as Michael was in the wrong, Anna's Polish swear words came out full bore.

During my very early days at Hamble, some of the jobs I got were to fly the taxi Fairchild Argus to take more senior pilots to collect their delivery aeroplanes. I went to various places, but one day I was told to go to the aerodrome at Chattis Hill, which I have mentioned before. This was the 'secret' aerodrome near Stockbridge, not far from Salisbury Plain. There were two camouflaged hangars hidden in the trees from which various things from Spitfires to American Fortresses emerged, but mostly Spitfires. There was one short runway, quite a lot of it between two woods, which made arrival and departure more interesting because of the veer of the wind off the trees.

The place was secret because earlier in the war it had become the dispersal spot for new Spitfires following the bombing of the Supermarine works at Woolston and Itchen. Dispersal of Spit production became a priority when Spitfires were urgently needed, and Chattis Hill was large enough to stick a factory without needing any major changes. The sheds were camouflaged by clearing just sufficient woodland to lay the foundations, pulling back the trees with ropes while prefabricated sections were assembled, then letting the trees spring back into their natural positions to break up the factory outline. As the airfield had fallen into disuse since the First World War, its main visitors had been racehorses, which were exercised on the old flying field. This continued during the war, in the hope that the 'gallops' would help obscure the new use of the old flying field, which had been a training depot station in the Great War.

No. 15 Ferry Pool's aircraft became a common sight at Chattis Hill, and when the possibility of an invasion by the Germans still prevailed, Chattis Hill was designated as Hamble's emergency base. Later in the war, when the need for secrecy declined, some of the trees were chopped down in order to improve the landing area.

The first couple of times I dropped pilots there, it was easy, because the more experienced pilots knew where it was. They also knew how to find it as someone had planted a field of lovely yellow mustard in an arrow shape. The head of the yellow mustard arrow pointed directly to Chattis Hill. Some secret! We all said the farmer must be a spy in league with the enemy.

One day, Alison from 'Ops' told me to take the Fairchild empty to pick someone up from this airfield. Off I flew, thinking to find the secret place would be, in RAF parlance, 'a piece of cake'. It wasn't. The field of mustard had been cut and my directional arrow had gone. I spent more than 20 minutes flying round the area before I finally spotted my destination.

The pilot I was to collect was 20 minutes tireder, crosser and colder.

◇   ◇   ◇

I haven't said much about my sister Virginia since our childhood, but I can bring her in now. Having gone to RADA, she had decided to become an actress, and had been seeing a young actor by the name of Morton Lowry. My mother had not approved and so took Virginia off to America to visit our relatives, where she got a part in a play in Hollywood opposite Pauline Frederick, a well-known actress of the day. The play ran on well, so Mama came back to England for Christmas. Virginia was 21, so Mama couldn't boss her about any more.

Virginia had left with Morton her gold and diamond cigarette case and her red MG car. Morton soon sold the case, borrowed £50 from Eddie Spielman, the antique dealer, and took the car to America on a ship 'steerage' (cheap), then motored to California, where he got a part as a junior lead opposite Virginia in the same play. They married in 1938 – on stage. My parents were dismayed. Virginia had a son, but the marriage was not a success and they divorced after the war when they returned to England.

Before all this, however, Virginia had had a great admirer by the name of Constaki Cawadias, brother of my Queen's College, Harley Street schoolfriend, Mary, who became the wife of Sir Nicolas Henderson, our Ambassador in Washington at the time of the Argentine invasion of the Falklands. Constaki used to call to try to see Virginia but if she was busy he got landed with her boring young sister – me!

During the Second World War, Constaki was in Greece. He was centred in Athens. He left his house hurriedly to escape the Gestapo, and went to the mountains to join the British Military Mission, where he stayed when not engaged in nefarious missions in small boats. The Germans entered his house to find him gone, but found a wonderful photograph of my now beautiful sister, with a suitably loving inscription to him written on it: 'To Con, My friend always'.

They badly wanted to catch Constaki. Thinking that Virginia was Greek, they plastered her photo all over Athens on a 'Wanted' poster. The Gestapo usually rounded up all the relatives and friends so they could unsqueamishly interrogate them to make them tell on the people they wished to capture. Virginia had not even been to Greece, and she was still safely ensconced in far-off Hollywood whilst the Germans were searching for her in Athens.

◆ *Chapter 12* ◆

A Unique Experience

IN SEPTEMBER 1944, Brussels, capital of Belgium, was liberated, with the Germans pushed back 15 miles to the east of that great city. The British 2nd Tactical Air Force, under the command of Air Marshal Sir Arthur Coningham KGB DSO MC DFC AFC, set up its headquarters there. Derek was still officially 'on rest' from operations after his four front-line tours, and had been appointed Personal Assistant to 'Maori' Coningham. He had got this nickname because he was a New Zealander, but later it got twisted into 'Mary'! Coningham had a fine record in the First World War as a successful fighter pilot and squadron leader, and he was a splendid air commander in the Second.

One morning, Derek arrived back at Hamble from Belgium with his invasion-striped Spitfire. I had four days' leave due to me, so hoped that we might be able to spend some time together. A forlorn hope with his new job.

Derek told me he had a problem that I would be able to solve. It sounded mysterious but during dinner that evening at the Clausentium Club in Southampton, he said that a photographic reconnaissance aircraft was needed in Brussels to take pictures of the latest German lines, but that he had no spare pilot to fly it over. Would I like to take it there for him the next day, whilst I was officially on leave?

Various squadrons were already in the Low Countries and Group support units were being set up, male ATA pilots being allowed to take aircraft across to them. However, the 'powers-that-be' in the ATA had decreed that no women pilots were to cross the Channel with ATA deliveries. We women, of course, longed to go. The RAF and that little strip of sea had stopped the enemy from getting to England and now the ATA hierachy were stopping the ATA women from going over. Psychologically it was a blow to us all.

For many years the women pilots had been flying – and dying – in the same aircraft types and in the same conditions as the men, yet now we were being denied these foreign trips. You can't imagine the dismay that we felt. We really believed we should be allowed to spread our wings abroad after being cooped up in the British Isles since the start of the war.

The ATA head boys gave themselves the first jobs overseas, whilst saying, 'Oh, no, *girls* can't go! There aren't any lavatories for them! Also there are still pockets of German resistance here and there. They might force-land and be captured by the dreaded Hun.' Seemed to me that we had been caught out in far more dubious circumstances in the British Isles, which also had a scarcity of loos sometimes. 'Silly excuses,' we said, 'unlikely to be equalled anywhere in Europe.' We really were very hurt and angry.

At first, therefore, I jumped at Derek's suggestion, but then said,

'I can't go. We're not allowed to.'

'Aha,' said Derek, 'you will be on leave, so this won't be an ATA job, it's an RAF one.' With a flourish he produced a letter signed by his boss, which I still have stuck in my flying log-book. It read:

> Headquarters,
> Second Tactical Air Force,
> Royal Air Force.
>
> 25th September, 1944.

This is to certify that First Officer D. B. Walker, Air Transport Auxiliary, has permission to travel to Brussels and to remain there for a period of four/seven days, as from 1st October.

She is proceeding by air and will be in uniform.

> A. Coningham
> Air Marshal Commanding Second Tactical Air Force

This seemed to make it official enough for me. Whether I was going to fly myself over rather than go in the back of some transport aircraft as a passenger seemed totally irrelevant at the time.

On 2 October we went to Northolt to fetch the aircraft, which turned out to be an invasion-striped Spitfire F.VII, serial number *MD174*. It had a pressurized hood that clamped you inside, so was not opened for either take-off or landing, like other Spits. It had criss-cross squares on the perspex for added strength, and felt somewhat claustrophobic.

The initials DGS were painted on its sides, as it was normally the aeroplane flown by Wing Commander Tactics, Fighter Command, Denis G. 'Splinters' Smallwood DSO DFC. He was often in Brussels with Derek. He later retired from the RAF as Air Chief Marshal Sir Denis – GBE KCB DSO DFC.

Derek's plan was for me to formate on his Spitfire as we flew to Brussels' Evere aerodrome. 'Whatever happens,' he warned, 'don't land anywhere else. If anything crops up, get yourself back to England.'

As mentioned earlier, the ATA did not fly in formation, we flew alone, so my idea of formation flying was practically nil. Still, it was a lovely sunny day, and my left wing was tucked in well beside Derek's right wing. It was exciting, to say the least, to see the White Cliffs of Dover being left behind after so long, then to see Cap Gris Nez ahead. Looking down, I could see the masses of bomb craters in the sandy strip of coast lying north–south up from Boulogne. I wanted to sing, throw the aircraft about in celebration of my freedom from my English bonds, but desisted as I had to watch my left wing-tip. I certainly didn't want to bump into Derek.

As we headed out over the Channel, I marvelled at the scene. This had to be a unique event: a husband and wife flying two operational Spitfires across to the Continent in wartime. Other husbands and wives may have flown together, but our set of circumstances left them all standing.

Brussels was still in gala mood when we arrived, having only been liberated a few days before. Everyone hugged and kissed everyone else, while the streets were full and noisy. There was the near distant rumble of guns, but no-one seemed to take any notice. I kept bumping into all sorts of friends from the Army as well as the RAF. Derek had already made friends with some lovely Belgian people, with whom we stayed at their 'House in the Woods'.

I was then allowed to fly the Spitfire around Evere and Brussels for a 'flight test'. I went and had a look at where I was told the Germans would be. It all seemed quiet to me, and I couldn't make out from high up where the so-called front line lay. Nobody took a pot shot at me. I wanted to press the camera button for a few seconds at the exact 15-mile distance, but it would have been a waste of film, as Derek said the RAF were going to use the aircraft anyway for their own PR work whilst it was there.

We had some glorious days of fun – and food. The Belgians had sugar, sweets, wine – all sorts of things that we in Britain hadn't seen for years. They had leather shoes and handbags in the shops, and no clothes rationing coupons anymore – their war was over! So was their blackout, it seemed. Everywhere the lights were on again.

After three days, down came The Great Fog. We went down to Evere each day, ever hopeful. The Spit VII had now been used for its PR job, and Derek said that both the film and the aircraft needed to be taken back to England. I was also due back at Hamble, but the weather was completely unflyable. Derek rang through on the RAF tie-line, enabling me to talk to Margot Gore, who, of course, had no idea where I was. As luck would have it, our ferry pool was not being overstretched at that moment, so I was allowed to add on two days of my next month's leave to my present leave.

Derek and I had now been together for longer than on our May honeymoon. In fact, this whole episode seemed more like a honeymoon for us, in a foreign country, foreign city with friendly foreign and British friends.

On the sixth day, 8 October, the weather was still extremely murky, but time had run out, so in the afternoon Derek and I decided to take off and do a circuit, to take a look at it. 'If it's no good, we'll come back to Evere,' he promised. Once one got airborne things often looked better, but on that day they didn't. To me they looked worse.

The weather on the ground had been bad enough, but my tummy sank down into my toes when we had words with the pilot of an RAF Anson just as we were getting started. This pilot confirmed that the weather was universally dreadful, having become even worse since he crept in. He didn't think we'd make it back to England.

Our plan was to do the same as we'd done on the way out: I would formate on Derek's wing as he had radio but I hadn't. (A radio was fitted in my Spit, but I had no helmet attachments, and no idea how to use a radio – I'd never had to learn.) Our destination was again RAF Northolt, just to the north of London.

In a Spitfire you see forward only a little triangle, as the nose and wings get in the way. Derek put up his cruising revs and boost to RAF settings, which were higher than ATA's fuel-saving settings. This produced a higher ground speed (as well as a higher petrol consumption). In that weather I would have preferred to be flying a bit slower in order to be able to map-read more easily, or even not to be flying at all, but Derek was undaunted, setting course 280°.

I could scarcely see anything except now and then a flash of light underneath from the water when we crossed over some dyke or canal. All the rest was just yellow muck. I was unable to map-read and formate at the same time, so I kept hoping Derek would stick to his word and turn back to Evere now he had had a look at it. But he plunged on, so I had to stay beside him.

After 20 minutes on a course of 280°, there started to be lumps of black muck in the yellow muck. Derek then disappeared into one beside me. When I looked again, he wasn't there! So, suddenly, I was on my own, but where in heaven was I? I went down low to circle, trying to pinpoint my position, but there were no features, only lovely open farmland. I didn't dare to stay in one place very long because I didn't know where the Germans were. No-one really knew. Some troops were holding out here and there as the main advance bypassed them, and I certainly didn't feel like being shot down.

I didn't even consider trying to find my way back to Evere, for I hadn't a hope of locating it without a radio. If I overflew it by just 15 miles – not that far by air – I would be well and truly over hostile territory.

I flew on again on a westerly course, even considering jettisoning the hood for better visibility as well as getting rid of the claustrophobic perspex squares.

The clouds in the muck came lower and lower. The hills of St Omer, lying in a ridge north/south, loomed up to try to meet them. I almost shut my eyes, squeezed through between the muck and those hills, before arriving over a bit of coast, lying north/south, which was pock-marked with craters. I could still hardly see anything at all, the visibility was so poor, but I wanted it to be that bit of coast just south of Cap Gris Nez, which we had flown over on our way out a week earlier. I decided that again I mustn't hang around, so set a course of 295°, throttling back to ATA cruising revs and boost.

In 7¹/₂ minutes I'll hit Dungeness, I thought to myself, but as I went out over the sea, I flew straight into sea fog. Low sea fog, right down on the water. I still wasn't much good on instruments but I went up, coming out at 4,000 feet in glorious sunshine over puffy white clouds. Down to the south I saw an aircraft, so turned towards it thinking it might be Derek. Almost at once I saw it was a twin-engined Dakota – going the other way.

I turned back, correcting my course. After 7¹/₂ minutes I looked down as the white clouds turned yellow. Then there was a little gap, through which I could see the sea. No land, no houses . . . something had gone wrong!

As I've said before, the ATA dictum was that pilots were worth more than aircraft because of their expensive training, so I thought the best thing to do would be to be quite sure I was over land, then bale out. The expensive cameras and the film could be forgotten.

I continued on for another three minutes, which seemed like hours. Still no land in the gaps, and I was also keeping one eye on the fuel gauges. Something really was wrong, so I tried to be logical about it all. Suppose I had not started from a point south of Gris Nez, but from some little north–south bit of the Belgian coast? I hadn't known the drift when Derek chose the course. If that was so, I might even be flying up the North Sea instead of across the Channel, in which case I'd run out of petrol before I got to England – before I got to the North Pole!

But just suppose I had left the pock-marked coast from further south than I originally thought? In that case I'd be flying right along the middle of the English Channel. This seemed almost impossible, but after another 15 minutes, with still no sight of land, I turned due north – 010° magnetic in those days – and went down low in the fog. For several minutes I saw nothing at all, then the wash of a large boat showed up white through the gloom. I was now at 200 feet.

Suddenly there was a little sheen of light ahead, a little line of white in the yellow. I peered at it anxiously; and yes, it was something. Land at last? The White Cliffs of Dover, perhaps? I flew on. It was not the White Cliffs of Dover, but an east to west line of lovely sandy beach. There, right behind it, looming up beside me with a rusty grin, was the huge gasometer at Bognor.

Tangmere wasn't far away, but I was determined not to mislay myself now that I had 'found' England, so instead of setting a six-mile course to Tangmere, I flew round the gasometer, crept up the river of Pagham Rife to Chichester, then turned right into the Tangmere circuit. My, it was foggy! All the runway lights were on, while green and white Very flares were being fired up through the murk. 'Just my luck,' I thought, 'they're bringing in a squadron of something, and I'll have to wait my turn.' It was now so thick that I stayed quite close to the circuit while keeping a good look-out for other aircraft, which I thought would jump out at me from the muck at any moment.

After a few minutes, not having seen any sign of other aircraft, I flew even closer. I certainly had no intention of going off anywhere else, so I decided it was now my turn, before I ran out of petrol.

When you have had a problem, it usually happens that the landing is absolutely perfect, and so it was this time. Perhaps one has been concentrating for so long that every fibre of you does things exactly as they should occur, beefed up by adrenalin. Feeling the ground beneath my wheels was terrific. I taxied in, parking by the Watch office, where, to my amazement, I saw Derek's Spitfire. As I arrived, he came running out, his face as white as a sheet. With an air of wonderment and relief, he called, 'How on earth did you get here? Do you know that this is the *only* airfield in the whole of the south of England that is open?'

I asked if the cascades of Very lights were for some other aeroplanes coming home to roost, hoping that I had not got in their way. No, he said, the bombardment had been for me alone.

We stayed in a pub in Chichester that night, I for one sleeping like a log. Derek, on the other hand, said he had heard the church clock opposite strike every quarter hour. At breakfast he quizzed me again about how I had managed to get to Tangmere; why had I chosen it? He had been guided to it over his radio, being given course and bearings, but without radio, how had I found the only airfield open in that dreadful fog? I reminded him that while he had had radio, I had had my guardian angel, and that Fellow Up Top was keeping an eye on me.

The fog cleared, so Derek flew back to his base while I took the Spitfire VII into Northolt, then headed back to Hamble. The following day, when I got back from flying, Derek rang up to ask if anything had been wrong with the Spit whilst I had been flying it. 'No,' I told him, 'no snags at all.' But then as I thought about it, perhaps it had sounded a little rough over the unknown sea . . . but when you've got the wind up, not relishing the idea of a swim, engines often do.

I asked him why he was enquiring. It was a very bad line but I thought he told me that the aircraft had blown up on take-off the next day. I didn't like to ask what had happened to the pilot because Derek sounded so upset. I just thought that my number had been on that aircraft, but that it had got someone else instead.

Forty years later, in 1984, I was invited to lunch by Air Marshal Sir Peter Wykeham KCB DSO OBE DFC AFC, in a 'caravan' at the Farnborough Air Display. Sitting to one side of me was Air Marshal Sir Patrick Dunn KBE CB DFC. Both had been distinguished fighter pilots during the Second World War, operating in Greece at the same time as Derek, although in other squadrons.

We watched the demonstration flying displays, talking about modern and ancient aeroplanes, when Paddy Dunn said that he had flown something that I had flown. Thinking that it was an aeroplane I had delivered, I asked what, when and where? 'It was a Spitfire VII, in October 1944,' he said, going into some details. He had collected it from Northolt, flown it to Bicester, had lunch with Laddie Lucas, but after lunch, the engine had failed on take-off.

So *he* had been the pilot whose neck that Spit VII had tried to break. For 40 years I had thought that whoever it was who had flown it next was dead instead of me! He went on to ask me if I would look up the aircraft in my log-book, to let him know the registration number, as he had been taken to hospital and hadn't put it in his log-book.

In a way, all this rather spoils my story, but at Farnborough that day, so long afterwards, a weight was lifted from me. I felt a whole lot better knowing that the next pilot of *MD174* was still very much around after all.

Our trip to Brussels, while unique, also caused a bit of a furore. A month later it was reported in the *Daily Mail* (17 November):

> . . . the beautiful daughter of the millionaire racing motorist, and her husband, Wing Commander Derek Walker DFC, have flown on a honeymoon trip to Brussels and back, each piloting their own Spitfire.

At this time a Parliamentary Committee wanted to go to Brussels to swan around and see the front line and so on. They were told it wasn't convenient. When the news of our flight came out in the newspapers, they were angry and made a fuss, so a white-washing court of enquiry followed. Derek lost three months' pay . . .

It was lucky we had been 'invited' over, or at least I had, by 'Mary' Coningham, who apparently believed it was good to give his people breaks from austerity. He had given Derek his break, as well as getting a Spitfire to Brussels which he wanted, so where was the harm? However, Air Chief Marshal Sir Wilfred Freeman, the then Chief Executive in the Ministry of Aircraft Production, and formerly Vice Chief of the Air Staff, even though he was a very great friend of my father and knew me well, thought Coningham's action 'quite monstrous', informing Sir Peter Portal, Chief of the Air Staff, about it.

Apparently, Coningham did live well at his HQ, which may have annoyed Wilfred, and he had brought Lady Coningham to Brussels, which annoyed him even more. He wrote to Portal, 'It is well known that Lady Tedder [wife of Sir Arthur Tedder, deputy Supreme Allied Commander of the Allied Expeditionary Force] is in Paris, Lady Coningham is in Brussels and that Lady Leigh-Mallory was accompanying her husband to Ceylon . . .' Trafford Leigh-Mallory and his wife were, in fact, killed on the journey when their aircraft crashed east of Grenoble on 14 November, their loss being assumed on the 21st.

However, it soon blew over. I for one would not have missed the trip for anything, even though I had had quite an adventure getting home.

Wilfred never said anything to my face about the trip and was always most friendly on his frequent visits to Ridgemead. I would often see him sitting in the garden, working on secret papers. The 1945 Easter weekend, Wilfred's wife Elizabeth and small children were also at Ridgemead. We arranged an Easter egg hunt in the garden. The kidlets shut their eyes whilst we scurried about hiding the eggs. I had brought them back from a recent trip to Brussels as there were few to be had in rationed Britain. We also had a couple of soft toys, a rabbit and a chicken.

When it was the turn of the kidlets to do the hiding with the next batch of eggs and toys, the grown-ups shut their eyes. When we opened them to start our hunt, there was the large blue fluffy rabbit sitting right in the middle of the lawn. I remonstrated with Wilfred's smallest child, saying, 'You haven't hidden it.' To this she replied, 'Oh yes I have, but I've hidden it in a very easy place . . .'

Another event, not directly attributable to me, was that soon after my trip, female ATA pilots were finally authorized to fly aircraft to the Continent. The Hamble girls were too far away to be part of the set-up, flights mainly going out from White Waltham. Very soon afterwards, however, I myself was posted back to White Waltham, and to No. 1 Ferry Pool, so was eligible for those trips – officially.

It should perhaps be said that RAF pilots were usually rested after a tour of operations, which consisted of so many fighter trips or bombing raids. They were rested by being given non-flying duties, or instructing, or less demanding jobs not incurring continual flying. This counteracted sustained fear on long-range bombing sorties over enemy territory, or short, frightening fighter forays. They needed it.

ATA pilots, on the other hand, were never rested, only laid off if they were ill. They flew every day, often several times a day. Some of the earlier entrants flew virtually non-stop for six years, with just three days' leave a fortnight, taken as one day during one week, and two days the following week. They never got stale because of the infinite variety of aircraft types, sorties and places of delivery, plus the frequent battles with indifferent weather. They went on for ever . . .

After the Low Countries were released from German occupation, RAF squadrons and their Group support units were set up in such places as Brussels, Ghent and Courtrai, to where the ATA regularly ferried aircraft.

The food rationing system in Britain was adequate to sustain life, but there were grave shortages, including sugar. In Belgium, as I said before, sugar did not seem to be a problem, while cakes and sweets were freely available in the local shops near to the various airfields. When we flew overseas, we generally came back loaded with delicious chocolates, plus other things we had not seen the like of during the war years.

The Belgians were short of cocoa, but this commodity was off ration in Britain: one could buy as much as one liked. Being a law-abiding girl, I would never go in for real smuggling, even though at the time there were no customs controls set up anywhere on any airfield. However, when faced with the dilemma that freely bought cocoa was needed overseas, and that there was a place in Brussels which would buy cocoa for cash . . . well, it didn't seem too illegal.

Cocoa was sold in England in flat tins $6^{1}/_{2}$ inches x $2^{1}/_{2}$ inches. It just so happened that 40 1-lb tins not only fitted into a parachute bag but the size and weight coincided with that of an actual parachute. All our aircraft had bucket seats, into which the parachute fitted and on which we pilots sat. The 'chute was strapped to our nether regions in case we needed to bale out. Instead of the parachute, the 40 lb of cocoa did quite nicely.

Flying without the silken, life-saving parachute was a bit of a risk, I suppose, not to mention a surprise if one had to bale out, having forgotten one had tins not silk. I imagine one's memory would soon be jogged when 40 tins flew up past one's ears. Nevertheless, it was a risk I was quite prepared to take, because the cocoa cash was enough for a good night out in Brussels, plus a bit left over for shopping for unrationed sweets and leather goods. During the latter part of my ATA career I must have sat on hundreds of pounds of cocoa.

Pilots did not know until they were issued with their 'chits' in the mornings by the Operations officer, whether they were to be given a job which entailed crossing the Channel, or to some location in the British Isles. So in case I was lucky enough to get a foreign trip, I kept a spare parachute bag full of cocoa tins in the boot of my aerodrome car. This was then a 14 hp Vauxhall. The Bentley that my father had given me for my 21st birthday present had long since been consigned to the back of the garage, because it only did 19 miles to the gallon, so with petrol severely rationed and the Bentley's successor, the Opel, broken, I was relegated to the Vauxhall.

I had saved up enough petrol to drive to London. We were in the middle of an extremely foggy spell of weather so we were released early one day as nobody could fly. Wendy Sale-Barker and I drove from White Waltham to London, staying at my flat in River House, from where we were taken out dancing by some friends. I parked the Vauxhall on a bomb site, of which we had plenty in London, at the junction of Tite Street and Royal Hospital Road, Chelsea. It seemed safer there off the road instead of risking someone driving into it in the fog. The miniscule car 'blackout' lights were still in use.

In the morning, the fog was so thick that I couldn't see the River Thames across the road from my window. Wendy and I rang Ops, who told us that there didn't seem to be a chance of any clearance, so flying was obviously off for the moment, but could we report in again, or ring back, at midday. We didn't say we were in London, pretending to be round the corner. In any case, Chelsea to White Waltham only took 40 minutes because there were scarcely any cars at all on the roads during the war.

We took a chance on the fog clearing and enjoyed a leisurely breakfast. Then the telephone rang. It was the Chelsea police, who said, 'Oh, Miss Barnato, we've got your car. Would you like to collect it?' I hadn't even missed it yet.

It transpired that during the night one of their patrol cars had seen four youths in the Vauxhall. I was pleased it had been recovered, but wondered what had made them suspicious? 'Well,' said the policeman, 'it just didn't look right to us.' So the squad car had chased after it with its bell ringing, whereupon the youths had 'baled out'. Three had got away but the fourth had been apprehended.

I was asked to go along to Gerald Road Police Station, where I was reunited with my little car. 'Is there anything missing?' the police asked. It seemed intact to me, but then I remembered the cocoa. It had disappeared. 'No, nothing missing,' I lied. I thought that the officer looked at me a bit sideways, but if he knew about the cocoa, he must have wondered how on earth I could use up 40 lb of it.

Later on, the police asked me to prefer charges about the car theft. I didn't want to do so for obvious reasons, but was eventually persuaded to. When the case came to court, the boy's father came along to speak up for his son. The father was an RAF flight sergeant who looked so small, crumpled up and sad. He was doing his bit for the war effort, and so was his wife, but while they were absent their son had run amok.

I felt really awful about having let the case come up at all, and felt very very sorry for the flight sergeant. I was relieved when the son got off with a caution. I had to admit I felt it should have been me in the dock – for cocoa running! I wonder what 'they' did with it all?

On 15 December 1944 I had a Mosquito Mark XXX (*NT241* 'G') to fly from Colerne to No. 456 Night-fighter Squadron at RAF Ford, by Beachy Head, now the site of Ford open prison. It was late in the afternoon by the time I took off, and I ran into a band of heavy snowstorms near the south coast. Although I had several tries to get through to my destination, in the end I gave up and flew back to Chilbolton, which was just between storms when I got into the circuit.

The aerodrome was covered in snow, and with daylight fast disappearing, the runway looked a bit short. Still, this was my chosen 'funk-hole', and it was far too late to go anywhere else.

Getting down safely, I mentally chalked up another plus for my guardian angel while taxying in extremely carefully because of a strong wind which had sprung up, in addition to the slippery ground. I was waved into a dispersal point by an American airman, and not for the first time did I see a man's jaw drop when he caught sight of a female form, as I dropped out from the underneath door. 'We ain't got no dames here, Ma'am,' he said, but promptly took me to his CO, a tall, blond, chunky colonel of the US Army Air Force.

The colonel told me that his station was to be 'gotton ready' for a large influx of American and Canadian Army and Red Cross nurses, but that things were not exactly fixed up yet. He only had a skeleton staff on the whole base. However, I was duly fed and watered in the Officers' Mess, in the usual American way – delicious tinned pork chops, runny sweet corn, biscuits with peanut butter, followed by ice-cream covered in maple syrup. Plus *real* coffee, with lots of unrationed sugar! All this was manna from heaven, or rather from the American PX – the equivalent of our NAAFI. Apart from one or two other US bases I'd been to, I hadn't seen such a feast for a long time.

After dinner, the colonel bade me goodnight, hoped I wouldn't be too uncomfortable in the nurses' quarters, and left. An American corporal took me out into the now heavy snowstorm, then across to a large Nissen hut. When we got inside, I saw 24 iron bedsteads in a row down one side of the hut, with another 24 down the other. The bare concrete floor was shiny with damp. Right in the middle of the hut, one of the beds was made up, with the three-part 'biscuit' mattresses and heavy grey army blankets. Peeping over the top was the frilled edge of a silk pillowcase and sheet, seeming somewhat incongruous. I had never slept in silken sheets before! 'They're the colonel's,' commented the corporal. The Yanks certainly did themselves proud.

The corporal said he had made up that bed as it was nearest to the stove, and what time would I like early-morning tea? Wonderful service, thought I. As soon as he had gone, I took a lot more blankets off the heaps on the other beds and put as many as possible on top of my bed. It was a very cold hut, with an even more freezing partitioned-off washroom at the end, which housed 24 basins in a long row, plus a dozen baths. The number of loos seemed uncountable. The water was icy, but my corporal produced a large enamel pail of piping hot water, covered by a beautifully initialled bath towel. The colonel's again, no doubt.

I climbed into bed, the sheets feeling marvellous, but I could hardly move because of the weight of all those extra blankets. Near the end of the bed, an iron boiler pipe went up through the tin roof of the Nissen hut, while the little iron stove glimmered away, although not seeming to make much difference to the overall temperature. Now and then there was a plop, followed by some sizzling noise, as a bit of snow slid down the pipe to land on the stove top.

I put the sheets over my head to keep out the plops and sizzles, as well as the noise of wind and beating snow outside, and fell asleep. I don't believe I moved all night – not surprising with the weight of the blankets on top of me.

I opened my eyes to see the corporal's anxious face peering at me beside my bed. He said, 'I'll soon get this lot off you, Miss.' I thought he'd gone barmy because of the 'No-Dames-On-the-Station' situation. Next, he produced a shovel which he started wielding around near to my ears. I then realized that I couldn't move at all! Horrors! I was going to meet my doom in an empty Nissen hut, on an army bed, albeit in silken sheets . . .

However, I was not faced with the danger of a shovel-wielding, sex-starved American airforce corporal – he was coming to my aid. It was morning, but during the night, part of the corrugated tin roof by the stove pipe had, unknown to me, collapsed in the storm. An enormous mound of snow had descended through the hole onto a heap over my bed, completely covering it! I had, in fact, been sleeping in an igloo.

By the time my hero had dug me out, the tea he had brought me was cold, so he went off and was soon back with another hot lot. I was taken to the CO again, whom I thanked for his station's hospitality.

He asked if he might have a look at the Mosquito as he hadn't seen one close-up before. Whilst we were sitting inside the cockpit and I was showing him all the knobs, gauges and switches, a US Army truck came alongside and the driver offloaded some PX cardboard cartons of stores which he then stowed in the Mossie. The colonel said it was the least recompense he could offer for nearly suffocating a sleeping lady guest.

I remonstrated at his generosity, although not very vigorously, saying that one American dinner had been kindness enough. He would have none of it, however, so off I flew. After an uninvited arrival, all those extra rations were more than adequate compensation for a leaky roof, but I was glad I'd piled on those extra blankets.

It also crossed my mind that I'd saved my CO the problem of making out a loss report on one of her pilots. Cause of demise: 'Frozen to death – in silken sheets!'

• *Chapter 13* •

Towards Peace

MY MOTHER RAN a 1,000-acre farm at Nutfield, in Surrey, throughout the war. I don't know how she managed to do so much work. She had the help of my stepfather, of course, although in the early war years he helped to organize the local Home Guard unit. There were also four wonderful 'land girls' (Women's Land Army), young women who had been called up but who had elected to work on the land instead of joining the Armed Forces, or working in a factory, or in the ATA like me. One of the land girls was the daughter of my friend Lois Butler.

The house at Nutfield – Kentwyns – was run by my old Nanny, who had become the general factotum after all the able-bodied men and women had been called up. There were always a lot of animals around. The farm consisted of a large herd of pedigree Guernsey cows, plus two flocks of sheep. Up at the house were two large white poodles, a Siamese cat, a marmalade cat, and a tame house-trained badger. There were also two large white geese.

I was always rather frightened of the geese: they didn't like strangers, nor apparently me either, for they always ran at me hissing, with an alarming 'keep off our patch' manner. I didn't get to know them well, but Old Nanny fed them and cleaned the stables for them, as well as having pet names for each bird. They followed her around whenever she went into the garden. Those two were going to be eaten up sometime, so I could at least look at them and think, 'I know something you don't know!', which gave me some satisfaction after they had chased me into the house. And one was scheduled for our Christmas (1944) fare.

White Waltham Operations very kindly arranged that my Christmas Eve job was to nearby Redhill. I had once again managed a Christmas Day off, which this year I was to spend with my mother. There was, naturally, no transport or petrol, so I was forced to trudge the five miles from the airfield, lugging my 40-lb parachute. As soon as the front door was opened by Nanny, I knew something was wrong, but she wouldn't let on what it was.

On Christmas morning, I went into the kitchen just before lunch, to find Old Nanny basting one of her geese with tears streaming down her face, saying, 'I can't eat a bit of it! I can't eat a bit of it!'

She didn't either . . . but I did.

◇ ◇ ◇

Lois Butler, who had tried to dissuade me from even joining ATA, was stationed at No. 15 Ferry Pool at Hamble for a short time. She was trim, strong-featured, with sleek blonde hair. She had beautiful hands, was a vision of sex appeal, and an extremely competent pilot.

On 29 December, in the winter of 1944, Margot Gore tannoyed for a few of us, including Lois, telling us that a certain RAF squadron along the coast had suffered losses in aircraft so we were to take a batch of new Mosquito XXXs (mine was *NT307*) to them from various MUs around the country. These new aeroplanes, which were of a later Mark, would have slightly different flying characteristics to those which they had recently lost, so the RAF crews would no doubt welcome seeing girls bring them in without any problems.

Margot said, 'You've got all day to do this one job . . ,' adding that she had chosen a good-looking bunch of us girls, so we should be sure to make ourselves as attractive as we could. 'Efficient and pretty, please,' she said finally, and added that she would later be sending transport for us all. She also said we could stay for lunch in the squadron's Officers' Mess and chat to everyone.

The plan was, of course, cooked up by Margot and the 'Mossie' squadron CO for the aircrews to see and talk to a load of girls who had flown in these new types, in order to allay some of the prevailing tension. It was most unusual for Margot to tell us to hang about, and even more so to be ordered to stay for lunch at an RAF station instead of gulping the issue bar of chocolate as we were being fetched, or taking another aeroplane on, as fast as possible. We certainly all liked the idea of the proposed outing.

Every one of us except Lois arrived safely, being certain to make careful – and beautiful – landings. The squadron CO had sent an RAF transport with some of his officers up to the airfield, (a) to ensure they saw us land, and (b) to drive us back to their Mess. Whilst we were awaiting Lois' arrival, we joked and flirted with the young pilots, who asked us who was coming in next. Lois had married at 16, and her daughter, also 16, had herself had a baby. So one of us chirped up, 'The flying grandmother!' The young men looked apprehensive but then we heard the sound of the approaching Merlins, and said, 'Ah, here comes Grannie in her Mossie.'

Lois did a dainty landing, taxied in, then emerged from the underhatch looking her usual immaculate self. She apologized for keeping everyone waiting. The RAF pilots, who had obviously expected some grey-haired, doddering old thing, were entranced at the apparition of femininity that had at last turned up.

We had a most enjoyable day. It was some days later before we learned that the Mossie crews had suffered severe losses and that the squadron

CO had confided to Margot that his men could do with some bucking-up. This was why we had been allowed so much leisure time on this delivery.

When we eventually got back to Hamble, a few pilots were still hanging around in our Mess. One was Joy Ferguson, a square, dumpy girl who wore her nondescript, roughly bobbed hair looped up either side of her large blue eyes. Without a spark of venom in her voice, she said, 'Oh, you pretty girls get all the nice jobs to squadrons.'

Now Joy was often teasing me about painting my nails, putting on lipstick and generally surveying my face in my powder-compact mirror, but always said it in a gentle way. She never did anything to make herself look more feminine or attractive, whilst the rest of us always tried to look as beautiful as possible whilst doing what was then called a man's job. So some of us turned on her, saying, 'Well, if you'd only do something about yourself, we'd be able to make quite a good-looking dish out of you! Take out your kirby grips, fluff up your hair, let your nails grow long; add some lipstick and nail polish, too.'

Would you believe it – after the war she turned into a man!

I saw her, or should I say him, after the war. He told me his story, after which I thought he was extraordinarily brave in facing up to such an appalling situation.

At the very moment that she was accepted as a woman pilot by ATA, Joy was told that it was possible for her to change her sex. She then thought that as she might well be killed doing the ferrying flights, it would be a waste of much-needed doctor and hospital time to have the operation then. She might just as well fly as a woman as a man, since she could do the same job as either gender.

She was extremely intelligent. She took a technical job after the war in one of the Ministries, to begin with as a woman. After her sex change, she went back into the very same job but called herself Jonathan instead of Joy, now dressing like a man. I just don't know how he/she faced up to it.

She had made a very ordinary-looking woman but, as has been said, she didn't really try. Later on we all understood why. He turned into a much better-looking man, confiding to me one day that it was sad that he couldn't have children. He was now hoping to marry a girl who had some of her own.

I saw him once in a while, then one day I rang up his office to be told that he had been shot dead in Hyde Park whilst driving along in his sports car. No-one knew why. What a waste of an extremely brave and kind person. And after all that.

30 April 1945 was a beautiful bright clear day, just the day for flying anything, but today it was my 27th Typhoon (*EK347*) from Lasham to Kemble, in Gloucestershire. There was a very bad draught in the cockpit, so, not wanting to end up with red eyes, I pulled down my goggles. Cruising along south of Swindon at about 2,000 feet, there was a sudden,

really almighty bang. I was instantly covered with tiny little bits of metal, while my map was blown from my hands.

I was sure, with all that noise, that the engine had blown up, so I pulled the throttle and boost levers back, stuck the nose down to retain my flying speed, whilst peering through the lower edge of the hood in order to choose a place for a forced landing.

There were any number of green Wiltshire fields to choose from. No problem, I thought – a piece of cake! Then, as I was about to turn off the fuel, I glanced down, horrified to see the ground between my legs and feet! No floor! There were the Typhoon's control wires and plumbing, but nothing else. The whole underside of the fighter had blown off in mid-flight, so it wasn't a dud engine after all.

I must confess to feeling a bit stupid, like a doctor must feel when his patient survives after a terminal diagnosis. I immediately opened up the still-roaring Sabre engine, dusted the bits off my goggles, thankful I had them over my eyes, and rescued my map, which had by now blown upwards, being flattened against the canopy above me by the inrushing gale.

I tested the elevators, which still worked. Thankfully, the large lump of underside had missed the tail-plane and rudder on its sudden and dramatic departure. Gingerly I climbed up high to see what my new stalling speeds would be without a clear airflow. Usually the stalling speed of a Typhoon was 88 mph, with everything up, but we began to fall out at 230 mph. This was much too much for flaps, and 30 mph too fast for even the undercarriage to be safely put down.

I cruised some more, keeping the speeds well above the ATA normal of 290 mph, just in case more bits came off which might increase the stalling speed even more. Reaching Kemble, I flew very low along the runway in use, doing this several times hoping that some sharp-eyed chap in either the blood-tub or crash-wagon crews might notice that some of my Typhoon was no longer there. Below me, nothing moved. No flurry of activity, no speeding ambulance or fire engine coming to my rescue. I supposed that with my speed, they all probably thought I was some lunatic doing a beat-up.

I decided that, come what may, the undercarriage was going to have to be lowered. I didn't fancy a belly landing with no protection at all underneath, with all the runway stones, dust, grass or earth being sucked up into the cockpit. I thought it might hurt.

There was also no protection from all the wind that was billowing around me: it was positively painful because my uniform was flapping against me all over my arms and legs, like a reefed tri-sail stuck in the cleets when you're luffed up trying to get it down in a storm.

I suddenly realized that I was very, very cold. As always happens when I get my own personal wind up, my teeth started to chatter – not only from the temperature.

I tightened the safety straps as much as I could, tried to catch and tuck in the extra long bits of canvas which were zipping about just missing my chin, then selected wheels down. I had slowed to just above the 230 mph stalling speed as the undercarriage came down. It didn't lock, so I had to swing the aircraft as I pressed the emergency pedals before the green lights showed on the instrument panel. All this was happening just above the stall. I hoped the undercarriage wouldn't be strained by excess speed at its lowering.

I landed without flaps, keeping the speed just above 230, squeezed the brakes on for a second at touchdown, then took them off again quickly so I wouldn't turn over. I used all the runway. When I had cleared the runway, I opened the hood, seeing that all the usually smooth sides of the Typhoon were torn and jagged, with bits sticking out all over the place from where the undersides had come adrift. I closed the hood fast, as all the little bits of metal got up my nose in the extra breezes. I taxied up to dispersal where we delivered our aircraft, hoping to be pulled together by the usual cup of strong tea that was always brewing.

The duty airman looked out of his shed with a startled expression on his face. 'What on earth happened, Miss Barnato? Why are you bringing us only half an aeroplane?' he gasped, surveying my sorry craft.

'I can't help it,' I answered, 'I didn't break it and it didn't happen on earth – it just fell apart in the air.'

In all I flew 31 Typhoons, but *EK347* was the only one that had a snag . . . Some snag!!

After an incident or accident, copies of the pilot's snag-sheets were sent to a multitude of departments, including the Air Ministry, the Accidents Branch, ATA HQ, the pilot's own pool, plus the airfield of delivery.

In 1985 I found out the previous history of Typhoon 1B *EK347*. It had had a tough life before I got my paws on it. Two squadrons, 485 (New Zealand) and 349 (Belgian), were planning to convert from Spitfires to Tempests. As Typhoons were similar in flying characteristics, the squadrons had been given six Typhoons in order to familiarize themselves with the type. There was a shortage of Tempests, hence the Typhoon stop-gap. In the event, neither squadron actually converted. 'Mine' had been one of the stop-gap machines.

Shortly after VE Day (8 May 1945), repair contracts were cancelled, so my Typhoon was not mended and never flew again. It was scrapped on 30 April 1946, exactly one year after our last flight together.

Twenty-six Typhoons were lost because of structural failure which was generally blamed on an elevator flutter. The flutter was cured, but there were still some accidents attributed to some sort of structural failure. The day after my incident, another Typhoon broke up over the New Forest.

No pilots came back or lived to report, except me. Thank you again, guardian angel. I hope you got those little bits of metal dust out of your wings.

◇ ◇ ◇

When VE Day (Victory in Europe Day – 8 May 1945) arrived, we didn't celebrate. Many of our friends were still out in the Far East fighting the

Japanese or were still in prison camps. Aeroplanes were coming out of the factories as production was at its height and they had to be moved. So our work went on. Not so many squadron replacement aircraft were needed now that the fighting on the European front had ceased, but many aircraft were littered about Europe and had to be brought back by us.

Not long afterwards, Margot told me that pools were being run down and pilots could easily be posted to other pools if they wanted. So towards the end of May, as I have said, I went back to White Waltham and No. 1 Pool because it was near my father's house and it was easier for Derek to get there than to Hamble. Derek was still with 12 Group HQ, but would soon get a posting to Cranwell for a Senior Commander's Course.

I must tell you something about River House, as I promised earlier. After my mother's divorce from my father, she wanted something to take her mind off the upset, so in 1924 she bought the fine, yellow brick, five-storey house on the corner of Tite Steet and Chelsea Embankment, London, overlooking the River Thames and Battersea Park.

My mother, who I must remind you was an American, converted River House into five self-contained flats, one on each floor. Unlike in America, few well-off British people lived in flats in those days – it simply 'wasn't done'. She did, however, put in central heating, which few houses over here had.

When the war began, she was living at Kentwyns, her house at Nutfield. Our London house in Elsworthy Road was promptly requisitioned by the Government for some unstated need. Meantime, the third-floor flat at River House had no tenant. Not knowing what sort of war we were going to have, nor able to imagine the extent of the forthcoming bombing, my mother had the whole flat painted out in the then fashionable pale yellow, curtained, carpeted over and filled with good antique furniture.

She became very busy with her 'war effort', running the large arable farm with its growing herd of Guernsey cows. Then the bombs began to fall on London, so she never stayed in the flat. For a while, whilst I was in the Red Cross, I shared a top-floor flat in Mount Street, Mayfair, with Moyra Butler, who married Charles Forester, who was taken prisoner at Calais shortly afterwards. I remember the bathroom there had a glass roof, but the bombs didn't crack it.

When I joined ATA in 1941 I moved into my mother's third-floor flat at River House, where I stayed whenever I was able to get to London. The rest of the time I was at my father's house, Ridgemead, as it was so close to White Waltham. As already mentioned, when I was at Hamble I shared a cottage with three other ATA girls that looked onto another river. I therefore led a very nomadic flying existence, having no less than four houses to receive me with lots of welcoming beds to sleep in if I wasn't 'stuck out' on some RAF aerodrome.

Derek and I took on the Chelsea flat after we married, renting it from my mother, but we often both stayed at Ridgemead, using River House only if there was a party to go to when we were both on leave. When the war ended, I continued to use River House, or stay with my mother at Kentwyns, or at father's Ridgemead, until he died in 1948.

The all-women's ferry pool at Hamble did not have enough female flight engineers, so we had posted to us, on secondment, a round, phlegmatic, blue-eyed man by the name of Flight Engineer John Robert Brown.

Nearly all the twin-engined aircraft we delivered were flown single-handed. The few exceptions included such things as the Hudson and the Whitley, where the pilot could not leave the flying controls in order to walk back – a very long way in the case of the Whitley bomber – to work any of the emergency services, such as undercarriage or flap lowering. In those two aircraft, we took a suitably briefed 'stooge' with us, usually a young Air Training Corps (ATC) cadet, or, very rarely, a fellow pilot.

With the four-engined aircraft, a flight engineer or fellow pilot was always carried. Commander T.H.N. ' Doc' Whitehurst took me with him in an American B24 Liberator when there was a dearth of flight engineers. He allowed me to fly it, too. It was the heaviest aeroplane on controls that I had then met.

With the American twin-engined tricycle B25 Mitchell bomber which, in addition to the inaccessibility of its emergencies and fuel cocks, was so heavy to fly that two hands were needed on the control column at take-off and approach, a flight engineer was also there, to even up the revs and boost on the throttles and boost levers, or put down the wheels or flaps, whilst the pilot hung on with, in my case, gritted teeth, as well as using maximum strength.

On 11 May 1945 – just three days after Germany surrendered, although we were still at war with Japan – I was given my fifth Mitchell, an RAF Mark II (*FK965*) which I had to fly from RAF Odiham to Hawarden, near Chester, so John Brown was assigned to me. The Mitchell had a lot of power from two 1,350 hp Wright double-row Cyclone engines.

We pointed towards Worcester, which would take us well clear of the Gloucester and Birmigham balloons. On the way, the weather became very poor with the visibility right down in fog. After passing Worcester, we had just superstitiously tipped our hats for good luck to the Wrekin, which we knew was there although we didn't exactly see her, when, CLANG! – something made an expensive noise which put paid to all our instruments.

All the blind-flying instruments, as well as the engine instruments, were also U/S. We checked the Venturi, but to no avail. We had no rev counters, no boost gauges, no oil pressures, no temperatures, fuel, altitude or air speed indicators. Nothing; just the compass.

When the bang occurred, I instinctively pulled back the power and pushed the nose down, but the comforting engine noises continued, so we gingerly opened up, although without instruments we didn't know where to stop the boost or rev levers. John Brown and I made a rough guess, and as we were not falling out of the sky, he evened up the engines by ear until there was no more extra torque on my rudder pedals. When he'd finished, we decided not to divert to Shawbury or High Ercall, which were closer, but to go on to our destination. We thought the RAF wouldn't thank us for an extra maintenance job – it was better for No. 3 Ferry Pool, Hawarden, to arrange to fix it.

The shining curves and snakes of the bends in the River Dee came up through the mist, reassuring us that we were right on course, but they were several minutes ahead of our ETA (Estimated Time of Arrival). The thought went through my mind that our engine revs and boost might be above the ATA cruise settings, but I wasn't going to fiddle around with the levers now that Brown had balanced the engines. My altitude seemed constant, as far as I could judge without instruments, as well as in the mist.

I adjusted my Hawarden ETA, but by the time we got there it was even foggier, with the addition of lumps of Liverpool smoke and muck drifting around as well. There was hardly any wind, and to my dismay, what little there was had gone right round to the south, so the shortest runway was in use. It is difficult enough to judge circuit height in a fog anyhow, but now, without the altimeter, I got it all wrong, finding myself far too high on the approach. Without the air speed indicator, I came in far too fast, realized the problem well before the threshold of the runway, and knew I hadn't a hope of making it. We might have made it on the long runway but not on the short.

I opened up the Mitchell to go round again, with Brown evening up the engines at climb power, but out of the corner of my eye I noticed, as I hung on to the control column, that he shook his shoulders, while wriggling his bottom from side to side on the seat. Poor chap, I thought, having to be flown by a girl. To make him feel better, I said comfortingly, 'It'll be alright next time,' but was not sure I had convinced him. He dug his chin into his collar, jerking his head sideways, then put his thumbs up. Who was reassuring whom, I wondered?

We made the low pass over the runway going round again, Brown retracting the undercarriage. How I missed my gyro in the hazy circuit! I stayed low on the next approach, wheels and flaps working like a treat. The landing was a daisy-cutter; as I've said before, they always are when one has a problem. We were still on the main wheels, just keeping the nose wheel off, when John Brown leant forward to put his hand in between my chest and the stick, pulling the safety pin from my safety straps. What in heaven was he doing when I was trying to finish off a difficult landing? As the nose wheel went down, I pushed the stick forward a little. Seeing there was an extra bit of space in which to work, his fingers rotated the circular 'chute catch and thumped me between my breasts to release the harness, as he hissed, 'Brake – quick, Diana, brake!'

I thought that the normally undemonstrative flight engineer Brown had gone potty, or, thinking he was about to die, had decided to go out groping the only woman handy. There was still masses of room along the runway while the landing, despite all our problems, had been a honey. I still hadn't even touched the toe-brakes, but then I shoved hard on them which brought us to a juddering halt.

In a flash, Brown switched off the fuel and engines, jumped up, grabbed me by the hand, yelling, 'Quick, quick – OUT!' Hauling me towards the exit, he then pushed me through the gap. I hit the ground and he landed on top of me, then clambered to his feet, while I, still in a daze, was wondering what all the rush was about. 'Quick – run – RUN!' He was pulling me away from the Mitchell. We ran a short distance, then he yanked me behind him onto the grass. His pale-blue eyes were now wide open, not relaxed as they had been when we said 'hello' to the invisible Wrekin.

Noises came to me now. Gathering some of my senses, I could hear ringing bells and the roar of car engines. Turning to look, I saw the fire engine and blood-tub roaring out along the runway behind us, making for the Mitchell which was . . . good heavens . . . which was on fire!

As I collected my thoughts, I could see that the Mitchell was burning on 'his' side, not on mine. The fire crew quickly put it out, covering everything with foam.

Since the big bang, when we'd lost our instruments, we had had no way of knowing what our engines were up to. We had obviously flown with too high or incorrect settings, so the engines had overheated, the exhaust stubs becoming red hot. The starboard ones, which could be seen by my flight engineer over his right shoulder, had got hotter than the port ones on my side. The Mitchell had large radial engine cowlings with one of the short exhaust stubs on the inboard side of the engines near the cockpit windows. The right-hand engine's stubs had so overheated that the last straw was my bodging the first landing attempt, having then to open up to go round again. The inboard stub had already been red hot, getting more than it had been designed to take, so it finally melted and fell off. Once that happened, the cowling had soon caught fire.

I hadn't seen any of this, as Brown's bulk beside me was in the way; anyhow, I had been far too busy to gaze out of his window. As the fire built up, he didn't say anything to me because he knew, if he did, that at that moment I had no real need of another problem. He had guessed, correctly, that knowing I had one engine on fire would have upset my already faulty judgement. No wonder he was groping me. He wanted to make sure I could get clear of the aeroplane in the shortest possible time, in case the whole thing went up.

He said later, 'It wouldn't have helped either of us. If we'd missed the second landing, that would have been curtains anyway!' I suppose it could have been, with a burning engine on finals, in a fog, and with no instruments. He knew I couldn't have suddenly got away with a single-engine landing in such conditions, so he kept quiet. Luckily the burning engine had kept going for long enough to get us down.

I thought about it all, deciding that we couldn't have baled out as we were too low when the fire took hold. Anyway, we couldn't have let the Mitchell go down without us, probably crashing into the hangars or onto some of those houses near and around the circuit.

Flight Engineer John Brown put his arm around my shoulders, his blue eyes twinkling again, then said, 'Come on, Diana. Let's go get us a cup of tea.'

Here is another tale of faulty communication plus pilot incompetence. Despite the end of the war, we were still flying. No-one knew for certain if the Russians would start something, so it was no time to relax fully. The war with Japan was still going on, too, although that only affected us indirectly. But planes were still required to be delivered and pilot training went on.

On 20 June 1945, just a few short weeks after the end of the war in Europe, I was dropped by road at Wisley, in Surrey, to take a twin-engined Vickers Warwick V (PN 710) up to Shawbury. A Warwick V (built as a replacement for the old Wellington) had two 2,520 hp Bristol Centaurus V engines, and, begging the maker's pardon, it looked rather like an elephant. Compared to some of the other lovely things that we flew, well, it rather flew like one too.

The famous Vickers test pilot, 'Mutt' Summers, an old friend, who had been down at Hamble testing Spitfires for Air Service Training, was now at Wisley. As this was to be my first Warwick, he kindly showed me the petrol tank cocks which were somewhat muddling to sort out, even with our ferry pilots' notes (in which it said, in large letters, 'all cocks must be checked before flight'). Mutt also pointed out the lines of the runways, although from dispersal, where the aircraft was parked, I couldn't see over the hump in the green grassy sward of the field. He said, 'Taxy straight up there,' so I did, then turned, as instructed, onto a wide grass runway.

Now, as I had been dropped by car and not flown in, I hadn't seen the aerodrome from the air, but I had seen a windsock behind me by dispersal, so knew which direction the wind was blowing, and which way I had to take off. I did my cockpit checks cross-wind, then turned into wind for take-off. There was still a rise in the ground ahead of me, and as I accelerated over it to get airborne, I was then able to see what was ahead. To my horror, there was another windsock absolutely bang in my path – in the middle of the runway.

I hauled the Warwick up over it, yanking the control column back, well below single-engine safety speed I admit, just missing the windsock by millimetres; I wonder my slipstream didn't blow it down. I daresay that Mutt Summers wondered what I was doing, flying one of his beloved aircraft in that way.

Aloft and in the circuit, I could see my error. I had taken off from the grass taxi-track, not from the main runway. Inadvisable with an elephant. Anyway, that was another thing I got away with, but I don't think Mutt thought I was much of a pilot. I must also stop being so attracted to windsocks!

Despite the war having ended, the aeroplane factories were still churning out aircraft, fulfilling Government contracts with desperation. The aircraft had to be cleared and dispersed to MUs or storage depots, as they had been for the past six years. Certain aircraft were still needed in the Far East but the urgency had gone out of our job and very few replacements were needed by RAF squadrons, so the ATA went on moving planes but they were also engaged in delivering supplies to our own troops and to our airfields in Europe.

On 21 July 1945 there was an Anson (*NK788*) to be taken from White Waltham via Down Ampney, in Gloucestershire, to RAF Buckeburg, a forward airfield near Hannover. Two of us were assigned, the other pilot being Leonard 'Thornie' Thornhill, an extremely tall, dark man with a lovely sense of humour, who 'talked with a plum in his mouth'.

The Avro Anson's payload was 1,987 lb, and apart from Thornie and me, it was all oranges. Crate upon crate of them! We decided Thornie should fly out, while I flew back on the homeward journey. It was a clear day, with good visibility, while the cloud base was at around 3,000 feet. When we were over Ashford, Thornie decided to go up higher to take advantage of a tail wind. I was sitting beside him as he put his head forward to go onto instruments for the climb through the cloud. He leant over the control column with his long back in a sort of arc to get his head down nearer to the instrument panel, whilst I remained looking around and generally dreaming.

The cloud tops were in pinnacles, like upside-down icicles. We came out of cloud 'my' side first. Being instantly shattered out of my reverie, dead ahead, and coming straight for us, was a huge four-engined aeroplane! Thornie, of course, still had his head down, as I yelled, 'Look, Thornie, look!' Although he was still on the climb, loaded to capacity with our freight, Thornie yanked the Anson up onto its tail, giving it full throttle. At the same time, thinking that we must collide, I ducked down.

I have no idea what I thought I would achieve by doing so; just a human reaction, I suppose, but I felt safer. However, I might have lost sight of the huge aircraft through the windscreen, but in ducking low, caught sight of it through the perspex nose of the Anson. Right in front of us was this huge great black mass of aeroplane tail fins, with the startled faces of the crew, then their rear gunner, eyeball to eyeball with me!

The Lancaster, for such it was, somehow went underneath us. I could not think but that its tail must catch ours – how could it miss? I continued to crouch down, put my hands over my face, prepared for death.

When, after a few seconds, there was no shattering bang, I looked across at Thornie. He was as white as a sheet. Pushing the stick forward, we flew along the top of the cloud with the pinnacles beneath us, then he turned to me, saying, 'Diana, am I as white as you are?' He was. Then we both started to giggle with relief.

You see, that Lancaster pilot must have been cloud-hopping, flying along just above the top of the cloud, in and out of the pinnacles, while we had been climbing up, coming out of one cloud stalagmite just as the Lanc was going in. Only I saw it, as 'my' side of the Anson broke cloud a fraction of a second sooner, whilst Thornie's side was still in cloud, and he still on instruments. His reaction to my warning yell had been instantaneous, and, luckily for us, the action taken was the correct one.

When he opened the throttle we billowed up on our tail, perpendicularly, just high enough to miss the other machine. If I had been flying, I know I would have shoved the nose down when I saw the other aircraft at our level, so, in that way, because we were on the climb, would have 'ballooned' right into the Lancaster.

Anywhere I meet them, I will always recognize those faces of the RAF crew.

We flew on over the Low Countries, the cloud breaking over the industrial Ruhr of Germany. It was the first time I had been so far into Germany since the war began. I was aghast at the miles and miles and miles of completely pinky-yellow dust and ruins. Not a whole building anywhere at all. How had anyone down there survived the might of Bomber Command?

Although there had been a few newspaper pictures of damage, they had not conveyed such devastation as I saw from the air on that lovely sunny, July day. Oh yes! We got our own back alright, for the bombing of Coventry, London, Exeter, and other of our major cities.

After a while we reached the Minden Gap, in a range of hills south of Hannover. The Minden Gap is literally a gash in those hills. There was a large white statue on the left-hand side as we flew past and she seemed to be welcoming and beckoning us as we flew through beside her to the green, peaceful, fertile valley beyond. I heaved a sigh of relief, saying a silent prayer of thanks for our recent deliverance. We both agreed that it was the nearest miss that anyone could have, and still be able to talk about it.

As we circled Buckeburg, the thought occurred to me that, with all those oranges, we could have made a nasty squashy mess somewhere. It would have made an awful lot of marmalade.

◆ *Chapter 14* ◆

Post War

DEREK AND I had been given a Rheoboam* of champagne as a wedding present, but we had decided to keep it to celebrate the end of the war. We put the bottle at the back of a cupboard in River House, resisting the temptation to drink it too soon.

The great VJ Day (Victory over Japan) arrived at last. First Germany and now Japan had surrendered. Derek asked my father to come round to celebrate with us. It was a beautiful sunny August day, so our low windows were wide open in the sitting room, which looked out onto the River Thames. The leaves rustled on the plane tree outside, while little boats sped up and down the sparkling water. Peace was here at last.

Champagne had obviously been impossible to import during the war, so we thought our Rheoboam must be nearly the last one left. With great ceremony Derek requested my father to open the huge bottle. We were all aware that this was an historic occasion.

My father opened it, sniffed it, then roared with laughter, shouting, 'It's corked!', and, with a magnificent gesture, threw the whole thing out of the window, where it smashed to smithereens amidst a sea of bubbles onto the pavement three floors below. He had not only a great sense of humour but also a great sense of drama. He knew champagne such as that was then nearly unobtainable, but also realised that by chucking it out of the window, it would heighten our realization of the momentous VJ-Day.

It did! Now, well over 45 years later, I remember the moment and occasion vividly. Would it have been so memorable if we had just raised our glasses of champagne and toasted ourselves and the world? Probably yes, but not with so much 'occasion'. My father played that act just for the effect it would have on us. It might also have had quite an effect on someone below the window had it hit them. Luckily, there was nobody there.

* *A Rheoboam is equal to six bottles.*

I am also quite certain that the bottle was *not* corked!

With the war over, the ATA hauled down its flag with a ceremony attended by well over 12,000 people. It was held at RAF White Waltham on a sunny 29 September 1945. There was an aircraft and flying display, while the late Lord Beaverbrook made a speech in which he said:

'Just as the Battle of Britain is the accomplishment and achievement of the RAF, likewise it can be declared that the ATA sustained and supported the RAF in battle. They were soldiers fighting in the struggle just as if they had been engaged on the battlefront . . .'

Someone had taken the trouble to count up the flights and times of all ATA pilots; they were impressive figures. The totals were:

Total aircraft ferried – 309,011
Total hours flown –   414,984

Other than 21,242 aircraft lumped under the general heading of 'light aircraft', the 'high scoring' aircraft deliveries had been:

Spitfires –	57,286	Hurricanes –	29,401
Wellingtons –	26,176	Oxfords –	14,367
Beaufighters –	13,603	Mosquitoes –	12,480
Lancasters –	9,805	Masters –	9,532
Halifaxes –	9,326	Blenheims –	8,569
Ansons –	8,528	Typhoons –	7,942
Barracudas –	7,039	Mustangs –	4,989
Whitleys –	3,786	Stirlings –	3,688

In 1944 there had been 659 ATA pilots who saw service during the war, of whom 108 were women. Some of the men had been RAF pilots seconded to us. No fewer than 174 people gave their lives, 16 of them women.

Our pilots came not only from the United Kingdom, but were of all nationalities. Among them were Americans, Canadians, South Africans, Australians, New Zealanders, Indians, Poles, French, Dutch, Danish, Czechoslovakian, Spanish, Irish, Argentinian, Norwegian, Swedish; we even had pilots from Siam, Chile, China, Ceylon, Estonia and Ethiopia.

Our Honours were impressive too: two CBEs, 13 OBEs, 36 MBEs, six BEMs, one George Medal, six Commendations, six Commended for Gallantry, and 18 King's Commendations for Valuable Service in the Air. In addition, our own Commodore signed 36 Certificates of Commendation to ATA members who performed some act of outstanding merit while in service. Five of the MBEs and four of the BEMs went to the ladies, as well as one Commendation and one King's Commendation for Valuable Service in the Air.

ATA had also received many fine accolades from very prominent people, some in the form of letters sent to 'Pops' d'Erlanger. For example, Rear Admiral D. W. Boyd CB CBE DSC, Fifth Sea Lord, wrote on 7 April 1944:

I wish to express my gratitude to you for the good service you have given to the Fleet Air Arm in ferrying aircraft, and in particular, the priority which you gave to the Barracuda which contributed to the signal success against the *Tirpitz*.

A letter from the Prime Minister, Winston Churchill, dated 28 May 1944, just prior to D-Day, read:

I am much impressed by the achievement of the Organisation under your command in making more than 200,000 aircraft ferryings on behalf of the Royal Navy and the Royal Air Force during the past four years; this is indeed a wonderful record.

That this formidable task should have been performed with so low an accident record rebounds greatly to the credit of both your pilots and ground staff. It was not to be expected that operations of this magnitude could have been undertaken without incurring casualties, and I note with regret and sympathy that 113 pilots have lost their lives in the course of their ferrying duties.

The time may come when many of your pilots will be delivering aircraft to the RAF bases that are to be established on the Continent, and I am confident that this important task, which is being entrusted to the Organisation under your command, will be carried out with the same efficiency and devotion to duty as has been shown by the personnel of the Air Transport Auxiliary since its inception.

Please convey to all my thanks for, and appreciation of, their past services, and my best wishes in the task that lies before them.

Another came from Sir Stafford Cripps, of the Ministry of Aircraft Production, dated 26 February 1945:

I have heard that on Wednesday, 21st February, the ATA ferried 570 aircraft, thus exceeding their previous record for one day by some 50 aircraft. Will you please convey to the ATA my hearty congratulations on this magnificent achievement. It is indeed encouraging to know that when bad weather has interfered so much with aircraft delivery we can rely on the ATA to smash all records when they are given a chance.

There are other impressive figures. During the period February 1940 to November 1945, there had been 1,152 male pilots, 166 female, 151 flight engineers, 19 radio operators and 27 air and sea cadet helpers, making a total of 1,515 air personnel. ATA's peak period was August

1944 when it had a total strength of 2,786 ground staff.

Everyone was trying to get back to normal life after their wartime experiences. I felt suddenly very weary, wanting keenly to sort out various small things such as daytime clothes, as I had been in uniform for so long. Clothing was still rationed, and our River House flat needed doing up, so it became then a choice between dresses or curtains. Perhaps, too, Derek and I could start a proper married life together.

Derek had just been given a post as Wing Commander Ops with Sector Headquarters at RAF Digby, a satellite of Molesworth, where most of the immediate post-war Meteor flying went on. The Station Commander at Molesworth was Group Captain John Wray DFC, and the Meteor Conversion Unit was on the station, commanded by Wing Commander H. 'Birdy' Bird-Wilson DSO DFC and bar. RAF Digby was just over 100 miles north of London. Until recently, Wing Commander Jas Storrar DFC had his Canadian Mustang Wing there, and when it disbanded, he gave his Mustang (*KM232*) to become a 'hack' for the use of the senior officers, John Wray's initials being painted on it. It also saved flying hours on the Meteor's precious Rolls-Royce Derwent jet engines. *KM232* had actually seen service with No. 442 Squadron RCAF in the last weeks of the war, before being attached to Digby's Station Flight. On 13 November 1945 Derek flew in to Hawker's factory at Langley, then came on to Ridgemead. He told me he had managed to get hold of a converted Nissen hut that we could live in until permanent quarters were available on his RAF station.

I was so tired of discomfort. Ridgemead was a wonderful, glamorous house, and our River House flat was warm and cosy. The sudden realization came over me that I would now have to cut my roots entirely in order to live the life of a serving RAF officer's wife, living permanently on one RAF station or another. And our first home was not going to be even a Wing Commander's married quarter, but a converted Nissen hut. It was also winter now.

Memories flooded back of times spent 'stuck out' on various aerodromes in uncomfortable, often freezing Nissen huts. That time I was almost buried in snow at Chilbolton, where I nearly got more than a chill. I responded badly to Derek's news, by saying, unwisely, that I thought a Nissen hut was a lousy idea. Derek explained its conversion which, no doubt, was adequate, but I didn't listen, saying grumpily that I didn't want to live in *any* sort of Nissen hut, however well it was converted. After all, to my mind a Nissen hut was still a Nissen hut. I'd had five years of them.

He was extremely upset, thinking that it must be that I didn't want to live with him anymore. That was silly. It wasn't that at all, but I couldn't make him understand. Nor did he say, until much later that evening, that the place was beautifully fixed up and ready for us to move in. This was our first 'tiff' – and our last!

The next morning we had made it up, agreeing that I would come up but that I really needed a short time to organize everything first. I needed to pack up as well as close down the flat. Derek gave me a kiss, then left to go back to his Mustang at Langley. Having been cocooned in concentration whilst flying each of the many aeroplanes I had met during the war, I was now going to live quite a changed life with Derek. ATA life had been full of banana skins – flying ones. Now everything would be different.

A little while later I went out for a ride on Tommy the Twin, the horse Bobby Loewenstein had ridden the day I met Norman Macmillan, along with Dick Fairey. It was a sunny but cold, clear day. I rode along the top of Priest Hill, Englefield Green, to the 'look-out', where the beautiful RAF Memorial to Missing Airmen now stands overlooking Runnymede. At that height I could see right over towards Langley aerodrome.

Tommy the Twin and I stopped. I was admiring the view and he was nibbling the nearby shrubs when suddenly something frightened him, making him leap forward a few paces. I pulled him up, patting him gently. He returned to his munching. At that moment I looked towards Langley again, seeing an enormous spume of black oily smoke coming up from where I knew the airfield lay. I was very frightened, being consumed with a terrible sense of premonition that something had happened to Derek in his Mustang. I cantered back home, rang the factory flying control, and was relieved to hear that '. . . the Wing Commander had booked out and taken off [safely] for Digby'.

I threw away my fearful thoughts, then drove up to the flat. My agèd Nanny was coming to stay for a couple of nights, using Derek's dressing-room. We joked, saying where would she go if he suddenly came to London, wanting to change in his own room? I tried to ring Derek that night but couldn't make contact. Anyway, I had only seen him that morning, and he knew where I was if he wanted to ring me.

Next morning I rang again. I was getting worried now, thinking it strange that he hadn't rung up. Surely he wasn't still angry with me? Nobody at Digby would tell me where he was.

Old Nanny departed early on the morning of the 15th, saying that the dirty, dreary London mists were no good at all for her asthma. Shortly afterwards my father rang, saying he was coming round to see me. Then I knew! I went cold. My mind was still working but I felt stunned. Everything became unreal. I knew something had happened. My father would never have said, 'I'm coming round to see you.' He would have said, '*You* come round and see *me*, Diana.' My premonition was correct. That spume of black smoke, the spooking of my horse, had presaged something dreadful. I had known about it then, but not when or where it was going to happen.

My father arrived, taking me into his arms. He didn't say anything; he didn't have to. For one thing, he thought someone else had already told me by this time. I told him of my ride two days earlier, describing what I had seen. But 'Oh no, Diana, it wasn't then; it wasn't until the next day!'

◇   ◇   ◇

The Air Ministry had not decided, so soon after the end of the war, just how many pilots were going to be kept on strength. There was, naturally, a certain amount of anxiety amongst the regular RAF officers like Derek about their future in the Service.

My dear friend Dick Fairey needed a test pilot for his Fairey Aviation Company, so Derek, who was interested, had arranged to meet Dick for lunch to talk about the proposed job. Derek was to fly into Heston on 14 November, where Fairey's had some factory hangars and Dick had his office. At midday, Dick was waiting in his car near the Watch office, seeing Derek overhead in his Mustang.

Heston had only just reverted from its former RAF status, being turned back into a civilian airfield. The new civilian controller would not allow Derek to land because of poor visibility. There was an inversion, which is a layer of misty visibility with clear weather on top. When one flies down into the mist from the clear on top, the visibility is sometimes not so good, especially the slant visibility. But that was nothing to upset a pilot of Derek's experience and capability. After all, he had been flying for over eight years, and had survived four tours of operations in Greece, the North African desert and from England. He'd flown Blenheims, Hurricanes, Spitfires, Typhoons, Mustangs – and now Meteor jets; a little inversion wouldn't worry the likes of him, certainly not in the middle of the day. But the new controller didn't know.

Derek flew back to Digby, from where he telephoned Dick to say that as he had not been allowed to land at Heston, he would be going down to Hendon after lunch instead. The CO at Hendon was a pal of his, so he frequently landed there. Digby to Hendon was 25 minutes by Mustang, from where he took the tube into London. In this way it took Derek about an hour to get from his station to our River House flat.

He and Dick arranged to meet for a drink at the Dorchester Hotel in Park Lane, London, that evening, but Derek did not arrive. Dick rang Digby, only to discover that Wing Commander Walker had booked out to Hendon, but had not been booked in there. Dick found out too that an aircraft had crashed in the circuit of RAF Hendon. Dick then rang my father later that night, but they decided to verify their forebodings before telling me.

My shock at the loss of my wonderful Derek was tremendous. Just the thought that he wasn't around any more, that never again would I hear his laughter, know his sureness, rely on his strength, filled me with dread. He had survived a terrible war, only to die in some senseless crash. He would have gone far in whatever post-war career he had decided upon, but now he was no more. I would never hug him again, never love him again, except in my heart.

I rang RAF Digby and talked to his flight sergeant. 'Was anything wrong with the Wing Commander's aircraft?' I asked, but he said no, then added, 'Oh, the oil pressure gauge wasn't working, that's all.' He went on to say that he had told Derek about the gauge and that Derek had said he would drop in at Molesworth on the way south to have it changed as Digby had no spares. But he didn't.

The Mustang was a clean aircraft, so when the Canadian-built, Packard-Merlin engine was throttled back, it took quite a time to slow down to wheels, flaps, and approach speeds. It was usual to throttle absolutely right back to lose speed, put everything down (maximum speed for flaps 165 mph), then open up 'round the corner' onto the final approach. Fighters always made curved approaches in those days, because of the poor forward visibility over the long engine cowlings. When the speed slowed and the angle of attack altered, this put the nose up in the way of the pilot's view forward, so on a curve, the pilot was able to peer out of the side instead, only losing sight of the runway when he/she finally straightened up for touch-down.

There is no doubt that Derek was a brilliant pilot. There is no doubt either that he flew with dash and flair. He was not ham-fisted nor ham-footed, but a Mustang IV stalled at 105 mph – or at 96 mph with flaps and wheels down – so there was very little leeway between a final approach speed of 110 mph and the stall.

Because of the 75-year rule, I have not, to this day, *officially* been able to get a sight of Derek's accident report or the enquiry. 'But the oil gauge wasn't working,' said his flight sergeant. Now – just supposing that it had been working and that it was registering correctly? Well then, there could have been something wrong with the oil flow, like a dirty filter or a faulty pump, which, when the Merlin was throttled right back then suddenly opened up again, made a great shortage of oil to the engine. This would cause it to blow up or falter, or 'hiccough', at a very critical speed on his low final approach – in poor visibility.

Well, that is one of my theories, but it doesn't really matter. He's dead anyway, so it doesn't really matter either *why* or *how* you die, because the result is the same. But how strange that I knew about it before it all happened. Did I really 'see' it from the hill above Runnymede?

A suggestion that Derek had got himself lost was stupid. He knew every inch of that bit of England like the back of his hand. He had also called up on the correct frequency for a vector into *Hendon* (not into Heston, which was a different frequency). The subsequent enquiry got muddled up between Heston and Hendon and the civilian controller who hadn't let him land at Heston before lunch was possibly anxious to clear his conscience about Derek's prang.

Derek went to Hendon because (a) he knew the CO there very well and often went there; (b) because he hadn't been able to see Dick for lunch (at Heston, as arranged and then cancelled) and was going to meet him in London instead. So Derek would *in no way* have gone or tried to go to Heston because by then Dick was not there. Anyway, he hadn't called up on the frequency to go into Heston, but on *Hendon's* frequency. To get to London from Heston was complicated, but from Hendon, very easy.

Derek was buried in the churchyard of St Judes, Englefield Green, where just 18 months earlier we had been married.

DEREK – NOVEMBER 1945

I saw you glistening in the sky
Like gleaming vapour flashing by,
I saw you next upon a marble shelf
A scorched grotesqueness of yourself.
The house you hit was still a smouldering shell,
That storm we had has turned my life to hell.

I went along to see
What could be done –
The smell of singeing flesh
And jagged, ugly hunks of metal
Still remained.
The wheels were there, and bricks
And burnt up privet hedges,
A single yellow rose
Was blooming on a blackened stem.
I stood and looked and wept,
My heart cried out to Him.

And as I stood, a little man
Came up and watched as well,
'Your house, Ma'am? And your Garden, Ma'am?
It will all grow again . . .'
But when I turned and looked at him
Just then he understood.
He picked the rose and gave it me:
'I'm sorry, very sorry, Ma'am,
I didn't know,' he said.
'Someone I love,' I cried,
'My heart sighs out for him.'

The years have passed,
My searing pains remained,
I went along again to look
And there, as in a dream,
A house of Phoenix stood,
Agleam and clean, with bright blue paint.
(The yellow rose was there.)
And underneath the hedge of privet lay a puppy
And a battered teddybear, and close by
Stood the pram.
'Life for a life,' cried I,
And wept for freedom from my Calvary.

◇   ◇   ◇

My father had given me a wrist-watch on Christmas Day, 1941. He said, 'You'll need a good watch for flying.' It was quite a watch, the epitome of precision engineering: anti-magnetic, shock-proof, with a copper-coloured face. I think it was made of white gold.

It was a stop-watch too, with an extra second hand and an extra minute hand in small circles on the face. It also had a movable bezel around the outside with the points of the compass on it, plus another rotating dial with conversion details, like a miniscule circular slide-rule. The whole thing was only just larger than a half-crown coin. I flew with it all through the war, when its accuracy in my DR navigation is proven by my survival.

You will remember that my father had a large, overheated swimming pool at Ridgemead. The pool was too warm all the year round, steam rising from it in the winter months when it was hotter in the water than out. One day in the late autumn of 1945, I dived into the pool, quite forgetting to take off my precious time-piece. After that, it didn't stop, but began to lose time, so Derek volunteered to take it to what he described as a 'brilliant' watchmaker near his station at Digby.

I didn't like to fly without my watch. I was superstitious. To me it was a lucky 'rabbit's foot', as was my gold map of Australia identity bracelet. This had been given to me by an admirer of mine early in the war, Rupert Clarke, an Australian baronet. We used to play backgammon for small stakes and, although we never settled up, kept a note of who had won what. Finally, over a long period of time, he owed me the princely sum of 10/6d, which he insisted he should give me before he went off to the African front. I argued against it and, in the end, to keep him quiet, I said I would settle for a tiny St Christopher's medal that cost 10/6d as an identity disc. He agreed, but then produced this gold bracelet in the shape of his native country, which he'd ordered from Asprey's, the Bond Street jewellers. There was a small ruby on one side which indicated where he lived, while my name and address were on the other, together with my wartime identity number – DMGM 65 2 – and my International Blood Group 'A'. I still have it. I thought that these things, the watch and bracelet, plus the 'Fellow Up Top', had helped to keep me alive during all those years of wartime flying.

In early November that watch was repaired and ready for collection. Derek said he would be picking it up, then bringing it back on his next trip. When he was killed, my watch failed to turn up amongst his possessions. It was later found in what was left of his badly charred uniform breast pocket. It hadn't done much for him.

◆ *Chapter 15* ◆

'B' Licence and the WJAC

I KNEW I had to do something positive to take my thoughts away from my sadness after Derek was killed. Flying had been my life for such a long time, so it seemed a good idea to go on doing it. I decided to take out a commercial flying licence, or 'B' licence as it was called in those days. I had acquired more than enough daytime flying hours to qualify, but I had not done any of the night flying that was needed. ATA pilots were supposed to land before dusk – although now and then we got caught out a bit late.

I did not think I could possibly do all the paperwork involved. I didn't know how to learn all the bumph for the examinations. I had flown quite successfully with ATA for years without needing a quarter of what was wanted for a 'B' licence.

I ran into Whitney Straight at a party. He was back from the Middle East. He said he was an out-of-work ex-Air Commodore. I said I was an out-of-work ex-ATA pilot, but that when I got my 'B' licence I hoped to go on flying for someone.

Whitney had led a scintillating life. I had first met him when I was 12; now he was 34 and I 28. He had been born in New York, the son of Major Willard Straight, an Oriental expert, who died in 1918. Whitney's mother, one of the wealthy Whitney family, remarried and came to England in 1925 where she and her new husband founded the educational, artistic and agricultural community at Dartington Hall, near Totnes in Devon.

When Whitney was at Trinity College, Cambridge, at the same time as the spies Philby, MacLean and Blunt, he used to drive racing cars at weekends. His tutors tried to stop him by disallowing him the use of his car, so he learnt to fly and flew to race meetings instead, both in England and abroad, where he became famous in his black and silver Maserati. He also owned aerodromes at Exeter and at Weston-super-Mare, giving up his car racing in 1935 to concentrate on running his Weston Airways, and became a British subject. By 1938, Whitney's business had expanded to cover 15 airfields and three airlines, with 100 aeroplanes and 1,500 staff.

In 1939 he joined the Royal Auxiliary Air Force, flying with 601 Squadron. In April 1940 he went to Norway, helping to set up a fighter base on the frozen lake at Lesjaskog, from where 263 Squadron operated Gladiator fighters. Whitney was injured in a bombing raid on the airstrip, and was repatriated to England. For his work in Norway he received the Military Cross. He became ADC to HRH the Duke of Kent for a short period, then returned to flying duties.

In the Battle of Britain he rejoined 601 Squadron, then became a flight commander in 1941. He won the DFC but at the end of July was shot down by ground fire near Fecamp, France. He evaded capture for some time, managing to get as far as the edge of the Pyrenees, in Vichy France, before he was arrested. He made out he was an army officer, and was imprisoned in the south of France, where he and another RAF pilot pretended to be seriously ill. The Germans thought they would be no good anymore for flying or fighting and repatriation was arranged, but before that, with the aid of the Resistance, Whitney escaped, returning via Gibraltar to England a few days short of a year after his forced landing in France.

For the rest of the war he had commands in both the Middle East and England, being released from service in late 1946. To his earlier decorations he had added the Norwegian War Cross, and been made a CBE and an Officer of the American Legion of Merit.

Whitney said he also wanted to get his 'B' licence, so decided to find a lecturer to teach us both at the same time. It was a freezing winter with lots of snow, but the government of the day had decreed that electricity had to be turned off for several hours a day and that private people could not turn on their lights or electric fires until after 4 pm when the factories began to close. This was because of the post-war fuel shortages. Industry had priority over citizens . . . Brr! Brr!

River House was on an old DC (direct current) system because my mother said to the electricity authorities that her contract with them would make them have to change all the lift machinery if they altered the cable to AC. Too expensive, they said, so they left it. As a hospital in Tite Street, also on DC cable, had to have constant electricity, so did we, although we stuck to the request of a 4 o'clock turn-on.

As I have already said, my mother had installed so-called central heating in River House. The boiler was an old Robin Hood contraption that burnt both coal and coke. Coal was rationed, but coke was available although in short supply. The enormous boiler was carefully and sparsely stoked by an old man who lived in the basement. It provided at least a background heat. My flat was warmer than other homes, and dry in spite of the Thames outside.

Whitney said his London house was absolutely freezing and the pipes were iced up, so, in January 1946, my River House sitting-room became our schoolroom, with an excellent teacher. Large trestle tables plus lots of maps, meterological charts, navigation instruments, slide-rules, etc, were littered about. Every day for a month lessons began at 4 o'clock when the fires could be turned on. We both passed the various exams and the medical. After that we spent a lot of time together. Barney is our son from that wonderful friendship.

All that remained now to acquire the coveted 'B' licence was the night flying. The only place to learn, so soon after the war had ended, was at Marshall's aerodrome at Cambridge. Mr Marshall had six lovely daughters, one of whom, Mollie Rose, had been a pilot at Hamble with me.

It was all laid on. Uncle Jim Joel lent me one of his fully staffed houses at Newmarket for a week where I was beautifully looked after and fed and nurtured. I got back into a Tiger Moth again at the Cambridge aerodrome. A line of gooseneck flares sort of showed the landing and take-off runs; anyway, they lined the grass runway. I think the flares were flickering oil-wicks in jam-jar contraptions – they certainly looked like it. They often went out, so to help me, they put on the hangar lights and left the doors wide open!

After flying, as dawn broke, I went back to Uncle Jim's house, was given a hearty breakfast, then went onto the gallops to watch the family horses and others, before going to bed for the rest of the day. One of the horses out one morning was an outstandingly beautiful tall grey colt by Precipitation. It was entered in the first post-war Derby, to be run again at Epsom. The wartime race had been run at Newmarket, which I believe was the only racecourse to operate during hostilities, despite a heavy bomber squadron operating from the place.

This horse had a springy flying stride. I thought it one of the most splendid animals I had seen in a long time. It belonged to Uncle Stanhope Joel's friends, John and Ena Ferguson. Uncle Stan had got the Fergusons interested in racehorses.

The colt was called Airborne, which seemed an appropriate name for such a mover. I decided to back it later on, as I was also airborne most of the time. Meantime, I finished the night flying course and returned to London, to River House, anxiously awaiting the dates for the night flying examination flights.

On Derby Day 1946, Uncle Stan and Gladys, his wife, took me to Epsom. We walked down to the paddock from their box in the grandstand with John and Ena Ferguson. We saw Airborne parading in the ring, looking truly wonderful to my eyes, but no-one else seemed to fancy him very much. I rushed back just in time to put five quid each way on him. Neither the Fergusons, who owned him, nor the Joels backed him, which I thought amazing. Airborne romped home. I got 66-1, a fortune for me in those days. It paid for all my night flying.

The night flying test date was finally announced, but it fell during Ascot week. Not at all put out, in spite of my father having a huge house party at Ridgemead – I don't remember feeling tired – off I went.

One of the night flights was from Croydon to Aldermaston. I didn't choose the date, but it really was cheating, for there was a full moon! There were no restrictions or air corridors to fly in as there are nowadays. Because of the moon's brilliance, it was easier than it had been sometimes when wartime flying, in daytime, in a fog. Aldermaston duly turned up, its long runway positively gleaming at me in the moonlight. I passed the test.

I hadn't landed there since my early training days – also in a Tiger. On that day a gale had been blowing stronger and faster than my approach speed. After throttling back, instead of being able to land I found that I was flying backwards over the runway a few feet off the ground. Two RAF men saw my predicament, wandered out and grabbed the wings, gently pulling the Tiger down, then hung on whilst I taxied in out of the draught.

◇   ◇   ◇

Soon after I got my licence, Gaby Patterson, one of the first eight women pilots to join ATA, asked me to fly for the Women's Junior Air Corps at weekends. The job required a B-licensed pilot to carry the cadets because they contributed towards their 20-minute flights, so it rated as a commercial venture.

The Women's Junior Air Corps, started way back in 1939, was a uniformed youth organization sponsored by the Ministry of Education. It was similar to the Air Training Corps, but, unlike them, was not considered a pre-entry preparation for the Royal Air Force, although some cadets did join the WAAF when they were old enough. The aim was to make the girls into good citizens, as well as to promote this with an air-minded flavour.

The Corps had its own aeroplane, an American Fairchild Argus II four-seater, high wing monoplane with a Warner Super Scarab 165 hp radial engine – the same type that ATA had used, along with Ansons, as taxi aircraft. It had been purchased with funds that had accumulated during the wartime years.

It was thought best to put it to good use by concentrating on air training and air experience flights. A competition had been held to decide the name of that first aeroplane, 'Grey Dove' being the chosen winner. As peace had barely come upon us, it was deemed appropriate.

In those early days, airline travel for the masses had not begun, so few children had been able to fly. One of the lures to join the Corps was the chance to get airborne for just 7/6d in their very own aeroplane. There were also several scholarships to be won which gave the lucky recipients of the award enough flying tuition to bring them up to their Private Pilot's Licence (PPL).

Some of the cadets did navigation tests as well as the 7/6d flights. They worked out a course, with the drift, variations, etc, to some not-too-faraway point, then gave me the headings to fly. I flew them, they map read, seeing if it all worked out. Very few of them got 'lost', although sometimes I pretended that they had 'lost' me, much to everyone's amusement – once they realized I was just kidding, of course.

The girls were aged between 13 and 21. At 21, if they were of the right calibre and so on, they could be considered to become officers. For most of them, getting airborne in the Fairchild was their very first flight. I had a patter that I drooled on about, but they had heard most of it in their ground instruction, so apart from noting the flying controls and the instruments, I think they hardly listened. The majority were far too excited with that new sensation of being in the air.

The Fairchild had dual control, so once we were up at about 1,000 feet, I sometimes let the girl in the front seat beside me try to fly. They had had lessons on the theory of flight, had learnt the operation of the controls, so most of them put their knowledge to reasonably good avail.

Once I was flying at Doncaster where there were several large units, so I did not know to which unit the various girls belonged. On one flight, a tall, heavy girl sat in front (I always put the lighter girls in the back), and when we were airborne and high enough up, she immediately asked to be allowed to try to fly. She took over, flew accurately straight and level, then we tried a turn, first one way, then the other, followed by a climb and descent. She had never been in an aeroplane before but she was absolutely flawless. A natural pilot, one might say, and had she had the chance, she could only have succeeded as an excellent flyer.

As the day ended and I was sitting ready to leave with the Fairchild, she came rushing up to me, thanking me profusely for letting her fly and handle the controls. Then she said, in a lovely North Country accent, 'Ah, if I'd had that, I wouldn't have gone wrong.'

I didn't know what on earth she meant, but only saw a large, happy face. Later, I asked what unit she was in, and was told, 'Oh, the one from the remand home!'

It seemed a worthwhile job for me to do, quite apart from enabling me to fly, so I continued with it for many years. During the week I stayed mostly in London leading a completely useless existence. Apart from some charity work, doing nothing but wearing beautiful clothes, going out to dinner parties, dances, theatres, film premières, restaurants and night clubs, seeing my friends and acquaintances at my home or theirs.

On Fridays I put away my glad-rags, put on my WJAC uniform, flew to the appointed venue of the various units and flew myself silly all Saturdays and Sundays, flying home on the Mondays to continue the social merry-go-round, interspersed with winter skiing and hunting, and sailing with Hugh Astor (Gavin's brother) on his beautiful yacht *Eostra*, or with Lois and Allan on one of their motor yachts (always called *Sylvia*).

There were about 10,000 young girls in the WJAC at that time, in units all over the British Isles. Each weekend, at nearly three flights an hour, I 'got through' a lot of cadets! Some weekends more than 100 girls would fly with me. I was in the Fairchild nearly all day, with efficient officers helping with the passenger change-over, getting them in and out quickly. The officers also needed to ensure that the seat-belts were done up, which gave me just a few minutes to relax at the controls between each flight.

We flew the units from small grass flying club aerodromes, or from large civil or RAF ones. We had summer camps at Blackpool (Squires Gate) or at Bournemouth (Hurn), where the Fairchild and I stayed for the fortnightly sessions, giving various flights and instruction and enjoying all the other entertainments. We did a Scottish tour too, when I left the Fairchild in the Highlands, staying with friends up there to avoid coming all the way south and back again for the following weekend.

We also went to units in Ireland. I always flew the very shortest route from the Mull of Galloway to Donaghadee. I knew my guardian angel was still with me, but I didn't want to give the devil any extra leeway to pull me down into the cold Irish Sea. In very bad weather, in that small single-engined thing, it was very reassuring to hear the, by then well-known, voice of the Preston Central Controller requesting my position if I was even a second late in reporting in to him. He gave me the feeling that I was the only person in the sky that he had to care for, even though he must have had many other aeroplanes to look after, just like my guardian angel, the Fellow Up Top.

Maybe the Controller was a relative of His?

During the whole of the war I had had only one aeroplane catch fire in the air, and that was the Mitchell, when Flight Engineer John Brown and I had flown up to Hawarden. However, soon after the declaration of peace, I had another fire which could have put a lot of people's programmes out of gear, not to mention my own personal light out, so to speak.

The WJAC Fairchild (*G-AIYO*) had been repainted a lovely shade of pale grey, in keeping with her new name, which had now been stencilled on her cowling. There was to be a 'christening' ceremony at RAF Hendon aerodrome on 17 July 1948, with Her Royal Highness Princess Marina, Duchess of Kent, pouring champagne over the engine cowling. Unlike a ship launch, to hurl a bottle at the tiny aeroplane would have dented it, which wouldn't have done it much good. Little did we know, when the plans were being made, that it would be somewhat dented by then anyhow.

There were going to be nearly 5,000 cadets present from units from across the breadth of Britain, and they were all going to sleep overnight in the wartime deep bomb shelters at Clapham. A few days before the ceremony was due to take place, I was to take the 'Grey Dove' from White Waltham over to Hendon so that a suitable platform could be constructed near the aeroplane, for the Duchess plus the various dignitaries and officials (and me) to stand upon. The arrangements were for me to do a flypast, then land, taxi in and park beside the platform ready for the champagne bit, whilst the Duchess was reviewing the cadet units.

On 11 July I duly arrived at my old stamping ground of White Waltham. The little Fairchild looked a picture, all shiny and bright in her new grey livery, polished inside and out.

I had brought my cairn dog P-nut with me, plonking her on the back seat. P-nut had done a lot of flying with me, usually quite unconcernedly peering out of the windows as we sped along. Perhaps she thought it was a particularly noisy car, somewhat higher off the ground than usual.

To save running down an aeroplane's own battery during starting up, most were plugged into an outside 'trolley acc' (accumulator). These were kept on a heavy metal frame, standing out on the aerodrome in all weathers. This contraption was wheeled up beside whatever aeroplane needed it. The mechanic in charge would then open a little flap in the engine cowling, usually with a penny piece, and plug in the battery from the 'acc' to the engine. The pilot then switched on, and, when the engine fired and was running nicely, changed over to the aeroplane's own battery system. The mechanic then pulled out the plug on the end of a heavy rubber-covered lead from the 'acc' and refastened the little flap, which had usually blown itself shut in the propeller's slipstream.

That day the Fairchild started first go. I switched over to its own battery while the mechanic did up the little socket flap as I sat there warming up, then ran up the engine when he was clear. I checked the various controls and instruments. Fine!

The Fairchild had an ammeter that registered a charge but could not show a discharge. When the battery was fully charged, the ammeter needle stayed at '0' (zero), but if the battery was low, then whilst the engine was running, the ammeter needle would move up off the '0' to show that the battery was being charged up. This time the ammeter needle stayed at '0'.

When I had checked with the mechanic he had told me that the battery had been on charge for days, so I was not expecting it to need to take in any more. It seemed to be reading correctly, as were all the engine instruments.

The weather was gorgeous and I felt in no hurry. I only had to pop across to Hendon. In those days, Heathrow was not the concrete monolith that we now know, so was hardly in my way. Much of it was still a grass factory aerodrome belonging to Fairey Aviation. This had been requisitioned post-war, under wartime rules, to make part of the new London Airport. So my course was nearly direct, taking me barely 15 minutes' flying time.

Hay was being made at White Waltham, so there was a circuitous route cut out by the farmer towards the runways, which had already been cut short. Ready for taxi-out, I combed my hair, powdered my nose, put on some more lipstick, patted the dog, arranged my maps, then slowly went towards the control waggon at the beginning of the runway. They were using the short runway from the south, towards the old ATA buildings, the Fairey Aviation hangars, and the London to Reading railway line. There was an Anson far away on approach, so there would have been plenty of time for me to swirl onto the runway and take off before he was on finals, but as I had oodles of time, I just sat and watched it come in to land, then lumber away off the runway. Was *somebody* telling me to waste a bit of time?

I was given another green light by the controller, so taxied forward onto the runway and took off. When I was at about 400 feet, right over the railway line, the left-hand side (my side) of the Fairchild suddenly burst into flames with a huge 'woomph' just beside my leg. Now it is extraordinary how super-training comes into play without one consciously thinking about it. I turned off the fuel cock, which was by my left elbow, situated on a small aluminium petrol pipe that ran down from the tank in the high wing above me, then went past the side of me, to disappear towards the engine. I leant over, seeing the other petrol cock on the other side was also off, then opened the throttle to use up any spare fuel in the carb. Starved of petrol, the engine stopped. I put the nose down to keep up flying speed, but ahead of me was a field of ripe, glowing, golden corn – on the *other* side of the railway line from the aerodrome. If I tipped over in that, by catching my fixed undercarriage legs, the whole lot would light up. What was also in my mind was that the White Waltham blood-tub and crash-wagon wouldn't be able to get over the railway line to help rescue me.

So I did what NO PILOT SHOULD EVER DO! I turned round to land back diagonally across White Waltham airfield. A pilot should always land dead ahead if he gets an engine cut on take-off. (In my particular case, I had stopped the engine because of the fire.) It is extremely easy to stall in such a situation, as one generally hasn't the height to achieve such a turn with safety. No end of pilots have been killed trying this manouevre, which, although a natural thing to try, is totally wrong. There again, it sometimes worked. I remember hearing about two Tempest pilots taking off from Volkel in Holland towards the end of the war. Both pilots had engine failure as they became airborne. The experienced leader crash-landed dead ahead, hit a low wall and was killed. The less experienced pilot turned back, bellied in – on his two external wing-tanks as well- and survived!

But I knew my little Fairchild. I had logged hundreds of hours in it, or one like it. There was hardly any wind, so a cross-wind dead-stick landing was not going to be a great problem. Smoke billowed around the cockpit, making P-nut in the back cough, as he didn't like it; neither did I, for that matter! I opened both side windows but I couldn't put my head out to my left because of the flames, while the other window was too far away on the other side of the front passenger seat. My precious nylon stockings began to scorch my left leg as they melted. (Nylons were still very difficult to get hold of; my pair had been brought over from America, given to me by a friend of my father who was a much travelled high-up in the USA administration at that time.) I wriggled away from the flames as much as I could without letting my feet get off the rudder bar.

We landed, braking hard in order to stop. I reached back, grabbed P-nut, then jumped out. It is terrible how fast an aeroplane fire gets going when it is fanned by all the slipstream in the air, but as soon as we had come to a standstill, the smoke abated, leaving just flame. The crash crews who had started out from their parking places when I came in across their aerodrome began to back away again to their standing. From where they were, they couldn't see the flames in the bright sunlight, although common sense should have told them to come and have a look. After all, it was so rare for them to have to do anything, they might have been grateful for the practice. Perhaps I'd interrupted a card game?

I jumped up and down, waved my arms, yelled . . . Yes, someone had seen me. The vehicles roared out again, heading in my direction. When they arrived they quickly covered my poor little plane with white foam, smothering the flames, thereby saving her from further damage. My pals on the fire engine said, 'You didn't give us any trouble during the war, Miss Barnato. What are you starting now for?'

But oh, what a nasty sorry mess my dear little shining WJAC gem had become! And she was due to drink champagne in three days' time. All the port side of the fuselage was mottled, melted or burnt, as well as some of the engine cowling. All the electric wiring on the panel by my left leg had gone up, and there wasn't a lot left of the door which had been beside me. By the time the fire had been put out, all the control wires had also been burnt through.

My favourite quarter-inch wartime map, with the balloon barrages still marked on it, had caught fire too, but the other maps in my bag were safe. Still, the dog and I were alright, except for my slightly scorched left leg plus one ruined pair of rare nylons. The right nylon had survived, though. If I could just find someone with an undamaged left one . . !

What happened to cause the fire? The Fairchild was an American aeroplane, so an adapter plug had to be used to make the outside trolley 'acc', which was British, fit into the American engine for the start-up. When the mechanic pulled out the large rubber hose with its own plug, plus an extra adapter plug added on, the little flap cover swung to, then he did it up.

Any amount of skill, training or inspections covered the safety factors of airframes and engines of all aeroplanes, but there were no rules for special adapter plugs. That plug could have been my Waterloo. It was made out of wood, with a metal plate at the points end. This plug had probably been lying around in wet weather for ages, so when the plug was pulled out of the engine by the mechanic, the metal plate came away from the wooden part, staying where it was, stuck across the prongs of my battery. The mechanic could not see it before he secured the flap, because the slipstream had already blown it shut. So the metal plate created a huge short, plus, presumably, sparks. With the engine running, no-one would hear the hissing sounds. As I said earlier, the ammeter wasn't designed to show any discharge, so I hadn't a clue about what was happening. Since starting up and during taxying and take-off, the sparks were arcing, which finally set the wiring alight. Simple, eh?

Now here is where my guardian angel showed that he was still around. Somebody relaxed me, 'told me' not to hurry before taking off. If I had taxied out and taken off without wasting so much time, I would have been much higher and well on my way before enough of the wires caught and burnt through that petrol feed pipe, causing the sudden conflagration. As I had only climbed to 400 feet, it didn't take so long to get back and down, albeit cross-wind, then get the fire put out. If, however, I had had time to climb to, say, 2,000 feet, the Fairchild's controls would undoubtedly have been all burned through before I could get it down. No controls, no controlled landing, no P-nut – and no Diana!

Nobody could explain my good fortune, or why the petrol had not exploded in the pipe above the fuel cock as well as below, when it would have blown up the rest of the fuel in the wing-tank on top of me. I commented, half-heartedly, that it was because I had turned the petrol cock off so fast, but even so, it could all have gone up in one ball of burning fuel.

I'd been lucky again. I hope my guardian angel didn't get His wings scorched. I suppose too, if it had exploded, my burnt man from the day of my first solo would have said, 'I told you so! I warned you.'

Everyone kept quiet about the incident. It was thought that if the parents of any cadets heard about the fire, they might not be too keen to allow their girls to fly (you bet your boots they wouldn't!!). That would have been detrimental to the whole of the WJAC, which was going so well.

The ground aircraft engineer at White Waltham Aero Club, Charlie Gorrod, worked night and day to patch up, repair, and repaint the 'Grey Dove'. The inside was more difficult, so he put hardboard, suitably painted, over the burnt-out electrics panel, and spare seat covers over the damaged upholstery, making the whole thing look more presentable. The machine was quite unflyable, so it was shipped over to Hendon on a lorry. To add insult to injury, the men dropped it onto its tail getting it off, which didn't improve matters either.

I went to Hendon on the morning of the ceremony in order to check over the aeroplane. It was a good thing I got there with plenty of time in hand. There were a lot of discrepancies. The burn marks and the dents where it had been dropped could easily be seen. I borrowed some flags and bunting and bedecked the Fairchild with them, covering the bits I hoped people wouldn't see. Because the control wires were non-existent, both the flaps and ailerons were in the down position on both sides, while the elevator was flopping downwards as well. I tried to get hold of some control locks, but finally a friendly RAF corporal lent me some huge red ones off a four-engined B24 Liberator. They were very large for the little Fairchild, but more flags and bunting soon helped cover them up.

On the great afternoon, Princess Marina arrived, looking quite stunning in a pale-blue suit with a lot of grey fox furs. I stood in my uniform on the platform beside the aircraft. The doors were locked so no-one could see inside, but with all the Union Jacks, etc, I don't believe anyone found out about our mishap. Several people asked me why the flypast hadn't taken place, but I just said it would have been difficult to taxi away from the platform without the people on it getting blown about too much. We got away with it.

The numerous units of the WJAC cadets marched past and saluted the Duchess, then the champagne was duly poured over the (very new) paint. The Duchess said a few words, speeches were made, but nobody guessed that the whole rally only came off by courtesy of my guardian angel. He really is a Heavenly Fellow.

Chapter 16

Through the Sound Barrier

MY FATHER DIED on 27 July 1948. Not only did I lose him as a father but also as a good friend. We had shared many things together, not least the courting of his third wife, in itself a rather unusual experience.

Early post-war months at Ridgemead were happy. I kept this wonderful friendship with my father, more like brother and sister really. He would talk to me about his girlfriends, I letting him know about my admirers.

Soon after the incident of Tony Bartley making such an obvious pass at Vera Scott in the garden at Ridgemead, an outstandingly attractive girl came to stay – Joan Southgate. My father was rightly smitten by her beauty, charm and amusing company. We got along fine, for she didn't try to usurp my position behind the teapot.

She had worked in the Fire Service in cold and damp wartime conditions, had developed pleurisy, but seemingly recovered her health. She was divorced from her first husband, who had been unkind to her, then she had pledged herself to marry a Norwegian Army officer 'after the war ended . . .' The war had now ended; my father had fallen for her, but had not declared his hand in asking her, in so many words, to marry him. She quite obviously did not want to become another Vera, who had in any case been trying to see her off the scene by various devious plots and plans. Luckily they hadn't come off.

One evening my father took me out to dinner in London and opened his heart to me. He was so in love, desperately wanting to marry Joan, but she had told him she had promised the Norwegian, and a promise was a promise. My father said he thought she would regret it, and begged me to get her to change her mind. Fancy a father sending his daughter as an envoy for so important a deed: to try and persuade another girl into marrying and becoming her stepmother. Unusual? This can't happen very often.

Joan sat on a sofa in her Wigmore Street flat over a doctor's consulting rooms. I tried all angles, I really did. Not only did I love my father and want him to be happy, but I was already fond of Joan, and my! how different she was from Vera . . . If I had been asked to persuade Vera, I wouldn't have tried at all. We talked and talked all around the subject. I thought I was winning, but she finally said she must keep her promise. I was amazed, thinking of my adorable father and all the material things he had to offer, but in the end she was adamant. I'd failed to persuade her.

My father was very cut up, to say the least. Joan went to Norway where very soon after getting married she realised it was a dreadful error. Things were not as she had been led to believe, or as she had expected. She didn't like smorgasbord either.

She returned to England, divorced the Norwegian, wasting six months before she and my father could marry. If only my powers of persuasion had been stronger. I rated her highly for keeping her word plus not being a gold-digger as far as my darling father was concerned.

They went to Bermuda for their honeymoon, where my father bought a large house on an island called Perrots Island. An 'investment', he said, to save death duties. Maybe he already suspected he was ill.

Sometime after their return, Joan went to have her fifth and final annual X-ray to see if she had avoided contracting T.B., which was a common chaser of pleurisy. She hadn't avoided it. The treatment then was to have part of a lung collapsed. By this time, Joan had realized that all was not well with her new husband's health. He had stronger and stronger pains and she persuaded him to have an X-ray. It was confirmed: he had cancer. A disastrous start to their lives together.

They had nearby rooms in the London Clinic, that nursing home where I had undergone such a traumatic time early in the war after my crash with Bobby Loewenstein's point-to-point horse. After four days I was told my father's operation had been a success, so I was allowed to see him. He was recovering so well that Joan was now to undergo her lung collapse. I arrived at the London Clinic laden with a huge quantity of flowers from the Ridgemead gardens, to be greeted on the doorstep by Matron, saying that my father had suddenly died from a post-operational thrombosis.

Worse was to follow. In those circumstances, although Joan had had her anaesthetic, it was decided at the last moment not to operate because the double shock would be far too great for her. Would I please tell her the sad news?

So there was my stepmother and friend recovering from what she thought was her operation out of the way, to be told by me that she had not yet been operated upon after all, so still had that hanging over her, and that her husband of six months, my father, aged only 52, had died. I had to tell another woman the same age as myself that she too was a widow. Holding back my own sadness, keeping up my outward spirits to comfort her was a task that I do not like to dwell upon.

Soon after my father's death, whilst Joan still had a period of hospitalization ahead of her, she decided to sell Ridgemead. It was far too big for her, and for most people too. It was sold for £25,000. The whole estate! It became an old people's home. The garden was cut up, the small lodges and the stables sold separately, another house built at the end of the line of lily-ponds, quite spoiling the view. So ended a glamorous era.

My father was buried in the plot right next to Derek. They had known each other for almost as short a time as I had known him but they had become good friends. My stepmother and I thought it fitting that they should lie side by side. It was not until the end of the ceremony of my father's burial that a long-faced Rabbi in his flowing black robes emerged from the crowd around the grave and said some Hebrew prayers, quietly pointing out to us that it was inappropriate for a Jew to be plonked in a Christian burial ground. Only then did we realize our mistake. In our grief we had not thought of that. Too late, he told us about a large Barnato/Joel burial place surrounded by railings at Willesden Jewish Cemetery in North London, where my late father should have joined the huge granite tombs of his parents, Barney and Fanny, and his various uncles and cousins and other relatives. We didn't know it existed. No-one had ever bothered to talk to us about it.

My father left me a tidy sum of money. My mother needed some money as her farm didn't pay, so she sold the whole of River House to me so some of the family cash went round the family. I finally moved down into Surrey and sold River House in the late 1960s. The end of another era.

During the post-war years I continued flying for the WJAC, and brought up my young son. Suddenly events occurred that were totally unexpected.

1963 was to be a momentous year for me, both good and bad. The previous year I had won the Jean Lennox Bird Trophy, which was presented annually to a British woman pilot. I received it for my work with the WJAC, so 1963 began for me in May with the presentation of the trophy by none other than Britain's premier aviator, Lord Brabazon of Tara – premier in that he was the holder of Aero Club of Great Britain's Aviator Certificate No. 1, awarded to him in 1910.

Jean Lennox Bird had been a Hamble ATA pilot during the war, and was the first woman to win RAF wings. She was killed piloting a Bristol Freighter aircraft in 1957 and the trophy was named in her honour and memory.

The second event of note concerned the offer to go through the sound barrier.

The Women's Junior Air Corps' aircraft was taken to a different airfield every weekend from March to November each year. We had some large units near Darlington and Middlesbrough, so I went to RAF Middleton St George twice during the season so that all the local cadets could have a chance to fly.

The second weekend that I was due to fly was an absolute stinker. On the Friday, I had a lot of trouble getting there in fog and had to use my X-ray eyes all the way. I should really have cancelled, but the Commandant of the WJAC units was not on the telephone and I didn't want the young people to take the trouble to get to the airfield, only to find their aeroplane had not turned up.

After dinner that night, I was in the bar of the RAF Officers' Mess. Several of the pilots of the Lightning Conversion Course that was based there pretended to be surprised that I had got there at all, and flattered me by saying it wasn't their weather. Well, it wouldn't have been in their fast Lightnings, and in truth, it really wasn't mine either.

Came Saturday morning and the fog was even thicker. Reams of kids arrived to fly: most of them had never been airborne before. Group Captain E. W. 'Bertie' Wootten DFC & bar, AFC (later Air Commodore CBE), the Station Commander of Middleton St George and a former Battle of Britain fighter pilot, a burly, friendly and supportive friend of my late husband Derek, had all the aerodrome lights turned on, and, terrified that I would lose the aerodrome, I flew the circuit all day. At least, I suppose I did, for I couldn't see a thing. The cadets didn't see anything either except the fog, but they all seemed happy with the idea of at least getting off the ground. I cancelled their navigation tests even though they worked out a course for me to fly for them.

That evening, the Wing Commander Flying, John de M. Severgne AFC (later Air Vice Marshal MVO and former Captain of Her Majesty the Queen's Flight), suggested that I should fly one of their Lightnings. Nothing I'd rather do, but, thinking that someone might get into trouble, I said, 'Only if it's made official.'

A lot of people in the air world knew me and would have shot me down as well. I had run into that sort of problem when wanting to fly a post-war Gloster Meteor to pick up the Women's Air Speed Record. All I was allowed to do on that occasion was to carry out all the technical and ground runs, plus taxying, but never allowed to actually fly. We could so easily have achieved that record for England then, but someone nobbled it by saying that the Meteor belonged to the Ministry of Aircraft Production (not the RAF) and therefore there was no insurance cover! In other words, someone still didn't want a woman in their post-war Meteors, although many woman had delivered them with ATA during the war.

'Well, who do you know?' persisted Johnnie.

'The Air Minister,' I told him, thinking it was all bar talk anyway.

Sunday was still thick pea-soup weather, but again the aerodrome approach and runway lights were all switched on and hordes of kids were all flown; but oh! was I tired from peering into the non-visibility for a glimmer of the aerodrome lights.

The next morning Johnnie Severgne came running out to my Fairchild just as I was warming it up to fly home. He yelled through the window,

'Don't forget to ask the Minister!'

The two airmen waiting to pull away the chocks stiffened, and looked as if they were about to salute me.

So I knew the flight was on, but only if I could get the tall, gaunt, strong-featured Minister of Defence (Air), the Right Hon. Hugh Fraser MBE PC MP, the younger brother of Lord Lovat ('Shimi') of Commando fame, to give me his permission. Hugh was subsequently knighted for his political services.

Hugh was an old friend of mine and I made an appointment to see him in his office at the Ministry of Defence on the following Monday at 9 o'clock. During the intervening week I went to a garden party dressed up to the nines in a green and black spotted full-skirted silk dress and with a shiny straw topper with a green chiffon scarf wound around it, plus lots of make-up and long trailing hair. Hugh came rushing up when he spotted me and said, 'Diana, I hear you are coming to see me on Monday. What's it all about?'

Now, here was I, all tarted up, and if I told him then of my yearnings to fly the Lightning, he would surely pooh-pooh the whole idea there and then. I wanted to let him see my other side; the more serious one. I murmured that I would rather not tell him until Monday, but he looked anxious and tried again.

'Is it anything to do with the Profumo/Keeler affair?' This scandal had been in the forefront of the news for some time, and Hugh knew that Jack and Valerie Profumo were very old pals of mine from pre-war and from when Jack had been the Secretary of State for War. I told Hugh it wasn't anything at all to do with that story and he looked very relieved.

I arrived early at the Ministry that Monday wearing my smartest uniform, with my hair rolled up off the collar and under my sidecap. Clutched in my clammy hand was a tiny card on which I had written 12 reasons why I wanted to fly that Lightning. I had to write them down as some of the reasons were so weak I could easily have forgotten them.

I was ushered into Hugh's lovely office – all dark green carpet and leather chairs. Hugh sat behind a huge desk backing onto a stupendous view of the Thames. I saluted and he looked somewhat startled – then he saw it was me. Standing at attention in my WJAC uniform, I prattled on to him with my 12 phoney reasons and finished up lamely with, 'I really do want to fly the Lightning.'

He said nothing, but pressed a bell and in came a smart Wing Commander. Hugh asked him to take a letter and said, 'She wants to fly a Lightning!' The Wing Commander looked suitably surprised. I held my breath and Hugh went on, 'I don't see why she shouldn't.'

I thought the uniform ploy had borne fruit. Hugh then said, 'But . . .', and my heart sank. 'But you will have to do a decompression test and be kitted out and so on.' I was over the first hurdle and hadn't fallen.

Hugh dictated to his Wing-Co secretary, calling out all of my 12 reasons in order and without forgetting one of them. Quite a feat when I had needed a sticky card even though I'd made them up. He then looked at me and said, 'Just one more thing . . ,' and my heart sank again. '. . . It fits in well: but do you mind publicity?' I said 'No. *Anything* to fly that aeroplane.' 'Full RAF publicity!' he emphasized. I agreed. The Ministry of Defence obviously had a 13th reason – the best. It was hoping to sell the Lightning abroad to many of our fairly friendly Eastern states, Hugh thinking that a woman flying one would make it seem easy and be of great commercial value.

During the next few days, arrangements were made for me to go to RAF Upwood to be medically checked up for high-altitude flying. I was put in a sort of railway carriage in a hangar accompanied by a doctor and an RAF officer. We were pressurized up to various heights and monitored on the way up and slowly down.

'You are now at 35,000 feet,' they said, which all seemed so silly when I knew that, including the wheels of the thing, we were barely five feet off the ground.

Having been fitted with a pressure helmet and other kit, and been taught how to pressure breathe, I made my way to Middleton St George where I stayed a few days and did quite a lot of hours on their Lightning simulator. During these weeks I had felt weak, for me, and had several symptoms that I didn't like at all. But I was determined to do this flight. I hoped my ill-health was only due to the excitement of the new turmoil in my flying career.

At last the great day arrived: 26 August 1963. The weather was perfect: blue sky, puffy broken cumulus at about 3,000 feet and wind straight down the main runway. I posed beside the Lightning, climbing up to it, sitting in it, standing on the steps waving, walking to it and away from it and back again! I loved all the attention from the surrounding press camera men but I was impatient to get going.

At last the great moment arrived. Squadron Leader Ken Goodwin AFC (now Air Commodore CBE and Regional Commandant of the Air Training Corps in the South West) came too as check pilot – for I was to fly a two-seat training version of the Lightning (*XM996*), not the single-seat fighter model. He really was kind and let me do it all. Ken, ten years my junior, was a pale-blue-eyed, fair-haired, tall young man, overflowing with good nature and friendliness; he was also a superb pilot. He was star of the RAF aerobatic team and flew individually or solo aerobatics. His son followed him into the RAF and flew operationally during the Gulf War.

After take-off in re-heat for 1½ minutes, I turned onto an easterly course to take me out over the sea. I was supposed to climb to 25,000 feet before turning north to do the timed run. It was decided to call my flight an attempt at the Women's Speed Record – not difficult to get that one in the Lightning.

First of all, in spite of all the simulator flying, it seemed to take ages to 'get around the corner' and onto my climbing course – not like my little Fairchild, which one could yank around, as it was nearly standing still anyhow compared to this supersonic thing I had now got my hands on. When I climbed – poof – in less than a second we were through the 3,000 foot based cumulus. I was using for my first time the vertical climb and descent indicator which showed black one side of the perpendicular and white on the other. I was amazed that I really was standing on my tail and the indicator was virtually off the clock.

I was concentrating on keeping my course accurate when Ken pointed at the altimeter. We were already at 42,000 feet after only a few seconds – not surprising when the Lightning climbs at 20,000 feet per minute, to 60,000 feet, its ceiling.

'We are a bit high,' Ken said, which was an understatement. We only had pressure helmets, not pressure suits which were needed at that altitude, and anyway, I had not been cleared at Upwood for that height. Ken jerked his head towards his left shoulder and continued, 'Turn onto course and start the run from up here.'

I turned north and with the afterburners lit again, off I went downhill in a shallow descent, building up speed to 1,500 mph to start the run at 30,000 feet. Oh, life was grand! The Mach-meter moved up, the instruments went haywire and the compressability 'cobbles' duly bumped, then went as we passed through the sound barrier, and the instruments came back to their normal readings again. Then suddenly, all was quiet – and I mean quiet. All our sound was left behind us. I could hear my neck creaking when I moved my head but that was all.

The sky was clear and blue and both the sun and the moon were hanging up there while far, far below, were the tops of the broken cumulus. Ken suddenly nudged me and said, 'We'll be in Norway soon!'

I hadn't realized how fast we were covering the ground, or rather the sea. I switched off what was left of the afterburners, which at full bore would burn for less than 20 minutes and which used 11,000 gallons per hour AvTag (nearly gasolene, not quite kerosene, but not so explosive or inflammable). In order to begin the turn, I slowed back through the sound barrier and regretfully turned towards the English coast, then flew down to Hartlepool Bay.

Oh, what an easy aircraft: light, power controlled and so manoeuvrable, and those wonderful twin Avon engines. Heading in over the River Tees with Middlesbrough below, I let down at Middleton St George to circuit height. Suddenly Ken said, 'I've got her,' and took over, then accelerated across the runway, dropping his own supersonic 'bang' I suppose, and doing a flick-roll as he went. Oh dear! I really wasn't ready for that and suddenly felt quite sick. 'You've got her now,' said Ken and I took a deep breath and pulled myself together for the approach (at 175 knots over the hedge) and the landing. I remembered the drogue 'chute too. This lets out behind the aircraft to help slow down the landing run.

I must confess I felt somewhat faint, not only with Ken's roll, but with all the excitement. I must not be sick or feel dizzy when I get out, I told myself, so I opened the hood for more fresh air as I taxied in, very, very slowly, taking a lot of deep breaths on the way. I hoped I'd last out and not pass out.

More photos were taken and the speed over the course was worked out. It depends on the indicated Mach number and the outside air temperature at whatever height you are flying. Then I was made a member of the 'Ten Ton Club', the 1,000 miles per hour club, and duly presented with a club tie – navy blue with a little Mach number in white on it – together with a certificate, which now hangs in my downstairs loo with other such certificates, such as my MBE, for example. A good place, the downstairs loo, to hang such things. Helps one's sense of proportion.

The other good news was that I had flown faster than any woman in the world at that time. I beat both the Jacquelines – Cochrane of the USA and Auriol of France. The official verdict was that I had flown at Mach 1.65 – an incredible 1,262 mph.

My exhilaration was short-lived, however. After I got home I was immediately put into hospital. My recent feeling of ill-health having returned. Just like my father, I had cancer.

I found myself in some little hospital near Paddington. I felt so weak from loss of blood that I suggested I might be topped up. Some woman came along – I don't know who or what she was – with the transfusion equipment but she didn't even know how to stick in the needle. So my old training as a Red Cross nurse and ambulance driver came in handy, giving her a quick lesson – on myself. As the first blood went in I suddenly felt alive again – perhaps like some of you do after a large double whisky, but I arranged to get out of that place as soon as possible, though with all those pints of blood going in, I wondered if I would take on the character of the donor.

Nicki Vansittart, the brother of Lord Vansittart, the famous foreign secretary who warned us about Hitler's build-up of arms and aircraft, kindly acting as one of my trustees, gave me the name of a new doctor, a female one, Doctor Christian Carritt. She agreed to take me on and became my lifeline all through that dreary period in my life. She was wonderful and reassuring, a tremendous comfort.

She came into the Middlesex Hospital, where I was next taken, every single day for weeks. I didn't belong to anyone and could not cope with decision-making on my own, so Christian did it all. I was very frightened and didn't think I'd come out. At first I kept my eyes closed most of the time as it was too much effort to open them, but I could hear alright. One day I heard my sister Virginia's voice. She said, 'She can't go on much longer, can she?' Tactless as usual.

The turning point came when I saw that the plastic hospital identity name tag on my wrist had the number 22297 on it. This was, you see, exactly the same number as my flying licences! This had to be a signal from above that some unknown spirit was keeping an eye on me – perhaps it was still that guardian angel who had seen me through the war.

The most gruesome thing in hospital was seeing a large body being wheeled out past my open door, all covered up and therefore dead. Not at all reassuring. Some terrible old woman patient kept on coming in to talk at me. 'I've got cancer too,' she would say. 'I've had both breasts off.' Very scare-making, the more so because at that time I was still vain about my body. She did not help my recovery at all, always leaving me fearsome and depressed. I eventually asked the nurses to keep her out of my room.

That November, whilst I was still in the Middlesex, the black-and-white TV news showed the assassination of President John F. Kennedy. What a way to go. Perhaps I wouldn't last much longer either. Although I didn't know it until later, the word was that I had little more than a month to go myself when I was first brought in.

Suddenly things seemed to improve. I was in the Middlesex for some time but was eventually allowed out. My dear old friend Tony Bartley came to drive me home. First we walked a few yards in Battersea Park, the other side of the River Thames from my house. I kicked at some of the fallen leaves and wondered if I would see another winter.

Coming out of the front door when we arrived was an enormously tall and large lady, frighteningly and completely dressed in black. She peered at me from under a pancake straw hat with a spotted veil. She was a friend of one of my mother's original tenants in the flat above mine. She paused on the front steps and said, 'Now don't you worry, my dear, you'll be alright. I had cancer 20 years ago and I'm still here.'

So all you faint hearts who may be ailing, I say to you: cancer is not necessarily a killer, especially nowadays. I don't want to boast too much, but I'm still above the ground over 30 years on and I have gloried in this extra time that has been granted to me to spend on this planet.

I even continued to fly for a few more years, and by 1969 had more than doubled the flying hours I had done when the war ended. I have flown over 120 different types and marks of aeroplanes, although there wasn't much difference between some of the marks. I wouldn't have missed a single type, a single hour or any one of those flights.

I have indeed been Spreading My Wings.

Epilogue

I RECOVERED FROM cancer after three operations. Later I became Master of the Old Surrey and Burstow Foxhounds for 13 seasons, which would be a book in itself. I continued to fly as Corps Pilot for the Women's Junior Air Corps, now renamed the Girls' Venture Corps.

I am now Commodore of the Air Transport Auxiliary Association. Together with the Hon. Secretary, Wing Commander Eric Viles MBE, who was a young ATC cadet attached to ATA at White Waltham and Aston Down in Gloucestershire during the war, I have become the epicentre of former ATA personnel, not only in this country but also for those who regularly fly in to Great Britain from abroad. The people of the 28 nations who flew with us retain their affection for Britain and keep up their friendships, plus their thoughts about their past exploits in the air. They did not have to volunteer for such a job.

My life is still a full one, much of it taken up with being a sheep farmer in Surrey. I didn't break my neck flying, nor did I break my neck hunting. I am lucky to be still able to walk around the garden, sniff the roses, bend down to pat P-nut's successor Mac (four dogs on), help sheep at lambing time and ride one of my horses round the fields – enjoyable pursuits for an elderly lady with a lot of past memories . . .

I do hope you have enjoyed my yarns as much as I liked writing them.

MY GERIATRIC SMILE

The past seems better than the present:
Some memories swirl then change to seem
A vivid happiness so clearly seen.

I know now why the agèd and the mindless
Seem quite content to dream their lives away
Within their many cells of sensitivity.
They hark back on what was or might have been
When they were young and free
Of all impediments and very fear of life,
And being vital, scoffed at thoughts of age.

The grave is open! Yes! but we're not told
Of what will happen when
The years creep on and we are old:

I think of carefree youth, and then I hide
Behind my craggy mask of sad senility.

DBW

ATA record of service

EFTS White Waltham	2 Nov 1941 – 22 Feb 1942
Cross Country Flight, White Waltham	23 Feb 1942 – 24 Mar 1942
Ferry Flight, White Waltham	25 Mar 1942 – 8 May 1942
No. 15 Ferry Pool, Hamble – junior taxi-pilot secondment	9 May 1942 – 3 Jun 1942
No. 1 Ferry Pool, White Waltham	4 Jun 1942 – 12 Jul 1942
No. 5 Ferry Pool, Luton	13 Jul 1942 – 25 Jul 1942
AFTS, Class II Conversion, White Waltham	26 Jul 1942 – 31 Aug 1942
Training Pool, White Waltham	1 Sep 1942 – 7 Nov 1942
No. 15 Ferry Pool, Hamble	8 Nov 1942 – 4 Dec 1942
No. 1 Ferry Pool, White Waltham	5 Dec 1942 – 14 Apr 1943
AFTS, Class III Conversion, White Waltham	16 Apr 1943 – 6 May 1943
No. 1 Ferry Pool, White Waltham	7 May 1943 – 22 Jun 1943
No. 15 Ferry Pool, Hamble	23 Jun 1943 – 2 Sep 1943
AFTS Class IV Conversion, White Waltham	10 Sep 1943 – 12 Oct 1943
No. 15 Ferry Pool, Hamble	13 Oct 1943 – 10 Apr 1944
AFTS, IV Class Conversion, White Waltham	11 Apr 1944 – 24 May 1944
No. 15 Ferry Pool, Hamble	25 May 1944 – 23 Feb 1945
Medical Pool (anaemia)	24 Feb 1945 – 17 Apr 1945
No. 15 Ferry Pool, Hamble	18 Apr 1945 – 26 May 1945
No. 1 Ferry Pool, White Waltham	27 May 1945 – 31 Aug 1945

◆ *Appendix 2* ◆

Aircraft types flown

Single-engined
Avro Tutor
Gloster Gladiator
Hawker Hart
Miles Magister
De Havilland Tiger Moth
Miles Master I
Miles Master II
Miles Master III
Miles Martinet
Westland Lysander
De Havilland Chipmunk
Percival Prentice
North American Harvard I
North American Harvard II
Hawker Hurricane I
Hawker Hurricane IIB
Hawker Hurricane IIC
Supermarine Spitfire IIB
Supermarine Spitfire IV
Supermarine Spitfire V
Supermarine Spitfire Vb
Supermarine Spitfire Vc
Supermarine Spitfire VII
Supermarine Spitfire VIII
Supermarine Spitfire VIII (retract TW)
Supermarine Spitfire IX
Supermarine Spitfire XI (PR)
Supermarine Spitfire XII (clipped wing)

Supermarine Spitfire XIV
Supermarine Spitfire XIX
Supermarine Spitfire XXI
Boulton Paul Defiant I
Boulton Paul Defiant II
Hawker Typhoon I
Hawker Tempest I
Hawker Tempest V
Piper Cub
Grumman Avenger Ic
Grumman Avenger II
Grumman Wildcat
Vultee Vengeance I
Vultee Vengeance IV
North American Mustang I
North American Mustang II
North American Mustang III
North American Mustang IV
Chance Vought Corsair
Fairey Swordfish
Blackburn Skua
Blackburn Roc
Curtiss Seamew
Fairey Fulmar I
Fairey Fulmar II
Fairey Barracuda I
Fairey Barracuda II
Fairey Barracuda III
Fairey Firefly I
Fairey Firefly II
Fairey Firefly III

Single-engined cont . . .
Supermarine Seafire I
Supermarine Seafire II
Supermarine Seafire III
Supermarine Walrus II
Supermarine Sea Otter
Hawker Sea Hurricane

Twin-engined
Airspeed Oxford
Avro Anson
De Havilland Rapide
Bristol Blenheim IV
Handley Page Hampden
Armstrong Whitworth Whitley
Vickers Wellington Ic
Vickers Wellington III
Vickers Wellington X
Vickers Wellington XI
Vickers Wellington XIII
Vickers Wellington XIV
Vickers Warwick V
Bristol Beaufighter
De Havilland Mosquito VI
De Havilland Mosquito XVI
De Havilland Mosquito XXX
De Havilland Mosquito XXXIV
De Havilland Mosquito XXXV
De Havilland Mosquito XXXVI
Armstrong Whitworth Albemarle
Lockheed Hudson I
Lockheed Hudson II
Lockheed Hudson III
Lockheed Hudson IV
Lockheed Hudson V

Lockheed Hudson VI
Lockheed Ventura
Douglas Boston IV
Martin Maryland
North American Mitchell I
North American Mitchell II
North American Mitchell III
English Electric Lightning T14 Jet

Civil aircraft
Bristol Freighter
De Havilland Puss Moth
Percival Vega Gull
De Havilland Hornet Moth
Wicko Warferry
Miles Mentor
Stinson Reliant
Percival Q.6 (Petrel)
Percival Proctor
Fairchild Argus II & IV
Fairchild Ranger
Airspeed Courier
Miles Messenger
Miles Gemini
Miles Whitney Straight
Jodel Musketeer
Jodel Ambassador
Tipsy B (Belgium)
Piper Commanche
Rollason/Druine D62 Conder
Cessna 172
Cessna 175
Forney F1A Ercoupe (USA)
Meta Sokol (Czech)

NB: Additional single-engined
British Taylorcraft Auster

Fairey Albacore

Index

Strickland, FO Claud 46-48, 67, 129
Strodl, 1st Off Vera 92
Summers, John 'Mutt' 185
Sweeny, Charles 95
Sweeny, F/Lt Robert 95

Tedder, Lord 170
Thornhill, 1st Off Leonard 186-7
Thurber, Dorothe 33
Thurber, Muriel (aunt and cousin) 33
Thurber, Col Philip 33
Thurber, Pomeroy 29-31, 33
Tuck, W/Cdr Robert Stanford 59, 139

Vansittart, Nicki 214
Veltheim, von 25
Viles, W/Cdr Eric 216

Wainwright, Dorothy Maitland née Falk (see Barnato)
Wainwright, R. B. 11-12, 31, 176
Walker, 1st Off Anne 140-1, 152-3
Walker, Barney Barnato 199
Walker, Derek 134, 140-4, 145-7, 164-170, 181, 188, 191-7, 209
Waller, Ken 35
Wilberforce, Cdr Marion K. 43
Wisdom, Tom H. 141
White, 'Whitey' 68, 154-5
Whitehurst, Cdr T. H. N. 77, 83-84, 182
Wolfson, Isaac 139
Wootten, A/Cdre E. W. 'Bertie' 210
Wray, G/Capt John B. 191
Wykeham, AM Sir Peter 169

Yarwood, Albert 77
Young, PO 58